*Muslims and Minorities*

# Muslims and Minorities

*The Population of Ottoman Anatolia
and the End of the Empire*

Justin McCarthy

New York University Press · New York *and* London
1983

Manufactured in the United States of America

Library of Congress Cataloging in Publication Data
McCarthy, Justin,
Muslims and minorities.

Bibliography: p.
Includes index.
1. Turkey—Population—History.   2. Minorities—
Turkey—History.   I. Title.
HB3633.4.A3M32   1983      304.6'09561      83-13165
ISBN 0-8147-5390-6

Clothbound editions of New York University Press books are Smyth-sewn
and printed on permanent and durable acid-free paper.

*To*
Justin Nicholas

# Contents

# Preface

I WOULD LIKE to acknowledge the financial support of the Social Science Research Council, the American Council of Learned Societies, the American Research Institute in Turkey, the National Science Foundation, and the University of Louisville. A grant from the University Committee on Academic Publications of the University of Louisville greatly helped to defer publication expenses. Many persons assisted me in writing *Muslims and Minorities*, particularly Stanford Shaw, Georges Sabagh, Charles Issawi, two anonymous reviewers, and my wife, Beth. The staffs of the UCLA Near Eastern Center, the Office of Population Research at Princeton University, and the Department of History at the University of Louisville admirably and efficiently provided the logistic support I needed to complete the manuscript. For the raw materials of research I depended on librarians and archivists in Turkey, France, England, and the United States. I thank them all.

# Introduction

THIS STUDY is an analysis of population gain and loss. Like all demography, it uses the statistical tools necessary to analyze the collective lives of millions of persons. Whenever possible, formulas and calculations have been relegated to footnotes and appendixes. Occasionally, however, basic calculations have proved to be essential to the presentation of an argument and have been included in the text. Certain conventions have been followed with all statistical materials in tables, text, and notes:

1. Numbers are printed as they appear in the source. Note will always be made of corrected or altered figures.

2. When figures are the result of calculations that have as their base exact numbers (e.g., $1,518,943 \times 1.3 = 1,974,626$) exact numbers are printed. This does not mean that the results are not approximations. In fact, the figure 1,974,626 may be just as much an approximation as two million would be. Exact figures are printed so that critics can check the calculations.

3. Approximate figures, such as two million, are used when there is no need or possibility to check calculations. They usually indicate that the figures are not precisely known. No number, such as a figure taken directly from a census, is ever printed in less precision than appears in the source.

4. All Ottoman dates, unless otherwise marked, are *hicra*, i.e., dates in the Muslim lunar calendar. If *mali* (financial year) dates are used, they are marked with an M (e.g., 1330 M). Conversions to western dates are given, but statistical calculations are made using the shorter Muslim year.

Throughout this book, Ottoman place names have been transliterated into Modern Turkish spellings. For example, "Mamuretülaziz," not "Mamurat ul ᶜAziz." All place names follow the conventions of Turkish grammar, in which a vowel is placed at the end of a compound in which one noun modifies another and a k often changes to a soft g (ğ). For example, the vilâyet (province) of Ankara becomes "Ankara Vilâyeti," the sancak (sub-province) of Biga becomes "Biga Sancağı," and the kaza (district) of Kastamonu becomes "Kastamonu Kazası." Turkish letters are pronounced as in English, with these exceptions:

c  j as in "jump"
ç  ch as in "child"
ğ  lengthens the sound of the preceding vowel,
    but has no sound itself.
ı  somewhat like the i in "first" or "dirt"
j  like the French g in "gendarme"
ö  like the German ö
ş  sh
ü  like the German ü

The diphthong "ay" is pronounced like the English word "eye," "ey" like the vowel in "hay." Circumflexes (ˆ) over vowels only slightly change the pronunciation of the vowel and can be safely ignored.

In any book of demography it is easy to view the statistics as an end in themselves, to try to find the perfect number. Even had such an approach been desirable, the data upon which this book is based are too imperfect to support such an excursion into the calculus of demography. No perfect numbers will be found here. The reader should be aware that each population number presented in this book, whether raw data from Ottoman population registers or analyzed and corrected figures, is approximate. I intend to present a picture of the Anatolian population in its rise and fall, and hope to provide accurate estimates of population that will be used by others. I also intend to put the lie to the often said statement that there are no population statistics of the Ottoman Empire.

*Muslims and Minorities*

# 1.
# Ottoman Anatolia

OTTOMAN ANATOLIA stretched from the Iranian border in the east to the Aegean and Marmara Seas in the west and from the Black Sea in the north to the Mediterreanean in the south. The bulk of the region was made up of central plateau—a dry area of harsh climate, pastoralism, and cereal crops—that extended into the mountainous east. On the sea-coasts, however, a mild climate and greater percipitation allowed varied and more productive agriculture.

Administratively, the Ottomans divided Anatolia into vilâyets in 1864. In most of the period from 1878 to World War One there were 14 vilâyets and two independent sancaks (in reality, small provinces) in Anatolia (see figure 1.1). Except in southern Anatolia, these provinces roughly conformed to the geographic/climatic regions of the country: north coastal—Kastamonu and Trabzon; west coastal—Hüdavendigâr, Aydın, İzmit, and Biga; central—Ankara, Sivas, and Konya; eastern—Van, Diyarbakır, Mamuretülaziz, and Bitlis. The southern provinces—Adana and Haleb—straddled different geographic regions.

The ethnic character of Ottoman Anatolia had been set by the Turkish invasions that began in the eleventh century. The conquests replaced much of the Orthodox Christian population of Anatolia with Muslim Turks; over the years of Ottoman rule, conversion to Islam cemented the Muslim predominance in the Anatolian population. Despite this, no major Christian religious group can be said to have disappeared. Anatolia remained a mix of Muslim and non-Muslim communities until World War I.

Following Islamic government practice, the Ottomans divided their population along religious lines into *millets* (literally nations). The Anatolian Muslim community was mainly composed of Turks and Kurds. Other indigenous Muslim groups such as the Laz were statistically insignificant, but a large influx of Caucasian Muslims had emigrated from Russia territory into Anatolia before 1878. The Greeks of Anatolia were found in the sea-coast provinces of the north and west. Jews were in western Anatolian cities. Armenians were in eastern Anatolia, but had spread into central and western Anatolia as well. In the east, smaller groups of Christians, especially Syrians (Catholic and Orthodox), Chaldeans, and Nestorians, had remained in their traditional homes.

In 1878, the population of Ottoman Anatolia had begun what was per-haps the best period of its history. Politically, the last of the nineteenth-century wars with Russia had ended and the Empire was at peace. Central-izing reforms begun under Sultan Mahmud II in 1826 had left the new sultan, Abdülhamid II, more in control of his empire than any Ottoman ruler since the sixteenth century, and central control meant relative peace internally, as well as internationally. Medically, the bubonic plague had ended in the middle of the century and the worst cholera epidemics were over. With the cessation of Russian imperial expansion, the typhus that accompanied the hordes of refugees into the Empire ceased also. New roads and railroads brought crops to market and supplies to areas beset by local famines. In short, conditions were very favorable for population expansion.

From 1878 to 1911, the population of Anatolia grew by almost 50 per-cent. By no means was the expansion shared equally between all groups and all regions, but for Anatolia as a whole the times were good. The Anatolian population increased at what might seem to be a very rapid rate of growth to those who are used to thinking of rapid population increase as a contem-porary phenomenon. The underlying fertility and mortality in Anatolia al-lowed the population to increase at approximately .015 a year. If it were not cut down by wars, bandit raids, and overtaxation, the population could have doubled approximately every 50 years.

Population increase in Anatolia was based on high fertility. Maternal mortality was great, but the woman who lived through her fertile period could have expected, on the average, to have six children. Of those six, three would die before they were five years old. Depending on the area in which he lived, the average Anatolian could have had a life expectancy of 25 to 35 years. However, life expectancy is an average heavily weighted by infant mortality. If a person survived to age five, he or she could expect to live an average of 45 to 50 years. When the Anatolian died it would probably have been of an endemic disease such as dysentery, tuberculosis, or malaria. Modern health care was nonexistent, except in a few cities. It would not be until the Turkish Republic that basic reforms in medicine and sanitation would significantly increase life span in Anatolia. The relative security of post-1878 Anatolia reduced death from wars, civil disorder, and famine, but did nothing to rescue the Anatolians from endemic disease.

The Anatolian population was enumerated in detail by the Ottoman government, and was estimated by others—European consuls, representatives of minority groups, and travelers. No one but the Ottomans, however, had

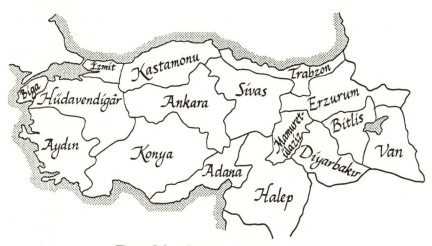

**Figure 1.1.** Ottoman Anatolia in 1895

any accurate knowledge of the size of the population. This was due to a common sense principle of demography that is often forgotten—the only way to know a population's size is to count the people. Only the Ottomans were in a position to have counted their people.

Ottoman population statistics are discussed in detail in Appendix 2, but it is necessary to give a brief description of the Ottoman statistical system and statistical publications if the analyses in later chapters are to be understood.

Ottoman population data was recorded by registrars in each Ottoman province. Though the ideal was total registration and continuous updating of population registers, the registers were understandably never perfectly kept. The accuracy of Ottoman population statistics on Anatolian Muslims varied greatly. In the provinces of northern and western Anatolia, where the authority of the central government was strongest, population statistics were well-recorded. This was less true in central and southern Anatolia, and the population records taken in eastern Anatolia were markedly inferior to those from other Anatolian provinces. The difference in statistical accuracy makes it desirable to consider each region and province of Anatolia separately. Also, the different geographic regions represented varying economic, ethnic, cultural, and demographic environments. Lower or higher standards of sanitation or economy caused fluctuations in the levels of mortality between regions.

Population registers were the basis of all Ottoman government population statistics. They were forwarded to Istanbul for inclusion in published and unpublished (for internal bureaucratic use) summary lists of the Empire's population, usually called "censuses." In addition, each province published its recorded population numbers in *salnames* or provincial yearbooks. Various tables of population numbers of single provinces or groups of provinces were also compiled for Ottoman government officials and are found in the Ottoman archives. All of these sources contained the same type of information on Ottoman population, drawn from the same source, the Ottoman population registration system.

Like all population records, the Ottoman population registers contained errors. These errors were generally of a type seen in modern censuses taken in developing countries, i.e., women and children were undercounted and an individual's knowledge of his or her age was imperfect. In order to arrive at more correct estimates of the populations of the Ottoman Anatolian provinces, it has been necessary to adjust the Ottoman figures for the undercount of women and children, using methods described in appendix 4. In this process, information on the male population of each province by age, as published in one of the censuses, the *1313 İstatistik*, has been compared to standard tables that show the extent of the undercount of children. A correction factor drawn from that analysis has then been applied to all Ottoman population records of that province. Because of the underregistration of women, the total population of the province has been taken to be the male population doubled. While doubling the males obfuscates some real differences in the male-female ratio, the result is the best available approximation of the total population of the province.

The standard tables that provide the correction factors for underenumeration of the population also give estimates of fertility and mortality—the

crude birth rate (the proportion of children born each year to the total population), crude death rate (the proportion dying each year to the total population) and the rate of natural increase (the excess of births over deaths).
These rates have been included in chapter 2 for each Anatolian province.

The standard tables themselves (the Coale and Demeny Stable Population
models) are invaluable tools for the historical demographer. Drawn from the
actual demographic experience of recorded populations, they allow one to
compare recorded, but imperfect, population statistics to theoretical data on
population, and in doing so to see where the errors lie in the recorded
population. The model tables have many complex demographic uses, but
they have been used here for a very simple purpose—to evaluate the total
population number of the Muslim and minority communities of Anatolia.
More detailed analysis of demographic variables such as internal migration
and fertility of subgroups in the population must await the discovery of data
more complete and detailed than the statistics presently available.

## Design of the Study

The following chapters will consider first the Muslim population, by region and province and by year, from 1878 to 1914, then the minority population, by province only. The Ottoman population records on the Anatolian Muslims became reliable long before those on minority populations.
Not until the end of the Empire were the statistics on Armenians, most of
whom lived in the most statistically underdeveloped areas of Anatolia, reliable. Records of Greeks and others suffered from the same disabilities, though
to a lesser extent. For this reason, the populations of minority groups have
been analyzed only for the period at the end of the Empire.

This study has divided Anatolia into five regions—north, south, east, west,
and central, roughly basing the divisions on those used by the Turkish State
Institute of Statistics. Because Ottoman population data was collected and
published on the provincial level, the boundaries of the regions cannot be
other than provincial boundaries, and of course political boundaries do not
necessarily conform to the cultural and economic boundaries of a country.
Nevertheless, the six regions do broadly represent real differences, as will be
seen below.

The Muslim community of Anatolia has been considered first, followed by the Armenian, Greek, and other communities. For each religious group the concern has been to arrive at accurate estimates of the total population, by province. After those population numbers have been analyzed and estimated for the period prior to World War I, the fate of the communities during and after the war has been considered, with the intent of finding how many died in the disaster.

# 2.
# Muslim Population

THE MUSLIMS of Anatolia were by no means a homogenous ethnic group. However, the Ottoman government refused officially to recognize ethnic differences among the Muslims of the Empire. To the Ottoman population registrars there were only Muslims, never Turks, Kurds, or Arabs. A researcher is forced to follow the Ottoman lead. There simply is no information on who was a Turk and who a Kurd and consequently demographic studies must speak of Muslims as if they were one unified group. The same difficulty arises with Christians. Arab Orthodox Christians, for example, were included with Greeks under the category Greek (i.e., Greek Orthodox), but for Anatolia this presents few problems, since Anatolian Greek Orthodox were also ethnically Greek.

One can theorize, based on evidence from the censuses of the Turkish Republic, that the Arab Muslims who lived in Anatolia were in the southeast, Kurds were in the east, Laz in the north, and the Caucasian minorities such as Circassians and Muslim Georgians in all parts of Anatolia. Except in southeastern Kurdish areas such as Siirt, Mardin, Van, or Hakkâri, Turks were the majority in the Muslim community.[1]

Perhaps because of the need of accurate records for conscription, Muslims were on the whole better registered than non-Muslims. Using Ottoman statistics, it is possible to create yearly estimates of the Muslim population of Anatolia in each province. In this chapter, Ottoman population statistics for each Anatolian province have been presented, corrected for underregistration, and compiled into tables that list estimates of the Muslim population for each year from 1878 to 1914.

## Western Anatolia

Western Anatolia included the provinces of Aydın (capital, İzmir) and Hüdavendigâr (capital, Bursa) and the independent sancaks of İzmit and Biga (also called Kale-i Sultaniye). Though Hüdavendigâr stretched into central Anatolia, these provinces were essentially coastal in orientation and, for Anatolia, fairly developed. The capitals of Aydın and Hüdavendigâr, İzmir and Bursa, were the largest cities in Anatolia; Bursa had over 70,000 and İzmir over 150,000 inhabitants. Izmir was, next to Istanbul, the leading port in the Empire.[2] Of the Anatolian provinces Hüdavendigâr was first in the number of teachers and students, Aydın second. Aydın had more physicians and hospital beds than any other province. Financially, Aydın and Hüdavendigâr were first in tax revenues to the central government. The western cropland was the best in Anatolia.[3]

Due to the relative modernization of these provinces, good sea and land communications, and effective control by the central government, population statistics from the western Anatolia region were numerous and relatively accurate. More so than for any other provinces, information from the long series of Hüdavendigâr and Aydın salnames can be used to illustrate both the population situation of Anatolia and the compilation practices of the Ottoman statistical offices.

### Hüdavendigâr Vilâyeti

The population information printed in the Hüdavendigâr salnames was unique. For all the other Ottoman provinces, the culling of population statements is a process of collecting, from various libraries and archives, all of that province's salnames and extracting the statistics from each. The 1325 (1907–8) Hüdavendigâr Vilâyeti salname, unique among salnames, presented a table of population totals from each preceding salname (table 2.1). This complete information illustrates the methods used by Ottoman provincial governments in compiling and publishing their population statistics.

In table 2.1 the Muslim populations have been listed as they appear in the 1325 salname. The figures for 1312, 1313, 1314, and 1315 indicate that population records were not updated each year. It is extremely unlikely that the Hüdavendigâr population would have risen by .0005 per year between

Table 2.1

Muslim Population of Hüdavendigār Vilāyeti

| Year | Population |
|------|-----------|
| 1287 | 817,076 |
| 1296 | 837,212 |
| 1306 | 1,038,761 |
| 1312 | 1,160,011 |
| 1313 | 1,166,115 |
| 1314 | 1,191,405 |
| 1315 | 1,200,012 |
| 1316 | 1,233,884 |
| 1317 | 1,269,683 |
| 1318 | 1,261,604 |
| 1319 | 1,267,385 |
| 1320 | 1,267,485 |
| 1321 | 1,279,478 |
| 1322 | 1,295,498 |
| 1323 | 1,359,612 |
| 1324 | 1,430,498 |
| 1325 | 1,430,198 |

SOURCE: 1325 salname.

1312 and 1313, by .0125 between 1313 and 1314, then by .0072 between 1314 and 1315, yet these rates are indicated if the populations given in the 1325 salname are correct. In fact, the population records from individual areas must have come into the central Nüfus Dairesi (Population Records Office) at various times; records for large numbers of villages may have been updated only every second, third, or fourth year.

The corrections for this problem and methods for manipulating the Hüdavendigâr population statistics will be considered in some detail here. The same methods will then be applied to all subsequent provincial populations. It would be needlessly repetitive to describe each step of the evaluative procedure for each province.

First, as described in appendix 2, the salname populations must be put in order and dated. We know from internal evidence[4] and from the examples of the dates of the Aydın salnames,[5] that the dates of the salnames did not necessarily reflect the time at which the information had been compiled. On the basis of the Aydın materials, it seems more likely that the statistics were printed three years after they were gathered. This is supported for Hüdavendigâr by the close proximity of the population given in the 1316 salname (redated 1313) and that of the 1313 İstatistik: 1,233,884 Muslims and 1,234,304 Muslims, respectively.

Population statements from the various "census" and archival sources must be integrated into the list of salname populations. This has been done in table 2.2, in which the "census" and archival populations are placed in their proper chronological place based on their relationship to the salname figures.

The great difference in magnitude between the populations, for example, of 1296 and 1306, and of 1324 and 1330, are due to changes in administrative boundaries. In 1306 the province of Karası (capital: Balıkesir) was broken into the sancaks of Karası and Biga. The former was made part of Hüdavendigâr province, while the latter became an independent sancak. Between 1324 and 1332, two-thirds of the province of Hüdavendigâr was detached from the main province and formed into four independent sancaks (Eskişehir, Kara Hisar-i Sahib, Karası, and Kütahya).

The populations in the final list must be corrected for undercounting in certain age groups and undercounting of women.[6] A correction factor of 1.1298 applied to recorded total (male plus female) population yields the corrected population.[7]

In table 2.2, the salname, "census," and archival populations of Hüdavendigâr have been used to create a series of populations, by hicra year, for 1295 (1878) to 1332 (1913–14). The most reliable population statements have been selected and placed in the list for their year. The rate of increase between each of these populations has then been calculated and applied to each intervening year, and a population estimate for each year recorded. For this process, knowledge of changes in administrative boundaries is es-

Table 2.2

Recorded Muslim Population of Hüdavendigâr Vilâyeti

| Source | Actual Year | Original Population | Corrected Population |
|---|---|---|---|
| 1306 Salname | 1303 | 1,038,761 | 1,173,592 |
| Census 1 | 1306 | 1,132,763 | 1,279,796 |
| 1311 Salname | 1308 | 1,155,580 | 1,305,574 |
| 1312 Salname | 1309 | 1,160,011 | 1,310,580 |
| 1314 Salname | 1311 | 1,191,405 | 1,346,049 |
| 1316 Salname | 1313 | 1,233,884 | 1,394,042 |
| 1313 İstatistik | 1313 | 1,234,304 | 1,394,517 |
| 1317 Salname | 1314 | 1,269,683 | 1,434,488 |
| 1321 Salname | 1318 | 1,279,478 | 1,445,554 |
| 1322 Salname | 1319 | 1,295,498 | 1,463,654 |
| 1323 Salname | 1320 | 1,359,612 | 1,535,090 |
| 1324 Salname | 1321 | 1,430,498 | 1,616,177 |
| Census 2 | 1321 | 1,430,498 | 1,616,177 |
| Census 3 | 1328 | 1,073,369 | 1,212,692 |
| 1330 Nüfus-i Umumî | 1330 | 474,114 | 535,654 |

sential.[8] The Hüdavendigâr salname of 1306, as listed in table 2.2, for example, represented the population as it was in 1303, but not the population of the area of the Hüdavendigâr Vilâyeti as it was in 1303. It rather represented the population in 1303 of the area that was taken up by the Hüdavendigâr Vilâyeti in 1306. The population of Karası Sancağı, which was only added to Hüdavendigâr late in 1306, must be subtracted in order to find the true population of Hüdavendigâr in 1303. Similar changes must be made for all boundary changes within the period 1878 to 1914. The final figures of the province's annual population have been modified to reflect the actual boundaries of the province in each year and have been listed in table 2.7.

The models used to evaluate the Hüdavendigâr population for underenumeration provide estimates of birth, death, and growth rates and life expectancy, as well as age structure. The model for Hüdavendigâr shows a growth rate of .017 per year. This growth arises from a birth rate of .049 and a death rate of .032. Hüdavendigâr's male life expectancy at birth was 32.5 years, one of the highest in Anatolia.[9] (Life expectancy at birth, $e_0^0$, is a deceptive statistic, since it is heavily affected by early childhood mortality. In Hüdavendigâr, if a child lived to age five, his expectancy of life was 49 years.)

## Aydın Vilâyeti

The population sources for the Aydın province must be collected one by one. No compendium such as the 1325 Hüdavendigâr salname exists for Aydın. However, Aydın salnames were published frequently, and their data was generally better than that of the Hüdavendigâr salnames. There are, for example, no repetitions of the same population in salnames of successive years, as occurred in the Hüdavendigâr yearbooks. The information in the Aydın salnames was more current. The Aydın salnames uniformly listed the year in which each population compilation took place, and this provides precise dating of the various statements of Aydın's population (table 2.3).[10]

The factor needed to correct the Aydın populations for undercounting of women and children, 1.2150, was higher than that of Hüdavendigâr (1.1298) (figure A4.6).[11]

The population model that most closely approximates the Aydın population has the following rates: birth, .049 per year; death, .035 per year; increase, .014 per year. The life expectancy at birth was 30 years, slightly lower than the 32.5 years expectancy of a child born in Hüdavendigâr.

The only major boundary change in Aydın Vilâyeti in the period came for the 1330 Nüfus-i Umumî population. Menteşe Sancağı was detached and made a separate independent sancak. This explains the drop in population in 1331 (table 2.3). Like other economically more advanced provinces, Aydın Vilâyeti was the target of in-migration of young males in search of work. This affects population totals somewhat and increases the proportion in the young adult ages of the population by a slight factor. As can be

Table 2.3

Recorded Muslim Populations of Aydın Vilâyeti

| Source | Actual Year | Original Population | Corrected Population |
|---|---|---|---|
| 1304 Salname | 1301 | 1,045,247 | 1,269,975 |
| Ist. U. Register | 1301 | 1,075,874 | 1,307,187 |
| 1305 Salname | 1302 | 1,091,129 | 1,325,722 |
| 1308 Salname | 1305 | 1,118,496 | 1,358,973 |
| Census 1 | 1305 | 1,119,323 | 1,359,977 |
| 1311 Salname | 1308 | 1,168,935 | 1,420,256 |
| 1312 Salname | 1309 | 1,175,637 | 1,462,588 |
| 1313 Salname | 1310 | 1,184,876 | 1,439,624 |
| 1315 Salname | 1312 | 1,202,175 | 1,460,643 |
| 1313 İstatistik | 1312 | 1,203,776 | 1,460,643 |
| 1316 Salname | 1313 | 1,221,946 | 1,484,644 |
| 1317 Salname | 1314 | 1,234,718 | 1,500,182 |
| 1320 Salname | 1317 | 1,270,355 | 1,543,481 |
| 1321 Salname | 1318 | 1,295,676 | 1,574,246 |
| Census 2 | 1320 | 1,313,011 | 1,595,308 |
| 1323 Salname | 1320 | 1,314,987 | 1,597,710 |
| 1326 Salname | 1323 | 1,313,561 | 1,595,777 |
| 1330 Nüfus-i Umumî | 1331 | 1,249,067 | 1,517,616 |

seen in table 2.4, the proportion of males in Aydın Vilâyeti would change somewhat if Ottoman citizens native to another area (*yabancılar*) were excluded from the totals. The difference is small, however, and few provinces published data on what numbers of their populations were yabancılar, so this differential migration has not been included in calculations of the population of Aydın or other provinces.

Table 2.4

Male and Female Proportions of the Total and Native Populations
of Aydın Vilâyeti Muslims

|  | Total | | Native* | |
|---|---|---|---|---|
| Males | 655,312 | (.5059) | 638,095 | (.5013) |
| Females | 639,954 | (.4941) | 634,791 | (.4987) |
| Total | 1,295,266 | | 1,272,886 | |

*I.e., not including yabancılar.

## İzmit Sancağı

There are fewer population sources for the İzmit independent sancak than
for any other area of Anatolia. İzmit issued no salnames and its population
appears only in the four "censuses" shown in table 2.5.

In the case of İzmit, the census populations have been dated by two pro-
cesses: First, by general comparison to the dates of the censuses for other
provinces, especially the contiguous provinces of Hüdavendigâr and Kasta-

Table 2.5

Recorded Muslim Population of İzmit Sancağı

| Source | Year | Original Population | Corrected Population |
|---|---|---|---|
| Census 1 | 1306 | 133,117 | 162,762 |
| 1313 İstatistik | 1313 | 155,565 | 190,209 |
| Census 2 | 1325 | 200,600 | 245,264 |
| 1330 Nüfus-i Umumî | 1331 | 226,859 | 277,380 |

monu. Second, by analysis of the rates of increase between the census years, assuming that they are relatively equal. This is necessitated by the lack of salname population materials which could be used to date the census data for İzmit. The process is not quite as precise as the use of salnames for dating purposes, but is relatively accurate, since the salnames have been used to date the censuses in the provinces to which İzmit is compared. The population as shown in the censuses have been corrected by a factor of 1.2227.[12] Mortality, fertility, and life expectancy were the same as in Hüdavendigar (.049, .032, and 32.5 years, respectively).

### Biga Sancağı

Unlike İzmit, the Biga independent sancak figured in one provincial salname, the *1305 Karası Vilâyeti Salnamesi*. Biga was one of two sancaks of the Karası Vilâyeti until Karası was split[13] in 1306 (1888–9). The presence of this dated salname population, assumed to be for a period three years earlier,[14] allows easier dating of the census populations. The actual years of these populations are given in table 2.6.

The undercounting of females in Biga (.518 males in the *1313 İstatistik*) probably was the result of migration, as well as the usual underenumeration.

Table 2.6

Recorded Muslim Population of Biga Sancağı

| Source | Actual Year | Original Population | Corrected Population |
|---|---|---|---|
| Ist. U. Register | 1301 | 98,998 | 110,502 |
| Census 1 | 1301 | 99,468 | 111,026 |
| 1305 Karası Salname | 1302 | 100,748 | 112,455 |
| 1313 İstatistik | 1313 | 121,327 | 135,425 |
| Census 2 | 1324 | 138,892 | 155,031 |
| 1330 Nüfus-i Umumî | 1331 | 149,903 | 167,322 |

Males from Hüdavendigâr Province very probably found work in the military and maritime area of the Straits.[15]

The Biga population was an anomaly in Anatolia. According to the population records of Biga in the *1313 İstatistik*, the province seems to have experienced lower overall fertility than the other Anatolian provinces. The Gross Reproduction Rate of Biga seems to have been closer to 2.5 than to the 3.0 of Hüdavendigâr, Aydın, or İzmit (i.e., an average of one less child born in the complete reproductive life of a woman who lived past age 45; five in Biga as opposed to six in İzmit or Aydın). Given the proximity of Biga to the European provinces of the Ottoman Empire and Biga's natural and economic ties to those provinces, it is possible that Biga did not follow the prevailing Anatolian fertility pattern. It must be admitted that such an analysis is tentative and based on limited data.[16] The correction factor is 1.1162.

The Biga population had a life expectancy of 30 years at birth. The birth rate was approximately .042 a year, the death rate .037, and the growth rate .005.

Biga was changed in 1306 from a dependent to an independent sancak, but the Biga boundaries remained unchanged during the 1878–1914 period.

Table 2.7, and the corresponding tables for each other region, are intended as a guide and approximation of the Muslim population of the province as it changed year by year. The table of course does not reflect small demographic changes that are not recorded in the sources. The Ottoman method of compiling registration records only every three or four years (or, in eastern provinces, less often) undoubtedly smoothed out many small variations in fertility and mortality over the period. This qualification is especially true of provinces which did not compile and print their populations very often. All boundary changes are reflected in the table.

## Northern Anatolia

The two provinces of northern Anatolia, Kastamonu and Trabzon, were similar in that they both bordered on the Black Sea. In many other respects, they differed. Trabzon Vilâyeti stretched in a long band from the Ottoman-Russian border to the east-west midpoint of Anatolia. It was bordered closely on the south by mountain chains—the Rize, Gümüşhane, Giresun, and Canik Mountains—and its population centers, commerce, and agriculture

Table 2.7

Muslim Population of the Western Anatolian Provinces, 1878 to 1914

| Year | | Aydın | Hüdavendigâr | İzmit | Biga |
|------|------|-------|--------------|-------|------|
| 1295 | (1878) | 1,243,028 | 833,304 | 127,409 | 99,848 |
| 1296 | (1878-79) | 1,254,518 | 845,308 | 130,278 | 101,550 |
| 1297 | (1879-80) | 1,266,114 | 857,485 | 133,210 | 103,280 |
| 1298 | (1880-81) | 1,277,817 | 869,837 | 135,209 | 105,540 |
| 1299 | (1881-82) | 1,289,629 | 882,367 | 139,276 | 106,830 |
| 1300 | (1882-83) | 1,301,549 | 895,078 | 142,411 | 108,651 |
| 1301 | (1883-84) | 1,313,580 | 907,972 | 145,617 | 110,502 |
| 1302 | (1884-85) | 1,325,722 | 921,051 | 148,895 | 112,455 |
| 1303 | (1885-86) | 1,336,714 | 934,319 | 152,247 | 114,371 |
| 1304 | (1886-87) | 1,347,798 | 951,670 | 155,674 | 116,320 |
| 1305 | (1887-88) | 1,358,973 | 969,343 | 159,179 | 118,302 |
| 1306 | (1888-89) | 1,379,101 | 1,240,196 | 162,762 | 120,318 |
| 1307 | (1889-90) | 1,399,527 | 1,263,227 | 166,426 | 122,369 |
| 1308 | (1890-91) | 1,420,256 | 1,286,686 | 170,173 | 124,454 |
| 1309 | (1891-92) | 1,428,399 | 1,310,580 | 174,003 | 126,574 |
| 1310 | (1892-93) | 1,439,624 | 1,328,916 | 177,921 | 128,731 |
| 1311 | (1893-94) | 1,450,095 | 1,346,049 | 181,926 | 130,925 |
| 1312 | (1894-95) | 1,460,643 | 1,370,069 | 186,021 | 133,156 |
| 1313 | (1895-96) | 1,484,644 | 1,394,517 | 190,209 | 135,425 |
| 1314 | (1896-97) | 1,500,182 | 1,420,470 | 194,282 | 137,100 |
| 1315 | (1897-98) | 1,514,478 | 1,446,905 | 198,442 | 138,795 |
| 1316 | (1898-99) | 1,528,911 | 1,473,833 | 202,692 | 140,512 |
| 1317 | (1899-1900) | 1,543,481 | 1,501,262 | 207,032 | 142,250 |
| 1318 | (1900-01) | 1,574,246 | 1,529,201 | 211,466 | 144,009 |
| 1319 | (1901-02) | 1,585,935 | 1,557,660 | 215,994 | 145,790 |
| 1320 | (1902-03) | 1,597,710 | 1,586,649 | 220,619 | 147,593 |
| 1321 | (1903-04) | 1,610,859 | 1,616,177 | 225,343 | 149,418 |
| 1322 | (1904-05) | 1,624,116 | 1,627,380 | 230,169 | 151,266 |
| 1323 | (1905-06) | 1,637,483 | 1,638,641 | 235,098 | 153,137 |
| 1324 | (1906-07) | 1,650,959 | 1,649,990 | 240,132 | 155,031 |
| 1325 | (1907-08) | 1,664,547 | 1,661,417 | 245,274 | 156,429 |
| 1326 | (1908-09) | 1,678,246 | 1,672,924 | 250,355 | 157,840 |
| 1327 | (1909-10) | 1,692,058 | 1,684,510 | 255,540 | 159,264 |
| 1328 | (1910-11) | 1,705,983 | 1,304,021 | 260,833 | 160,701 |
| 1329 | (1911) | 1,720,023 | 1,313,052 | 266,236 | 162,150 |
| 1330 | (1911-12) | 1,734,179 | 535,654 | 271,751 | 163,613 |
| 1331 | (1912-13) | 1,517,616 | 539,364 | 277,380 | 165,089 |
| 1332 | (1913-14) | 1,530,106 | 543,099 | 283,126 | 166,578 |

were on the coast. Kastamonu stretched much farther inland and was not tied to the sea in the same way as Trabzon. Much of its area was geographically, agriculturally, and climatically closer to Sivas and northern Ankara than to Trabzon, and, like the central Anatolian provinces, it was a cereal-growing region. Trabzon's agriculture was unlike any other in the region, mild climate and high precipitation allowing crops such as tea, citrus fruits, and tobacco.[17] The population of Kastamonu was two-thirds that of Trabzon, yet Trabzon's income to the Ottoman state was three times greater.[18] Trabzon was by far the more developed province.

## Kastamonu Vilâyeti

The populations given in the salnames (table 2.8) of Kastamonu are consistent, useful demographic sources. At first glance they do not appear to be so. The salname population figures appear to state that the population rose and fell capriciously. The figures are actually affected, though, by changes

Table 2.8

Recorded Population of Kastamonu Vilâyeti

| Source | Actual Year | Original Population | Corrected Population |
|---|---|---|---|
| 1294 Salname | 1291 | 802,312 | 937,261 |
| Ist. U. Register | 1295 | 845,940 | 988,227 |
| Ist. U. Register | 1296 | 851,468 | 994,645 |
| 1306 Salname | 1303 | 919,703 | 1,086,721 |
| Census 1 | 1306 | 929,300 | 1,098,061 |
| 1311 Salname | 1309 | 958,146 | 1,132,145 |
| 1312 Salname | 1310 | 925,244 | 1,093,268 |
| 1314 Salname | 1311 | 922,180 | 1,089,648 |
| 1313 İstatistik | 1308 | 945,192 | 1,116,839 |
| 1317 Salname | 1314 | 959,670 | 1,133,946 |
| 1321 Salname | 1319 | 1,001,723 | 1,183,636 |
| Census 2 | 1326 | 1,072,240 | 1,266,959 |
| Census 3 | 1328 | 696,466 | 822,944 |
| 1330 Nüfus-i Umumî | 1332 | 737,302 | 871,196 |

in the Kastamonu administrative boundaries. In 1309 (1891–2) Kalecik Kazası went from Kastamonu to Ankara Province, followed by İskilip Kazası in 1313 (1895–6). In 1328 the sancak of Bolu became independent. These changes further illustrate the difficulty of finding yearly populations, such as are presented in table 2.10 for Kastamonu, for the Ottoman provinces. First the years for the salnames and other sources must be ascertained, then the populations corrected and placed in their proper place in the yearly population table. These populations are, however, not always the actual populations of the province for those years; the geographic area they cover may not be the same as the area of the province in that year. For example, the Kastamonu 1312 salname records the population of the area of Kastamonu in 1312 as it was in 1310, but in 1310 the Kastamonu Vilâyeti was larger than in 1312; thus an adjustment must be made. This adjustment projection of the vilâyet population and the population of the area lost or gained must be made before the year-by-year populations are correct.

The correction factor for Kastamonu is 1.1816.

The growth rate for Kastamonu was .014 (birth rate, .049; death rate, .035). This is very close to the observed rate of increase in the sources (e.g., the 1328 to 1332 rate of increase is .014), and there was probably little or balanced migration in Kastamonu. Expectation of life at birth was 30 years.

### Trabzon Vilâyeti

The Trabzon province population appears to have been the healthiest and best recorded in Anatolia. Its inhabitants enjoyed the highest life expectancy in Anatolia, 35 years at birth.[19] The exact reason for the greater health of the populace may have derived from economic factors, climate, or a level of medical sophistication greater than that of the rest of Anatolia. Of these three, climate and economy seem the most likely. The climate of Trabzon was milder and less subject to extremes of heat and cold than other parts of Anatolia. In a country in which rainfall is slight, the Trabzon Vilâyeti had the highest rate of precipitation. Agriculture and horticulture were considerably different in Trabzon, with meadows, pastures, and orchards taking significantly more acreage than in other parts of Anatolia.[20] What is known of the standards of health care in Trabzon, though, does not indicate that Trabzon was particularly well-equipped with doctors or hospitals,[21] so any

Table 2.9


Recorded Population of Trabzon Vilâyeti


| Source | Actual Year | Original Population | Corrected Population |
|---|---|---|---|
| 1296 Salname | 1293 | 729,596 | 730,107 |
| Ist. U. Register | 1294 | 731,638 | 732,150 |
| 1305 Salname | 1304 | 798,623 | 817,950 |
| Census 1 | 1308 | 857,280 | 878,026 |
| 1311 Salname | 1309 | 869,727 | 890,774 |
| 1313 İstatistik | 1313 | 933,718 | 956,314 |
| 1318 Salname | 1317 | 963,157 | 986,465 |
| 1319 Salname | 1318 | 972,981 | 996,527 |
| 1320 Salname | 1319 | 990,267 | 1,014,231 |
| 1321 Salname | 1320 | 1,006,192 | 1,030,542 |
| Census 2 | 1325 | 1,071,988 | 1,097,930 |
| Census 3 | 1328 | 865,695 | 886,645 |
| 1330 Nüfus-i Umumî | 1332 | 921,128 | 943,419 |

differential in medicine must have been on the folk medicine level. It is true that a relative abundance of free-flowing water may have aided sanitation. Whatever the exact reason, Trabzon was healthy.

No other province recorded its population so well. The dates of the populations given in the Trabzon salnames (table 2.9) are seldom more than one year behind their publication dates. Unlike many other sets of provincial salnames, the populations in the Trabzon salnames were updated for each publication year.

The accuracy and consistency of the Trabzon population figures makes the analysis and correction of the Trabzon population comparatively easy. The recorded populations need only very minor adjustment (recorded population × 1.0242 = corrected population.) Much of this correction comes from the undercounting of women.[22] Males in Trabzon were recorded as a greater percentage (.508) than might be expected in a province with accurate registration. Some of the excess of male numbers may have come from refugees from Trabzon's contiguous areas that were lost to the Russians in 1878.

The administrative boundaries of Trabzon Vilâyeti changed only slightly from 1295 (1878) to 1327 (1909–10). Kelkit and Şiran kazas (districts) were passed to Trabzon in 1306 (1888–89). After 1327 a major division took place. Canik Sancağı (capital: Samsun) was detached and formed into an independent sancak. The figures in table 2.10 take these changes into account.

The model indicates that life expectancy in Trabzon was 35 years at birth—the highest life expectancy in Anatolia. Mortality was .029 per year and fertility .048 per year.


## Central Anatolia


In Ottoman Anatolia, the provinces that can be styled as most developed were all on the northern and western coasts. The sea provided moisture for agriculture and the best available lines of communication. Benefiting from this, the mortality situation of the inhabitants of the north and west coasts was relatively good. Provinces such as those of central Anatolia, which were not on the sea, were often less developed, both economically and demographically. Except for a small and extremely fertile area on the Mediterranean coast of Konya Vilâyeti, the entire area of Ottoman central Anatolia was made up of mountains or high plain. The region was subject to extremes of heat and cold, with temperatures reaching a maximum of 40° C. (104° F.) in summer and −25° C. in winter.[23] Precipitation averaged about 350 mm (14 inches) per year, well below the national average for a relatively dry land.[24] In Ottoman times, farming centered almost exclusively on cereals.[25]

In terms of demographic statistics, the central Anatolian provinces fell between those of the north and west, on one hand, and the east on the other. They shared the same general fertility and mortality as the eastern provinces, but their records were better kept and their data more reliable. Since data from the central region is fairly reliable, it can be used to make accurate comparisons with better-developed provinces when, due to faulty

Table 2.10


Muslim Population of the Northern Anatolian Provinces, 1878 to 1914


| Year | | Kastamonu | Trabzon |
|------|------|-----------|---------|
| 1295 | (1878) | 988,227 | 740,308 |
| 1296 | (1878-79) | 994,645 | 748,558 |
| 1297 | (1879-80) | 1,007,305 | 756,889 |
| 1298 | (1880-81) | 1,020,126 | 765,334 |
| 1299 | (1881-82) | 1,033,110 | 773,862 |
| 1300 | (1882-83) | 1,046,260 | 782,485 |
| 1301 | (1883-84) | 1,059,577 | 791,205 |
| 1302 | (1884-85) | 1,073,063 | 800,021 |
| 1303 | (1885-86) | 1,086,721 | 808,936 |
| 1304 | (1886-87) | 1,103,924 | 817,950 |
| 1305 | (1887-88) | 1,121,400 | 823,622 |
| 1306 | (1888-89) | 1,139,152 | 872,498 |
| 1307 | (1889-90) | 1,150,819 | 878,548 |
| 1308 | (1890-91) | 1,162,605 | 884,640 |
| 1309 | (1891-92) | 1,132,145 | 890,774 |
| 1310 | (1892-93) | 1,093,268 | 906,725 |
| 1311 | (1893-94) | 1,089,648 | 922,962 |
| 1312 | (1894-95) | 1,099,990 | 939,940 |
| 1313 | (1895-96) | 1,116,839 | 956,314 |
| 1314 | (1896-97) | 1,133,946 | 937,399 |
| 1315 | (1897-98) | 1,143,714 | 953,477 |
| 1316 | (1898-99) | 1,153,567 | 969,831 |
| 1317 | (1899-1900) | 1,163,504 | 986,465 |
| 1318 | (1900-01) | 1,173,527 | 996,527 |
| 1319 | (1901-02) | 1,183,636 | 1,014,231 |
| 1320 | (1902-03) | 1,195,195 | 1,030,542 |
| 1321 | (1903-04) | 1,206,867 | 1,043,680 |
| 1322 | (1904-05) | 1,218,653 | 1,056,986 |
| 1323 | (1905-06) | 1,230,554 | 1,070,462 |
| 1324 | (1906-07) | 1,242,571 | 1,084,109 |
| 1325 | (1907-08) | 1,254,706 | 1,097,930 |
| 1326 | (1908-09) | 1,266,959 | 1,112,635 |
| 1327 | (1909-10) | 1,279,332 | 1,127,537 |
| 1328 | (1910-11) | 822,994 | 886,645 |
| 1329 | (1911) | 834,750 | 900,510 |
| 1330 | (1911-12) | 846,726 | 914,592 |
| 1331 | (1912-13) | 858,874 | 928,893 |
| 1332 | (1913-14) | 871,196 | 943,419 |

data, statistics from the eastern provinces would not be reliable. Such comparisons show a better standard of mortality, i.e., a longer life span, for the people in the western provinces than those in the central region. This, of course, is what one would expect, since all indicators of physical development show that the Ottoman western provinces were better developed than those in central and eastern Anatolia. The population data for Sivas, Ankara, and Konya demonstrate that the variance in economic status in the Anatolian provinces was accompanied by a variance in mortality, as well.

## Sivas Vilâyeti

From 1308 (1890–91) to 1321 (1904–04) no salnames were issued by the Sivas Vilâyeti. This makes the task of dating Ottoman population figures fairly difficult. There is, nevertheless, a coherent picture of population and population change in the Sivas sources. The magnitude of the population change is hidden, however, by changes in administrative boundaries. In 1313, Osmancık kazası was given to Ankara, as was Mecidözü in 1330. Bunyan-i Hamid Kazası was also detached from Sivas in 1331 and given to Kayseri independent sancak.

Table 2.11

Recorded Population of Sivas Vilâyeti Muslims

| Source | Actual Year | Original Population | Corrected Population |
|---|---|---|---|
| 1293 Salname | 1290 | 711,286 | 821,678 |
| Ist. U. Register | 1290 | 711,574 | 822,010 |
| Archival Docmt. 8 | 1299 | 735,448 | 870,476 |
| Archival Docmt. 2 | 1299 | 735,489 | 870,575 |
| Archival Docmt. 1 | 1299 | 737,074 | 872,401 |
| Census 1 | 1304 | 766,558 | 907,298 |
| 1313 İstatistik | 1310 | 807,651 | 955,936 |
| Archival Docmt. 2 | 1308 | 809,704 | 958,366 |
| 1321 Salname | 1317 | 853,425 | 1,010,114 |
| Census 2 | 1324 | 972,788 | 1,151,392 |
| 1325 Salname | 1322 | 968,786 | 1,146,655 |
| Census 3 | 1327 | 975,888 | 1,155,061 |
| 1330 Nüfus-i Umumî | 1330 | 939,735 | 1,112,270 |

One population source, the 1325 Sivas salname, gives a population that does not fit into the list. The date of population registration as given in the volume, 1322 (1904–05), makes a population that large an impossibility (e.g., the yearly increase between the populations of the 1321 and 1325 salnames would be .030, almost three times the expected figure). The 1325 salname figure thus has been excluded as a bureaucratic or printing error.

The population of Sivas experienced a yearly birth rate of approximately .050, a yearly death rate of .039, and a yearly rate of growth of .011. Life expectancy at birth was 27 years.

## Ankara Vilâyeti

Table 2.12 gives the original and corrected populations of the salnames, "censuses," and archival population sources for Ankara Vilâyeti. Analysis of the figures is slightly complicated by changes in the administrative bounda-

Table 2.12

Recorded Muslim Population of Ankara Vilâyeti

| Source | Actual Year | Original Population | Corrected Population |
|---|---|---|---|
| Ist. U. Register | 1296 | 660,616 | 767,305 |
| Archival Docmt. 2 | 1300 | 689,635 | 812,942 |
| 1308 Salname | 1304 | 723,247 | 852,564 |
| 1311 Salname | 1307 | 735,736 | 867,286 |
| Census 1 | 1308 | 749,046 | 882,975 |
| 1313 İstatistik | 1313 | 895,196 | 1,055,257 |
| 1318 Salname | 1314 | 896,672 | 1,056,997 |
| 1325 Salname | 1322 | 1,003,927 | 1,183,429 |
| Census 2 | 1323 | 1,011,556 | 1,192,422 |
| Census 3 | 1324 | 1,014,557 | 1,195,960 |
| 1330 Nüfus-i Umumî | 1331 | 877,285 | 1,034,144 |

Table 2.13

Recorded Muslim Population of Konya Vilâyeti

| Source | Actual Year | Original Population | Corrected Population |
|---|---|---|---|
| 1299 Salname | 1296 | 788,540 | 996,005 |
| Ist. U. Register | 1301 | 822,406 | 1,038,781 |
| Ist. U. Register | 1303 | 835,396 | 1,055,189 |
| 1310 Salname | 1303 | 829,946 | 1,054,778 |
| 1312 Salname | 1303 | 829,946 | 1,054,778 |
| Census 1 | 1307 | 877,232 | 1,114,874 |
| 1313 İstatistik | 1312 | 942,932 | 1,198,372 |
| 1317 Salname | 1314 | 967,606 | 1,257,174 |
| Census 2 | 1322 | 1,137,238 | 1,445,316 |
| Census 3 | 1323 | 1,145,713 | 1,456,087 |
| 1330 Nüfus-i Umumî | 1330 | 750,712 | 954,080 |

ries of Ankara Vilâyeti. In 1313 (1895–96), İskilip and Osmancık kazas were added to Ankara. Mecidözü was added in 1330 and Kayseri, Develi, and İncesu kazas taken away in 1331.

The population of Ankara experienced a birth rate of .050 per year, death rate of .039 per year, and a growth rate of .011 per year. Life expectancy at birth was 27 years.


## Konya Vilâyeti

As is indicated in table 2.13, population registers for Konya Vilâyeti were regularly updated. The province boundaries remained constant from the beginning of the period until 1331, except for the addition of the Ermenak Kazası in 1324.[26] The addition of Ermenak does require a certain amount of mathematical manipulation, but major changes in boundaries came only in 1331, when the sancaks of Antalya and Niğde were detached to create two independent sancaks. The effects of all boundary changes have been calculated into the figures in table 1.13.

The population of Konya had a birth rate of .049, a death rate of .035, and a growth rate of .014. Life expectancy was 30 years at birth.

## Southern Anatolia

Adana and Haleb (Aleppo), the two provinces included in the southern Anatolia region, were coastal provinces. The ports of Mersin and İskenderun, as well as numerous lesser ports, were gateways to southeastern Anatolia, and, before the cross-Anatolian railroad to Diyarbakır was constructed, sea transit and transshipment at a southern Anatolian port was the most practical way to reach the southeast. In fact, all along the southern coast, the road network was a feeder system from the interior to the southern ports. (If it were not for the necessity of dividing this study by Ottoman provincial boundaries, the southern section of Konya Vilâyeti would be better placed as a part of the southern region. The port of Antalya and the Antalya Sancağı of Konya Vilâyeti fit better economically with the coastal regions of Adana and Haleb.) Because of their coastal nature, Adana and Haleb might be expected to have shared the demographic characteristics of the coastal provinces of western Anatolia. This was not the case. Away from the coast, both Adana and Haleb stretched far inland, and the inhabitants and environment of the inland areas differed greatly from those of the coast. The mortality levels of the inland areas dominated the demographic picture of the southern provinces.

Northern Adana province touched all three vilâyets of central Anatolia. The fertile, well-irrigated (and malarial) areas of the Çukurova gave way on the north, northeast, and west to high mountains, dividing the province of Adana into two extremely different agriculture zones. Ethnically and linguistically, the Muslims of Adana Vilâyeti were Turks.

Due to its odd geographic configuration, Haleb Vilâyeti contained coast, mountains, and both high and low desert. Muslims in Haleb were Turks in the north of the province, mixed Turks and Arabs in the center (southern Maraş and Urfa sancaks and northern Haleb sancak), and Arabs, including large numbers of Beduin, in the south.

The sanitary and economic conditions that affect population size, mortality, and fertility were very mixed in Adana and Haleb. Generalized statements of demographic conditions by province should thus be understood,

Table 2.14

Muslim Population of the Central Anatolian Provinces, 1878 to 1914

| Year | | Sivas | Ankara | Konya |
|------|------|-------|--------|-------|
| 1295 | (1878) | 851,058 | 756,302 | 987,826 |
| 1296 | (1878-79) | 857,534 | 767,305 | 996,005 |
| 1297 | (1879-80) | 863,602 | 778,468 | 1,004,252 |
| 1298 | (1880-81) | 869,713 | 789,794 | 1,012,568 |
| 1299 | (1881-82) | 875,867 | 801,284 | 1,020,952 |
| 1300 | (1882-83) | 882,065 | 812,942 | 1,029,406 |
| 1301 | (1883-84) | 888,307 | 822,744 | 1,037,929 |
| 1302 | (1884-85) | 894,593 | 832,664 | 1,046,524 |
| 1303 | (1885-86) | 900,923 | 842,703 | 1,055,189 |
| 1304 | (1886-87) | 907,298 | 852,864 | 1,069,804 |
| 1305 | (1887-88) | 919,797 | 857,644 | 1,084,621 |
| 1306 | (1888-89) | 932,468 | 862,452 | 1,099,643 |
| 1307 | (1889-90) | 945,313 | 867,286 | 1,114,874 |
| 1308 | (1890-91) | 958,366 | 882,975 | 1,131,095 |
| 1309 | (1891-92) | 966,713 | 901,521 | 1,147,551 |
| 1310 | (1892-93) | 976,271 | 920,457 | 1,164,247 |
| 1311 | (1893-94) | 983,994 | 939,791 | 1,181,187 |
| 1312 | (1894-95) | 991,778 | 959,531 | 1,198,372 |
| 1313 | (1895-96) | 978,803 | 1,055,257 | 1,213,949 |
| 1314 | (1896-97) | 986,545 | 1,056,977 | 1,229,729 |
| 1315 | (1897-98) | 994,350 | 1,072,031 | 1,251,060 |
| 1316 | (1898-99) | 1,002,216 | 1,087,279 | 1,272,761 |
| 1317 | (1899-1900) | 1,010,144 | 1,102,743 | 1,294,838 |
| 1318 | (1900-01) | 1,023,777 | 1,118,428 | 1,317,298 |
| 1319 | (1901-02) | 1,037,594 | 1,134,336 | 1,340,148 |
| 1320 | (1902-03) | 1,051,598 | 1,150,469 | 1,363,394 |
| 1321 | (1903-04) | 1,065,791 | 1,166,833 | 1,387,043 |
| 1322 | (1904-05) | 1,080,175 | 1,183,429 | 1,411,103 |
| 1323 | (1905-06) | 1,094,753 | 1,192,422 | 1,426,876 |
| 1324 | (1906-07) | 1,109,528 | 1,195,960 | 1,442,824 |
| 1325 | (1907-08) | 1,124,503 | 1,207,347 | 1,458,951 |
| 1326 | (1908-09) | 1,139,680 | 1,218,842 | 1,475,258 |
| 1327 | (1909-10) | 1,155,061 | 1,230,447 | 1,491,748 |
| 1328 | (1910-11) | 1,168,647 | 1,242,162 | 1,508,422 |
| 1329 | (1911) | 1,182,393 | 1,252,989 | 1,525,282 |
| 1330 | (1911-12) | 1,196,300 | 1,265,929 | 1,542,331 |
| 1331 | (1912-13) | 1,210,371 | 1,034,144 | 964,744 |
| 1332 | (1913-14) | 1,138,995 | 1,043,990 | 975,525 |

especially for Haleb, to have allowed a great deal of variation among areas within the provinces.

## Adana Vilâyeti

The population sources (table 2.15) for Adana were based on a registration system that, as in many other provinces, was completely updated only

Table 2.15

Recorded Muslim Population of Adana Vilâyeti

| Source | Actual Year | Original Population | Corrected Population |
|---|---|---|---|
| Ist. U. Register | * | 163,080 | 191,913 |
| Ist. U. Register | 1292 | 293,208 | 374,866 |
| Archival Docmt. 1 | 1305 | 336,914 | 435,057 |
| Census 1 | 1306 | 341,376 | 440,819 |
| 1313 İstatistik | 1310 | 355,912 | 459,589 |
| 1312 Salname | 1308 | 348,824 | 450,436 |
| 1316 Salname | 1314 | 378,446 | 488,713 |
| Census 3 | 1328 | 435,169 | 561,934 |
| Census 2 | 1328 | 435,825 | 562,881 |
| 1330 Nüfus-i Umumî | 1330 | 341,903 | 441,499 |

* Before 1878.

every few years. This is demonstrated by the appearance of the same population figures in the 1316 and 1318 salnames. Because of the system, population figures in salnames may have been recorded from two to four years before their publication date, as shown in table 2.15. The population totals in the sources are consistent, indicating that the underregistration was fairly constant.

The population of Adana had a life expectancy at birth of 27 years. Its birth rate was .050, death rate .038, and growth rate .012.

## Haleb Vilâyeti

The major problem in evaluating population figures for Muslims in Haleb Vilâyeti concerns nomads. Haleb salnames occasionally mentioned that many *aşair* (nomads) were not counted, but gave no estimates.[27] Most of the nomads in the provinces would have been in the southern, non-Anatolian portion of Haleb. In any case the consistency of the Haleb population sources (table 2.16) demonstrates that whatever nomads were uncounted remained uncounted from beginning to end of the period.

The Haleb population sources are remarkably consistent. The Haleb Vi-

Table 2.16

Recorded Muslim Population of Haleb Vilâyeti

| Source | Actual Year | Original Population | Corrected Population |
|---|---|---|---|
| Archival Docmt. 2 | 1294 | 663,416 | 777,656 |
| Archival Docmt. 8 | 1294 | 663,416 | 777,656 |
| Archival Docmt. 1 | 1294 | 663,416 | 777,656 |
| 1299 Salname | 1295 | 675,822 | 787,062 |
| 1305 Salname | 1303 | 659,875 | 773,505 |
| 1307 Salname | 1303 | 664,677 | 779,134 |
| 1309 Salname | 1305 | 660,651 | 774,415 |
| 1310 Salname | 1306 | 658,330 | 771,694 |
| Census 1 | 1309 | 684,599 | 802,487 |
| 1313 Salname | 1309 | 697,044 | 817,075 |
| 1315 Salname | 1311 | 698,494 | 818,745 |
| 1313 İstatistik | 1313 | 718,895 | 842,689 |
| 1317 Salname | 1313 | 712,585 | 835,292 |
| 1318 Salname | 1314 | 734,581 | 861,076 |
| 1319 Salname | 1315 | 742,760 | 870,663 |
| Census 2 | 1315 | 750,212 | 879,396 |
| 1322 Salname | 1318 | 764,429 | 896,064 |
| 1323 Salname | 1318 | 764,429 | 896,064 |
| 1324 Salname | 1320 | 771,400 | 904,235 |
| 1330 Nüfus-i Umumî | 1331 | 576,320 | 675,562 |

lâyeti administration published many salnames and in only one instance did it not update the population for a new year, i.e., between the 1322 and 1323 salnames. In some cases, such as the 1313–1315 salnames, the Haleb administration obviously did not completely update the registration lists, but, in general, the series of Haleb population sources was one of the best in Anatolia.

The major difficulty in evaluating the Haleb population comes from changes in provincial borders. In 1302 (1884–5), Zor Sancağı was dropped from Haleb and made an independent sancak. Meskeni Sancağı was taken from Haleb in 1306 (1889–9) and Rakah added. In 1328 Urfa Sancağı was detached and made independent and Viran Şehir Kazası was given to Diyarbakır. Finally, Maraş Sancağı was made independent in 1331. These boundary changes make analysis of the yearly Haleb population difficult, especially since districts such as Zor were areas of very poor statistics. Nevertheless, the administrative boundary changes have been included in the compilation of the figures in table 2.17.

The Haleb life expectancy (37 years) and the rates (birth, .050; death, .038; growth, .012) were the same as those in Adana.

## Eastern Anatolia

Ottoman population statistics, and thus this study as well, did not differentiate between different types of Muslims. Ottoman statistics reflected the theocratic nature of the state, and all population was listed not by ethnic or linguistic group, but by religious community. For Muslims of the eastern provinces, this religious criterion disguised the basic ethnic and linguistic split between Turks and Kurds.

Ottoman population records of the type used here never mentioned the words Turk or Kurd. Separate Kurdish data appeared only when Ottoman officials estimated the size of tribal groups in official reports, but these reports were too incomplete and fragmentary to be the basis of serious population study. Thus, by default, the researcher must follow the Ottomans and study Muslims as a group, ignoring linguistic differences.

The five provinces in eastern Anatolia—Erzurum, Mamuretülaziz, Diyarbakır, and Van—were the least statistically developed provinces of Ottoman Anatolia. Their data is often inexact and needs to be carefully ana-

Table 2.17


Muslim Population of the Southern Anatolian Provinces, 1878 to 1914

| Year | | Adana | Haleb |
|------|------|-------|-------|
| 1295 | (1878-80) | 387,972 | 787,062 |
| 1296 | (1878-79) | 392,441 | 792,202 |
| 1297 | (1879-80) | 396,962 | 797,376 |
| 1298 | (1880-81) | 401,535 | 802,583 |
| 1299 | (1881-82) | 406,161 | 807,824 |
| 1300 | (1882-83) | 410,840 | 813,100 |
| 1301 | (1883-84) | 415,573 | 818,410 |
| 1302 | (1884-85) | 420,361 | 823,755 |
| 1303 | (1885-86) | 425,204 | 779,134 |
| 1304 | (1886-87) | 430,102 | 784,222 |
| 1305 | (1887-88) | 435,057 | 789,344 |
| 1306 | (1888-89) | 440,157 | 771,694 |
| 1307 | (1889-90) | 445,316 | 782,797 |
| 1308 | (1890-91) | 450,536 | 794,060 |
| 1309 | (1891-92) | 455,040 | 805,485 |
| 1310 | (1892-93) | 459,589 | 817,075 |
| 1311 | (1893-94) | 466,703 | 825,525 |
| 1312 | (1894-95) | 473,927 | 834,063 |
| 1313 | (1895-96) | 481,263 | 842,689 |
| 1314 | (1896-97) | 488,713 | 851,218 |
| 1315 | (1897-98) | 493,664 | 859,883 |
| 1316 | (1898-99) | 498,665 | 868,536 |
| 1317 | (1899-1900) | 503,717 | 877,326 |
| 1318 | (1900-01) | 508,820 | 886,206 |
| 1319 | (1901-02) | 513,975 | 895,175 |
| 1320 | (1902-03) | 519,181 | 904,235 |
| 1321 | (1903-04) | 524,441 | 914,971 |
| 1322 | (1904-05) | 529,754 | 925,835 |
| 1323 | (1905-06) | 535,121 | 936,828 |
| 1324 | (1906-07) | 540,524 | 947,951 |
| 1325 | (1907-08) | 546,018 | 959,206 |
| 1326 | (1908-09) | 551,549 | 970,595 |
| 1327 | (1909-10) | 557,137 | 982,120 |
| 1328 | (1910-11) | 562,781 | 799,393 |
| 1329 | (1911) | 567,994 | 808,885 |
| 1330 | (1911-12) | 573,256 | 818,489 |
| 1331 | (1912-13) | 445,589 | 675,562 |
| 1332 | (1913-14) | 449,717 | 683,583 |

lyzed. When considering Muslim population of eastern Anatolia one must, in addition to accounting for general inexactness, remember that nomadic groups were poorly counted, if they were counted at all. In addition, the borders between provinces and between the Ottoman Empire and Iran were extremely porous. A group counted in one enumeration may have been in another province or country at the time of the next.

That the Ottoman statistical system was a registration system provides some assurance that the groups of persons counted in one enumeration were the same groups of persons counted in another, i.e., whole villages counted one year were not excluded the next, nor were whole sections of a village or city, since population registration is a matter of updating already existing registers.[28] In the Ottoman system, population members were registered by household and name, not counted simply as a number. The inhabitants considered here are those who were registered. The summary date drawn from registration records may or may not have been "improved" by Ottoman bureaucrats. The consistency or inconsistency of the data demonstrates whether or not this was done.

### Bitlis, Mamuretülaziz, and Diyarbakır

Throughout the period 1878 to 1914 the provinces of Bitlis, Mamuretülaziz, and Diyarbakır were separate. They theoretically had exact provincial boundaries, yet before 1306 (1889–9) their boundaries changed and often cannot be distinguished. Sancaks shifted back and forth between vilâyets and the changes are not always found in the imperial salnames. Indeed, the imperial and provincial salnames were sometimes at considerable variance with each other as to what areas are included in each eastern province. This happened rarely in the other provinces. Perhaps because of a lack of effective government control, the boundary situation was much more confused in the east than in other parts of Anatolia.

Changes in kazas are difficult to follow in all Ottoman provinces. They are impossible to follow in Bitlis, Mamuretülaziz, and Diyarbakır for the period before 1306. Kaza names changed often and there is no way to trace them, and no way to know to which province their populations were attached from one year to the next.

An example of the boundary change chaos lies in the recorded sancaks of Diyarbakır province. The Diyarbakır salnames of 1293, 1294, 1299, and 1302 listed the Diyarbakır sancaks as follows:

1293　Diyarbakır, Mamuretülaziz, Malatya, Siirt, Mardin
1294　Diyarbakır, Malatya, Mardin, Siirt

1299 Diyarbakır, Mardin, Ergani, Malatya
1302 Diyarbakır, Mardin, Ergani

Malatya eventually went to Mamuretülaziz, Siirt to Bitlis province.

Boundaries as given in the "censuses" are also unreliable. The Census of 1311, called here Census 1, was completely wrong in its administrative boundaries. It listed four kazas for Mamuretülaziz Vilâyeti—Mamuretülaziz, Malatya, Hozat, and Mazgirt—a collection that in no way represents the Mamuretülaziz administration boundaries in 1311 or, as far as can be seen, any other year. Sancaks were listed as kazas, some sancaks were not listed, etc.

Table 2.18

Muslim Population of
Bitlis, Diyarbakır, and Mamuretülaziz

| Year | Population |
|------|-----------|
| 1295 (1878) | 1,114,862 |
| 1296 (1878-79) | 1,125,544 |
| 1297 (1879-80) | 1,136,344 |
| 1298 (1880-81) | 1,147,262 |
| 1299 (1881-82) | 1,158,300 |
| 1300 (1882-83) | 1,169,461 |
| 1301 (1883-84) | 1,180,744 |
| 1302 (1884-85) | 1,192,153 |
| 1303 (1885-86) | 1,203,689 |
| 1304 (1886-87) | 1,215,352 |
| 1305 (1887-88) | 1,227,147 |
| 1306 (1883-84) | 1,238,763 |

Source: Salnames, censuses and archival documents from each province. Since the boundaries between the three provinces are not properly known, their populations have been combined.

After 1306, boundaries as listed in the imperial salnames (yearbooks of the Empire) are recognizable. Before that date, the only way properly to count the populations of Diyarbakır, Mamuretülaziz, and Bitlis is to count them together. In this way, any problem of unknown boundary changes between the three provinces is obviated. Table 2.18 is the result of pooling the corrected populations of the three provinces from 1295 (1878) to 1306 (1884–4). The sources and procedures used in drawing up the table's populations are explained in the following sections.[29]

### Bitlis Vilâyeti

Two salnames were issued for the province of Bitlis, 1310 and 1316, ten years apart. Both gave the same population (table 2.19). From this one can

Table 2.19

Recorded Muslim Population of Bitlis Vilâyeti

| Source | Actual Year | Original Population | Corrected Population |
|---|---|---|---|
| Ist. U. Register | * | 163,080 | 191,913 |
| Archival Docmt. 2 | * | 167,054 | 220,244 |
| Census 1 | * | 167,054 | 220,244 |
| Archival Docmt. 8 | * | 167,055 | 220,245 |
| Archival Docmt. 1 | * | 167,213 | 220,454 |
| Ist. U. Register | * | 187,544 | 220,702 |
| Census 2 | * | 197,906 | 260,919 |
| 1310 Salname | 1305 | 204,941 | 270,194 |
| 1316 Salname | 1305 | 204,941 | 270,194 |
| 1313 İstatistik | 1311 | 224,772 | 296,339 |
| Census 3 | 1316 | 246,047 | 324,388 |
| 1330 Nüfus-i Umumî | 1330 | 309,999 | 408,703 |

* Not known.

assume the provincial government's idea of the province's population was somewhat deficient. Yet, when placed in a series with "census" and archival records, a somewhat coherent picture of the population from 1305 (1887–8) to 1330 (1911–2) does appear. The pre-1305 sources in table 2.19 seem consistent only because they have been arranged in ascending order. It is probable that they represent the population of Bitlis at certain times as accurately as do the post-1305 materials, but the confused state of the administrative boundaries makes it impossible to know which areas they represented and when. Because of this, the pre-1305 population, included in the three-province totals, has been found by projecting the 1305 population back in time, using the rates of increase that have been observed for the period 1305–1330.

The growth rate of Bitlis was .01155 (birth rate, .05006; death rate, .03853). Life expectancy was 27 years at birth. The amount of migration among the recorded population was probably small. An amount of in-migration is indicated by the rate of change (1305–1330, .0166 a year), but the quality of the data does not allow any migration conclusions or generalizations.

After 1305 the boundaries of Bitlis Vilâyeti were stable. The populations in table 2.19 are all for the same geographic area.

### Mamuretülaziz Vilâyeti

The same series of population sources for Mamuretülaziz is more consistent than that of Bitlis (table 2.20). In general, population records were better kept in Mamuretülaziz.[30]

The main difficulty with the Mamuretülaziz population material is dating. Two of the salnames have populations dated before 1306, though one was published in 1307. These salnames listed the same population, even though a large sancak, Dersim, was added to the province in 1306, between the publication of the two volumes, an event that should have affected the province's population. The 1305 and 1307 salnames thus cannot be used. Dates for the post-1306 populations must be set by assuming that the 1313 İstatistik and the 1330 Nüfus-i Umumî populations fell roughly in the same years as they did for all the other provinces. This assumption results in a

Table 2.20

Recorded Muslim Population of Mamuretülaziz Vilâyeti

| Source | Actual Year | Original Population | Corrected Population |
|---|---|---|---|
| 1301 Salname | * | 273,690 | 345,889 |
| Census 1 | * | 300,188 | 379,378 |
| Archival Docmt. 2 | * | 300,194 | 379,385 |
| Archival Docmt. 1 | * | 300,194 | 379,385 |
| 1305 Salname | * | 342,286 | 432,581 |
| 1307 Salname | * | 342,286 | 432,581 |
| Ist. U. Register | * | 346,652 | 421,148 |
| Ist. U. Register | * | 360,838 | 438,382 |
| 1312 Salname | * | 375,668 | 474,769 |
| 1313 İstatistik | 1311 | 380,092 | 480,360 |
| Census 2 | 1314 | 390,794 | 493,885 |
| 1330 Nüfus-i Umumî | 1330 | 446,379 | 564,164 |

* Not known.

reasonable rate of increase between the two years (1311–1330, .0085 per year).

The 1306 to 1330 populations have been projected to provide the yearly populations given in table 2.20. The projection also furnished the Mamuretülaziz input into the three-province pre-1306 totals, seen in table 2.18.

Table 2.24 takes into account the change in population caused by the loss of Kuzicane Kazası to Erzurum in 1310 (1892–3). The population of Kuzicane in the 1312 salname is projected to 1310 and subtracted from the projected province total for that year.

The birth (.050), death (.038), and increase (.0012) rates of the Mamuretülaziz Vilâyeti were the same as in Bitlis, as was the life expectancy at birth, 27 years.

## Diyarbakır Vilâyeti

Because of the problems of the pre-1306 administrative boundary changes, only the last six sources in table 2.21 can be used in analyzing the Diyarbakır population.

It is interesting to note that the time needed for compiling and printing the Diyarbakır populations was considerably greater than that of the more western Anatolian provinces. Moreover, the yearly rates of increase given in the sources for Diyarbakır province were clearly impossible. The yearly rate between the recorded populations of the 1317 and 1321 salnames, for example, is .0323 per year, almost three times the expected rate. The rates demanded by the other sources are equally absurd. Rates of increase of approximately .0320 are higher than those experienced by almost any country in the world today, and the area of eastern Anatolia from 1878 to 1914 surely did not experience conditions that in any way qualify it to compare to today's areas of high fertility. The only possible explanations for the high rates of increase necessitated by the populations given in table 2.21 are high in-migration or large-scale errors in the sources.

There is no evidence for intense migration into Diyarbakır. The only possible explanation for the high rates of increase is that, as the control of the central government over the Diyarbakır Province improved in the latter part of the nineteenth century, more and more previously unenumerated persons were counted for the first time and included in the population totals. If this is true, the rates of increase would reflect the increase in statistical capability, not natural population growth or migration.[31]

For Diyarbakır Vilâyeti, only the 1330 Nüfus-i Umumî has been taken here as approaching accuracy for total population. The population as listed in the 1330 Nüfus-i Umumî has been projected back (table 2.24) at the rate of .007 per year, allowing, in the projection, for the addition of the kaza of Viran Şehir from the Haleb Vilâyeti in 1328. The .007 rate was chosen because it was felt that the age pyramid (figure A4.20) of Diyarbakır indicates a gross reproduction rate of between 2.5 and 3.0 and a mortality level of 5. The .007 rate of yearly increase is proper for that gross reproduction rate and mortality level.[32]

Diyarbakır had fertility of .049 and mortality of .035 per year and a life expectancy of 27.5 years at birth.

Table 2.21

Recorded Muslim Population of Diyarbakır Vilâyeti

| Source | Actual Year | Original Population | Corrected Population |
|---|---|---|---|
| 1293 Salname | * | 611,121 | 690,458 |
| 1297 Salname | * | 219,120 | 249,008 |
| Ist. U. Register | * | 250,284 | 284,423 |
| Ist. U. Register | * | 249,880 | 283,964 |
| Archival Docmt. 1 | * | 240,574 | 292,827 |
| Archival Docmt. 2 | * | 240,574 | 292,827 |
| Archival Docmt. 2 | * | 240,574 | 292,827 |
| Census 1 | * | 289,591 | 352,590 |
| 1312 Salname | 1308 | 314,720 | 383,077 |
| Census 2 | 1309 | 315,569 | 384,111 |
| 1313 İstatistik | 1310 | 329,843 | 401,485 |
| 1317 Salname | 1310 | 330,000 | 401,676 |
| 1321 Salname | 1317 | 375,528 | 457,093 |
| 1330 Nüfus-i Umumî | 1330 | 492,101 | 598,985 |

* Not known.

## Van Vilâyeti

The population of Van Vilâyeti is the most difficult to analyze of all the Anatolian vilâyets, and conclusions drawn about the Van population are the least exact. Ottoman figures are the only remotely accurate population statistics for the province. However, one must assume that the Ottomans were unsuccessful in counting a certain amount of the tribal population of Van. Because of this, and other reasons given below, the present analysis of the

Van population must be regarded as very possibly an undercounting of the actual Muslim inhabitants of the province.

This study has made use of correction factors drawn from the recorded population of each province to adjust undercounts in the province's children and females. For Van this has not been possible.[33]

The overwhelming inaccuracy of the Van data leaves no choice but to draw the correction factors used on the Van population from other sources. Van is the only Anatolian province for which this is necessary. Based on comparisons to similar provinces, a correction factor of 1.3 has been chosen for Van. This falls between the factor of Mamuretülaziz (1.2638) and Bitlis (1.3184). The application of the 1.3 correction factor to Van should result, once again, in a slight underestimate, since it is likely that Van's registration system was approximately as deficient as that of Bitlis.

Of the sources listed in table 2.22, the *1315 Van Vilâyeti Salnamesi* is

Table 2.22


Recorded Muslim Population of Van Vilâyeti

| Source | Actual Year | Original Population | Corrected Population |
|---|---|---|---|
| Ist. U. Register | * | 49,052 | 63,768 |
| Ist. U. Register | * | 52,028 | 67,636 |
| Archival Docmt. 2 | * | 54,582 | 70,957 |
| Census 2 | * | 54,582 | 70,957 |
| Census 1 | * | 59,412 | 77,236 |
| 1313 İstatistik | * | 76,956 | 100,043 |
| Archival Docmt. 8 | 1298 | 202,786 | 263,622 |
| 1315 Salname | 1312 | 207,833 | 270,183 |
| 1330 Nüfus-i Umumî | 1330 | 179,380 | 233,194 |
| 1330 Nüfus-i Umumî | ° | 241,017 | 313,322 |

* Not known.

° Hakkâri Sancağı counted correctly.

the best. The *1330 Nüfus-i Umumî*, which is the best source for the populations of every other Anatolian vilâyet, is deficient for Van, particularly for the Hakkâri Sancağı, an almost completely Kurdish area. The Census of 1311 (Census 1 in the table) does not even give the Hakkâri population. In order to draw the year-by-year projections in Table 2.24, the deficiencies in the *1330 Nüfus-i Umumî* have been corrected by assuming that Hakkâri Sancaği was the same proportion of the population of Van Vilâyeti in 1330 as in 1315. These two populations have been used to find the rate of increase between 1312, the assumed actual date of the 1315 salname figure, and 1330, the assumed date of the *1330 Nüfus-i Umumî's* figures.[34]

Changes in administrative boundaries have further complicated the creation of table 2.24. İmadiye Kazası was part of Van Vilâyeti until 1310, when it was transferred to Mosul Vilâyeti. Because, however, no count of İmadiye's population has been found, Imadiye has been completely excluded from the Van population as it appears in table 2.24. Van and Hakkâri were separate vilâyets until 1302 (1884–5) and are listed as such in the table. They have been divided so that their percentages are the same as in the 1315 salname.

Mortality in Van (.035 per year) appears to have been slightly lower than mortality in Diyarbakır or Mamuretülaziz. Fertility was .049 per year and life expectancy 30 years at birth.

### Erzurum Vilâyeti

The populations given in the Erzurum salnames offer further evidence of the Ottomans' policy of updating their registration lists only every few years. Four salnames are listed in table 2.23—1312, 1315, 1317, and 1318. As was true with the salname population lists from Aydın Vilâyeti, mentioned earlier, the population registration records of Erzurum were not properly updated each year. If this were not the case, the rates of increase of Erzurum's population would be impossibly strange: 1312–1315, .0007 per year; 1315–1317, .0047 per year; 1317–1318, .0332 per year. For these rates to be true the population of Erzurum must have risen 40 times faster from 1317 to 1318 than from 1312 to 1315.

Except for occasional yearly updating, based probably on births and deaths

Table 2.23

Recorded Muslim Population of Erzurum Vilâyeti

| Source | Actual Year | Original Population | Corrected Population |
|---|---|---|---|
| 1299 Salname | 1294 | 427,710 | 478,308 |
| Ist. U. Register | 1303 | 431,802 | 482,884 |
| Archival Docmt. 1 | 1305 | 441,686 | 527,682 |
| Archival Docmt. 2 | 1305 | 442,055 | 528,123 |
| Archival Docmt. 8 | 1305 | 442,055 | 528,123 |
| 1310 Salname | 1307 | 445,074 | 531,730 |
| Ist. U. Register | 1304 | 475,594 | 531,857 |
| Census 1 | 1307 | 445,548 | 532,296 |
| 1313 İstatistik | 1309 | 513,446 | 613,414 |
| 1312 Salname | 1309 | 514,829 | 615,066 |
| 1315 Salname | 1312 | 515,861 | 616,299 |
| 1317 Salname | 1314 | 520,822 | 622,226 |
| 1318 Salname | 1315 | 538,402 | 643,229 |
| Census 2 | 1316 | 551,506 | 658,884 |
| Census 3 | 1326 | 632,668 | 755,848 |
| 1330 Nüfus-i Umumî | 1330 | 673,297 | 804,388 |

reported to the population registration officials (*nüfus memurları*), the officials only re-registered the entire population at intervals of, in Erzurum, at least six years. This explains the small rise in the recorded Erzurum population between 1312 and 1317 and the sudden jump in 1318. The populations given in the salnames and "censuses" must be examined carefully to find the ones that list the population soon after a new registration.

The population for Erzurum had a growth rate of .014 per year, roughly the average for Anatolia. Comparison between the rate of change of the recorded populations (.01413 per year from 1296 to 1332)[35] and the ex-

Table 2.24

Muslim Population of the Eastern Anatolian Provinces, 1878 to 1914

| Year | | Bitlis | Mamuretülaziz | Diyarbakır |
|---|---|---|---|---|
| | | | Three Provinces Combined | |
| 1295 | (1878) | | 1,114,862 | |
| 1296 | (1878-79) | | 1,125,544 | |
| 1297 | (1879-80) | | 1,136,344 | |
| 1298 | (1880-81) | | 1,147,262 | |
| 1299 | (1881-82) | | 1,158,300 | |
| 1300 | (1882-83) | | 1,169,461 | |
| 1301 | (1883-84) | | 1,180,744 | |
| 1302 | (1884-85) | | 1,192,153 | |
| 1303 | (1885-86) | | 1,203,689 | |
| 1304 | (1886-87) | | 1,215,352 | |
| | | | Three Provinces Separated | |
| 1305 | (1887-88) | 270,194 | 469,945 | 487,008 |
| 1306 | (1888-89) | 274,395 | 473,939 | 490,429 |
| 1307 | (1889-90) | 278,661 | 477,968 | 493,874 |
| 1308 | (1890-91) | 282,993 | 482,030 | 497,343 |
| 1309 | (1891-92) | 287,393 | 486,127 | 500,837 |
| 1310 | (1892-93) | 291,861 | 490,259 | 504,355 |
| 1311 | (1893-94) | 296,399 | 480,360 | 507,898 |
| 1312 | (1894-95) | 301,797 | 484,827 | 511,465 |
| 1313 | (1895-96) | 307,292 | 489,335 | 515,058 |
| 1314 | (1896-97) | 312,888 | 493,885 | 518,676 |
| 1315 | (1897-98) | 318,586 | 498,009 | 522,320 |
| 1316 | (1898-99) | 324,388 | 502,167 | 525,989 |
| 1317 | (1899-1900) | 329,786 | 506,360 | 529,684 |
| 1318 | (1900-01) | 335,274 | 510,588 | 533,404 |
| 1319 | (1901-02) | 340,851 | 514,851 | 537,151 |
| 1320 | (1902-03) | 346,525 | 519,150 | 540,925 |
| 1321 | (1903-04) | 352,291 | 523,485 | 544,724 |
| 1322 | (1904-05) | 358,153 | 527,856 | 548,551 |
| 1323 | (1905-06) | 364,113 | 532,264 | 552,404 |
| 1324 | (1906-07) | 370,172 | 536,708 | 556,284 |
| 1325 | (1907-08) | 376,332 | 541,189 | 560,192 |
| 1326 | (1908-09) | 382,594 | 545,708 | 564,127 |
| 1327 | (1909-10) | 388,961 | 550,265 | 568,090 |
| 1328 | (1910-11) | 395,433 | 554,859 | 590,658 |
| 1329 | (1911) | 402,013 | 559,492 | 594,807 |
| 1330 | (1911-12) | 408,703 | 564,164 | 598,985 |
| 1331 | (1912-13) | 415,504 | 568,875 | 603,193 |
| 1332 | (1913-14) | 422,418 | 573,625 | 607,430 |

Table 2.24 (continued)

| | | Erzurum | Van | Hakkâri |
|---|---|---|---|---|
| 1295 | (1878) | 488,799 | 105,686 | 129,223 |
| 1296 | (1878-79) | 499,521 | 106,559 | 130,291 |
| 1297 | (1879-80) | 510,477 | 107,439 | 131,368 |
| 1298 | (1880-81) | 521,646 | 108,327 | 132,454 |
| 1299 | (1881-82) | 533,117 | 109,222 | 133,548 |
| 1300 | (1882-83) | 544,811 | 110,125 | 134,651 |
| 1301 | (1883-84) | 556,761 | 111,035 | 135,764 |
| 1302 | (1884-85) | 569,973 | 111,952 | 136,886 |
| 1303 | (1885-86) | 581,453 | 250,895 | |
| 1304 | (1886-87) | 594,206 | 252,968 | Merged With Van |
| 1305 | (1887-88) | 607,240 | 255,058 | |
| 1306 | (1888-89) | 575,784 | 257,166 | |
| 1307 | (1889-90) | 588,064 | 259,291 | |
| 1308 | (1890-91) | 600,605 | 261,434 | |
| 1309 | (1891-92) | 613,414 | 263,594 | |
| 1310 | (1892-93) | 629,459 | 265,772 | |
| 1311 | (1893-94) | 637,224 | 267,969 | |
| 1312 | (1894-95) | 645,025 | 270,183 | |
| 1313 | (1895-96) | 653,044 | 272,416 | |
| 1314 | (1896-97) | 661,100 | 274,667 | |
| 1315 | (1897-98) | 669,256 | 276,936 | |
| 1316 | (1898-99) | 677,512 | 279,225 | |
| 1317 | (1899-1900) | 685,870 | 281,532 | |
| 1318 | (1900-01) | 694,331 | 283,859 | |
| 1319 | (1901-02) | 702,897 | 286,204 | |
| 1320 | (1902-03) | 711,568 | 288,569 | |
| 1321 | (1903-04) | 720,346 | 290,954 | |
| 1322 | (1904-05) | 729,233 | 293,358 | |
| 1323 | (1905-06) | 738,229 | 295,783 | |
| 1324 | (1906-07) | 747,336 | 298,227 | |
| 1325 | (1907-08) | 756,556 | 300,691 | |
| 1326 | (1908-09) | 765,889 | 303,176 | |
| 1327 | (1909-10) | 775,338 | 305,681 | |
| 1328 | (1910-11) | 784,903 | 308,207 | |
| 1329 | (1911) | 794,586 | 310,754 | |
| 1330 | (1911-12) | 804,388 | 313,322 | |
| 1331 | (1912-13) | 814,311 | 315,911 | |
| 1332 | (1913-14) | 824,357 | 318,522 | |

pected growth rate shows very little migration, or balanced in- and out-migration. The birth rate was .049, the death rate .035, and the expectation of life at birth 30 years.

Erzurum's total Muslim population by year (table 2.24) is changed by the loss of Kelkit and Şiran kazas in 1306 (1888–9) to the Trabzon Vilâyeti and the addition of Kuzicane kaza from Mamuretülaziz in 1310 (1892–3). The projections in table 2.24 have been adjusted to include these changes.

The mortality and fertility shown by the model chosen for Erzurum were the same as those in Van (mortality, .035 per year; fertility, .049 per year; life expectancy at birth, 30 years).

## NOTES

1. See the section "Population by Provinces and Mother Tongue" in any census of the Turkish Republic, e.g., pp. 182–187 in the 1965 census (*Census of Population, Social and Economic Characteristics*, Ankara, 1969).

2. In 1912.

3. For statistics on the western provinces, see Justin McCarthy, *The Arab World, Turkey, and the Balkans: A Handbook of Historical Statistics* (Boston: G. K. Hall, 1982). Hereafter referred to as McCarthy, *Statistics*.

4. In the Hüdavendigâr salnames, financial data was often dated and uniformly showed dates two or three years prior to the cover date of the salname. The Aydın salnames stated that the population tables represented the population three years before the publication date of the salname (see Appendix 2) and one Kastamonu salname gave a date for its population tables that was two years before the date of the salname.

5. See appendix 2.

6. See the methodology section, appendix 4.

7. Using the methods described in appendix 4: the recorded total population was 1,454,294 (732,525 males and 721,769 females). Once corrected for underregistration of young males, the resulting corrected total population is 1,643,046 (821,523 males doubled). The correction factor used on all other recorded total population statistics for Hüdavendigâr is thus 1.1298 (1,643,046 / 1,454,294). If the source yields only male population, as is often the case with early population statements, the correction factor will be smaller. For example, that for Hüdavendigâr is 1.1215 times the doubled male population: 1,643,046 / (males × 2).

8. Because of this, Imperial Salnames for each year of the study were consulted, along with other records of administrative boundaries (see the bibliography).

9. Level 7, GRR = 3.0.

10. Under the theory of the compilation of the "censuses," advanced in chapter 1, the dates of compilation of the census populations for geographically and economically similar provinces should have been similar. Both Hudavendigâr and Aydın should have provided their population figures quickly to the census bureau in Istanbul. These figures would have waited for those of more tardy provinces to arrive before publication. The years of compilation of the Aydın and Hüdavendigâr sections of the censuses are indeed close (Census 1: Hüdavendigâr 1306, Aydın 1305; Census 2: Hüdavendigâr 1321, Aydın 1320).

11. The rate of increase per year of the Muslim population was not as high as the model population would suggest (.010 instead of .014 per year). This is a minor factor, however, and the closeness of male and female populations is undoubtedly

mainly due to accurate registration. The same cannot be said for the registration of children (see figure A4.6), who were obviously much undercounted.

12. In the *1313 İstatistik:* males 120,425; females 108,018; total 228,443. Correction factor: 228,443 / (120,425 × 2) = 1.2227. The yearly rate of increase that corresponds to the model that describes the İzmit population (L. 7, GRR = 3) is .0165. While increase in fertility could account for some of the difference between .0165 and .021, it could not account for it all.

13. Karası Sancağı went to Hüdavendigâr Vilâyeti.

14. See appendix 2 and the section on Hüdavendigâr in this chapter.

15. Since these extra migrant males were counted in the correction formula for Biga and not for their home provinces, they make the female underenumeration look greater in Biga and smaller in their home provinces. The home provinces are not known and there is no remedy for the statistical problem, unless data on migration in the area is found in the future. Consequently, the populations of provinces such as Biga will be slightly overstated and the populations of home provinces slightly understated after the correction factor is employed. For example, if Biga had the recorded male-female ratio of Hudavendigâr, the corrected population in 1313 (table 2.6) would be 132,102, instead of 135,425, a decrease of 2.5%. The home province, probably Hüdavendigâr, would show a much smaller percentage increase, less than 1%, due to its much larger size.

16. The age pyramid for Biga corresponds to a 2.5 GRR, but the recorded natural increase in the province (1301 to 1331: .0137 a year) corresponds much more closely to a 3.0 GRR. The 2.5 GRR has been selected here mainly because all the GRRs for the Anatolian provinces have been selected on the basis of the age pyramid method and because Biga was a prime area for possible distortion due to migration. In addition, the resemblance of the Biga population to a GRR = 2.5 model might also be the result of a much more extensive age distortion than that seen in Aydın, Hüdavenidgâr, or İzmit. Given the geographic proximity of the four provinces and their equivalent closeness to the central government, this seems unlikely. The anomaly remains.

17. See the various sources of historical statistics on the area, including McCarthy, *Statistics,* the *1313 İstatistik,* and the *İhsaiyati-i Maliye.*

18. *İhsaiyat-i Maliye* 1326, pp. 2 and 3.

19. Based on the model drawn from the age pyramid (see appendix 4).

20. SIS., *Statistical Yearbook of Turkey, 1971.*

21. In the *1313 İstatistik,* "Memalik-i Mahruse-i Şahane'de mevcud hastahanelerine mustahdem memürin ve hadım ve saire'nin mikdarı" ("The amount of officials, helpers, and others employed in hospitals in the Ottoman Empire.") Other tables in the same source give other medical figures. In none of them is Trabzon particularly distinguished. In all categories, it is well below the medical standard of the provinces of west Anatolia.

22. See "Sex Ratios" in appendix 2. The rates of increase demanded by the model population are somewhat lower than the growth rate of the recorded population.

This may be explained by Trabzon's traditional position as a source of manpower for Istanbul. The difference in rates is, in any case, not great: model: .019 per year; observed: .016 per year. As can be seen in table 2.10, as the period advanced, the observed rates of increase went up. For evidence of the out-migration pattern on the Black Sea see Justin McCarthy, "Age, Family, and Migration in Black Sea Provinces of the Ottoman Empire," *IJMES* 10 (1979), pp. 309–323.

23. Average temperature in January, c. O° C. (32° F.); in August, c. 22° C. (72° F.). SIS, *Statistical Yearbook of Turkey,* 1973, pp. 14–18.

24. Ibid., p. 22.

25. See Vital Cuinet, *La Turquie d'Asie,* v. 1 (Paris, 1890) on agriculture and industry in Sivas, Ankara, and Konya.

26. The Devlet salnames are in error on the addition of Ermenak Kazası. They do not show it in Konya in 1324, but the *1324 Konya Vilâyeti Salnamesi* shows it, and its population, as already in the province in 1324.

27. See, for example, the *Haleb Vilâyeti Salnamesi,* 1299, p. 461. This problem was by no means confined to Haleb. An archival document states that the governors of Bağdad, Basra, Mosul, Van, Bitlis, and Erzurum all complained of nomads crossing their borders, particularly nomads from Iran. (Yıldız 18–553/202–93–35)

28. See McCarthy, "Age, Family," for examples of population registers.

29. The pre-1306 population of Dersim Sancağı was, to my knowledge, listed nowhere. It has been included in these totals by projection from later dates.

30. As indicated by the age pyramid.

31. It is possible that the nomads would have been counted in one census and not another, but the counting of nomads would probably be a function of increased central authority, even more than would the enumeration of the settled, and so this is not likely.

32. The age pyramid indicates negligible migration.

33. See appendix 2.

34. Dated 1330 Maliye, 1332 Hicra.

35. This yearly rate of increase would be very slightly affected by changes in administrative boundaries, i.e., the loss of Kelkit and Şiran kazas and gain of Kuzicane Kazası.

# 3.
# Armenian Population

T HE ARMENIAN POPULATION of the Ottoman Empire has been the subject of considerably more estimates and debates than the population of any other Ottoman millet. During the late nineteenth century, various Europeans provided population figures on Armenians in the Ottoman Empire. The Armenians later provided their own figures, as did the Ottomans. Professional historians, politicians, and propagandists have used the various estimates of Armenian population to buttress moral and political arguments, each side often taking figures that best fit its argument. Little has been done, however, to evaluate logically and statistically the material on Armenian population.[1]

## Armenian Sources

Armenian groups and individuals had been furnishing estimates of Armenian population of the Ottoman Empire since the 1880s,[2] but their most important and detailed figures were presented immediately after World War I. These figures were intended to convince the delegates to the Versailles Peace Conference, and world opinion, that before World War I there had been more Armenians than Turks in the Armenian areas of eastern Anatolia, and that there was in 1919 a large enough population of Armenians to create a stable Armenian state. Armenian sources always recognized that, through death and migration, the Armenian population of eastern Anatolia in 1919 had become very small. They asserted, however, that to apply the principle of self-determination to the population as it was in 1919 would be to reward the Turks for what they stated were the Turks' evil deeds during

Table 3.1

Population of the "Six Vilâyets" in 1912, Patriarchate Statistics

| | Erzurum | Van | Bitlis | Harput | Diyarbakır | Sivas | Total |
|---|---|---|---|---|---|---|---|
| Turks | 240,000 | 47,000 | 40,000 | 102,000 | 45,000 | 192,000 | 666,000 |
| Circassians (immigrants) | 7,000 | -- | 10,000 | -- | -- | 45,000 | 62,000 |
| Persians | 13,000 | -- | -- | -- | -- | -- | 13,000 |
| Laz | 10,000 | -- | -- | -- | -- | -- | 10,000 |
| Gypsies | -- | 3,000 | -- | -- | -- | -- | 3,000 |
| Sedentary Kurds | 35,000 | 32,000 | 35,000 | 75,000 | 30,000 | 35,000 | 242,000 |
| Nomadic Kurds | 40,000 | 40,000 | 42,000 | 20,000 | 25,000 | 15,000 | 182,000 |
| Kızılbaş | 25,000 | -- | 8,000 | 80,000 | 27,000 | -- | 140,000 |
| Zazas et. al. | 30,000 | -- | 47,000 | -- | -- | -- | 77,000 |
| Yezidi | 3,000 | 25,000 | 5,000 | -- | 4,000 | -- | 37,000 |
| Armenians | 215,000 | 185,000 | 180,000 | 168,000 | 105,000 | 165,000 | 1,018,000 |
| Nestorians, Jacobites, and Chaldeans | -- | 18,000 | 15,000 | 5,000 | 60,000 | 25,000 | 123,000 |
| Greeks and other Christians | 12,000 | -- | -- | -- | -- | 30,000 | 42,000 |
| Total | 630,000 | 350,000 | 382,000 | 450,000 | 296,000 | 507,000 | 2,615,000 |

Source: Population Armenienne de la Turqiue Avant la Guerre, Statistiques etablis par le Patriarcat Armenien de Constantinople, Paris, 1920.

the war. They further asserted that peace and a high Armenian birth rate would soon increase Armenian numbers.[3]

Though various estimates were offered, the population data that was at the heart of the Armenian claims was drawn from statistics supplied by the Armenian Patriarchate, as they had appeared in a prewar book by Marcel Leart (Krikor Zohrap), *La Question Arménienne à la Lumière des Documents*.[4]

The statistics supplied by the Armenian Patriarchate were avowedly based on records of baptisms and deaths kept by ecclesiastical officials. Registration was founded on the canonical need for Armenians to be baptized, married within the Church, and to have a religious funeral.[5] Moreover, it was stated that the Patriarch kept records that were used to impose an ecclesiastical tax and that were used to fix the number of deputies from each district to the Armenian political and religious assemblies.[6]

The Patriarchate statistics gave figures for the years 1882 and 1912. For 1912, the Armenian population of the "Six Vilâyets" (Erzurum, Van, Bitlis, Mamuretülaziz or "Kharpout," Diyarbakır, and Sivas) was given by province, accompanied by estimates of the populations of other groups. The figures were not based on the Ottoman provincial boundaries. Instead, the Patriarchate figures were "*A l'exclusion des parties de ces provinces ou les Armeniens ne sont pas en nombre.*" The excluded areas were: "*Hekkiari dans le vilayet de Van; Le Sud de Sighert dans le vilayet de Bitlis; Le Sud du vilayet de Diarbekir; Le Sud de Malatia dans le vilayet de Kharpout; Le Nord-Ouest et l'Ouest du vilayet de Sivas. Le nombre des Armeniens qui habitent ces parties est de 145,000.*"[7]

The Patriarchate did not give detailed population statistics for areas outside of the six vilâyets, nor did it present data on other groups of the population (table 3.2) for those areas.

The Armenian Patriarchate figures were summary statistics. Problems arising in their analysis are many, some of them insoluble. Since no major Armenian population survived in Anatolia at the time of the modern Turkish Republican censuses it is impossible to compare the Patriarch's data to more modern material. No age or sex breakdowns were presented in the Patriarchate tables, so it is impossible to analyze the figures demographically, as has been done above for Ottoman governmental statistics. In fact, there is no completely satisfactory way to evaluate the Armenian Patriarchate materials on Armenian population.[8] It is possible, however, to evaluate the data given for Muslim population in the same tables. Doing so sheds some light on the accuracy of the Armenian statistics.

It can be easily demonstrated that the Patriarchate figures for Muslim population are extremely low (table 3.3). As seen before, the Armenian figures covered an area smaller than that of some of the Ottoman provinces listed above. The Patriarchate figures for the Sivas Vilâyeti, however, shared the same geographic area as the Ottoman figures and can serve as a good point of comparison. Taking Sivas as an example, one can readily see that the Armenian figures are much lower than either the Ottoman figures or

Table 3.2

Armenian Population of the Ottoman Empire in 1912

Armenian Patriarchate Statistics

| | |
|---|---|
| Turkish Armenia | 1,018,000 |
| Other parts of the "Six Vilâyets" | 145,000 |
| Cilicia | 407,000 |
| European Turkey | 530,000 |
| Total | 2,100,000 |

Source:  Population Armenienne, Paris, 1920.

the corrected figures for Muslim population computed earlier.[9] We know, as well, that the 1927 Turkish census listed the population of the geographic area of the Ottoman Sivas province as 964,989.[10] As demonstrated in appendix 1 the figures of the 1927 were, if anything, too low. Were the Armenian Patriarch's figures for Muslims accurate, the Muslim population of Sivas Vilâyeti would have increased threefold from 1912 to 1927, an impossibility, especially considering the mortality of World War I and the Turkish War of Independence and the lack of mention in any source of a great migration into the province. We are left with the conclusion that the Armenian Patriarchate figures only listed 25% of the Muslim population of Sivas.

Patriarchate figures for other eastern provinces were low, as well. A small part of the discrepancy arose from those members of the population who were listed as "Muslims" by the Ottomans, but as "Other Religions"—"Kizilbashis [sic], Zazas, Tchareklis, Yezidis"—by the Patriarchate.

It is impossible to know whether the Patriarchate figures on Muslim population were intentionally or unintentionally incorrect. The Armenian ecclesiastical authorities had no way themselves to count the Muslim population and they refused to accept Ottoman figures. Most likely, they simply guessed.

Table 3.3

Muslim Population of the "Six Vilâyets" in 1912

|  | Armenian Patriarchate | Ottoman | Corrected Ottoman |
|---|---|---|---|
| Erzurum | 345,000 | 673,297 | 804,388 |
| Van | 122,000 | 179,380 | 270,518 |
| Bitlis | 127,000 | 309,999 | 408,703 |
| Mamuretülaziz | 197,000 | 446,379 | 564,134 |
| Diyarbakır | 100,000 | 492,101 | 598,985 |
| Sivas | 287,000 | 939,735 | 1,112,270 |

Sources: Population Armenienne, Paris, 1920, and 1330 Nüfus-i Umumî.

The diminution of Muslim population may have been conscious or unconscious, although it was the case of course that the undercount of Muslims met the political aims of those who desired Armenian independence.

The figures of the Armenian Patriarchate were presented to the Versailles Peace Conference along with other statistics on the populations of Armenians in Russian Transcaucasia and Ottoman Cilicia.[11] In each case, the population estimates presented by the Armenian delegates was considerably at variance with populations as recorded in the censuses and registration records of the respective governments. Table 3.4 gives the Armenian and Russian government figures.[12] Though not as great a discrepancy exists as

MUSLIMS AND MINORITIES

Table 3.4

Muslim and Armenian Population of Russian Armenia

|  | Armenian Statistics, 1912 | Russian Statistics, 1897 |
|---|---|---|
| Armenians | 1,296,000 | 891,704 |
| Muslims | 673,000 | 933,313 |

Sources: Armenian Question, Annex 3, and the 1897 Russian census. See also Great Britain, F.O. 608.108, "The Population of Trans-Caucasia."

Table 3.5

Population of Cilicia

|  | Armenian Statistics, 1914 | Ottoman Statistics, 1912 |
|---|---|---|
| Armenians | 205,050 | 91,855 |
| Greeks | 40,000 | 5,607 |
| Other Christians | 41,000 | 3,224 |
| Muslims | 156,000 | 405,757 |
| Others | 48,000 | N.A. |

Sources: Armenian Question, Annex 2, and 1330 Nüfus-Umumî.

Note: No specific source for the Armenian figures is listed in Armenian Question, although they are obviously based on the Patriarchate statistics.

between Ottoman and Armenian figures, a similar pattern does emerge. If the figures of the Russian census approached accuracy, then the Armenian figures would seem to have overcounted Armenians and undercounted Muslims.[13] It will be seen below that this pattern of over- and undercounting was true for all Armenian statistical estimates.

The Armenian figures for Cilicia, like those for the "Six Vilâyets," selected those areas that were centers of Armenian population, the sancaks of Adana, Maraş, Kozan, and Cebelibereket. In the statistics Muslim population was undercounted by a very large factor. Armenian population was listed as twice that shown in the Ottoman statistics. Interestingly, the Armenian estimate of the number of Greeks and other Christians were even more at variance with the Ottoman statistics than were the estimates of Armenian or Muslim population.

## Patriarchate Statistics for 1882

The Patriarchate estimate of the Armenian population in 1882 was much farther from the mark than that for 1912 (table 3.6).

The 1882 figures need little comment, as they are obviously large-scale overstatements of the actual Armenian population. The two sets of Armenian Patriarchate figures show, for example, a drop in the Armenian population of Van of 54% from 1882 to 1912. The Patriarchate figure for 1912 was itself too high. If a more correct figure[14] (130,500) for 1912 Van Armenians is substituted the drop in population becomes even more sensational, 67%. There were indeed Armenians killed in the troubles of 1895–6, but not even the most exaggerated count[15] of mortality records such a loss for the entire Ottoman Empire, much less for one province. Migration was also an impossibility. Between 1882 and 1912 Van was on no international borders, nor was any sizable Armenian migration from Van recorded by Ottoman or European consular sources during those years.

The data for provinces other than Van was obviously also much exaggerated. The only remote possibility of accuracy for the 1882 data is that the statistics were meant to be records of a much earlier period, early in the nineteenth century, before the migration and death that came with the Russo-Turkish wars in the east, but even this is very unlikely.

Table 3.6

Armenian Patriarchate Statistics:
Armenian Population in 1882 and 1912

|                              | 1882      | 1912      |
|------------------------------|-----------|-----------|
| Van                          | 400,000   | 185,000   |
| Bitlis                       | 250,000   | 180,000   |
| Diyarbakır                   | 150,000   | 105,000   |
| Erzurum                      | 280,000   | 215,000   |
| Mamuretülaziz                | 270,000   | 168,000   |
| Sivas                        | 280,000   | 165,000   |
| Adana                        | 280,000   | N.A.      |
| Haleb                        | 100,000   | N.A.      |
| Trabzon                      | 120,000   | N.A.      |
| Hüdavendigâr                 | 60,000    | N.A.      |
| Aydın                        | 50,000    | N.A.      |
| Ankara, Kasta-<br>monu, Konya | 120,000  | N.A.      |
| İzmit                        | 65,000    | N.A.      |
| Total                        | 2,425,000 | 1,018,000 |

Source:  Population Armenienne, Paris, 1920.

## Summary: The Patriarchate Statistics

The difficulties with the statistics provided by the Armenian Patriarchate can be summarized as follows:

1. The form of the Armenian Patriarchate statistics naturally leads to questions as to how they were created. Statistics of any actual population count or enumeration are usually listed in odd numbers, not rounded to the

nearest 100,000. The Patriarchate statistics are in the form of an answer to the question "Approximately how many Armenians would you say were in the eastern vilâyets," not in the form of a compilation of baptismal records.

2. No examples of detailed Armenian parish records have ever come to light. The only detailed person-by-person records of Ottoman minority population ever seen and reported are in the Ottoman archives.[16] Nor have specific rules from the Patriarchate for the collection of baptismal, marriage, and death records in Istanbul been discovered. It is doubtful that the Ottomans, suspicious as they were of Armenian community action and publicity, would have allowed the type of massive collection and checking of data necessary for such records.

3. No detailed breakdowns of the Armenian population were presented by the Patriarchate. Statistics by sancak, kaza, and village could have been analyzed for correctness, as could data subdivided in other ways—for example, year of baptism—but they were never published.

4. The Patriarchate figures were obviously in great error on points other than the 1912 Armenian population. For example, they listed some provinces' Muslim populations as only 25% of the real totals and much overstated the 1882 Armenian population.

5. No official from the Armenian Patriarchate ever wrote commentary on the statistics or on how they were collected and compiled. We have only non-Patriarchal sources that infer the completeness of the Patriarch's knowledge. The only population statistics actually attributable to an Armenian Patriarch were published by the ex-Patriarch Malachia Ormanian in an appendix to his book on the Armenian church.[17] He made no statement concerning baptismal records and gave no indication that his figures, often widely at variance with the 1912 "Patriarchate Statistics," were anything but estimates.

6. The Armenian Patriarchate statistics, and all the statistics that followed from them, were uniformly presented as sections of polemic documents, not a part of a normal publication of statistical documents. They were used solely as supports for Armenian Independence.

That some form of baptismal records existed for Ottoman Armenians in their villages and towns is undoubtedly true. There is at present no way to know whether or not these were collected by the Patriarchate in Istanbul nor, if they were collected, whether they were complete and whether death records accompanied them. Would the records have accurately have listed the fates of the Armenians who died in 1878 and 1895 or of the many who followed the Russian evacuation from the eastern provinces, or of those who migrated to the United States or Europe? If so, why have none of these records ever appeared? Krikor Zohrab, who first published the Patriarchate statistics, could only come to an estimate of Armenian deaths and migrations by subtracting the Patriarchate 1912 statistics from the 1882 statistics. Had deaths of Armenians been recorded, these figures themselves could have been presented. Even if baptisms were somewhat accurately recorded, deaths were almost surely not, and underestimating the numbers of deaths and migrants would have made population estimates higher than the real numbers.

In fact, the Armenian Patriarchate population statistics were more or less informed guesses, more informed for western Anatolia, less for the east. This does not necessarily mean that the Patriarchate statistics were always wrong. Guesses can be good guesses or bad guesses. The best Patriarchal estimates (e.g., Sivas) of Armenian population may have been based on hard data, including Ottoman figures and house counts. That the Patriarchate statistics were estimates does, however, necessarily mean that Ottoman statistics, data for which we have detailed, age-specific counts, available examples of population registers, printed rules, and more, were of an order of magnitude better as population sources than were the Armenian data.

Lest it be thought that erroneous guesses were the province of any one group in the Ottoman Empire, it should be noted that whenever the Ottomans themselves strayed from their collected population data they were also capable of making absurd statements on population. To demonstrate this one might cite the section in the 1330 *Nüfus-i Umumî* that stated that perhaps 40% of the Muslim population of Van Province had not been counted, but that all the Armenians had been entered,[18] or the problems of the estimates of the Ottoman geographers, mentioned in appendix 2, or perhaps the "official" publication *La Turquie à l'Exposition Universelle de 1867*,[19] which gave the same type of rounded, inaccurate estimates (e.g., listing as total population less than half of the population of the eastern provinces) for which the Armenian Patriarchate has been criticized above. Erroneous European statistics can fill many books, as the multivolume collection of population estimates by Michoff attests.

With the exception of the wildest chance correlation, *any* estimate of a large population not founded on census, survey, or registration data must have been inaccurate, whether made by Armenians, Ottomans, Europeans, or Americans. Detailed census and registration figures in a statistically underdeveloped area like the Ottoman Empire are usually somewhat incorrect due to undercounting, but the undercounts can be corrected. Only census and registration data can give an accurate picture of the Ottoman population.

## Ottoman Statistics

The Ottoman government kept statistics of the Armenian population as part of its regular registration system and as taxation records for the military exemption tax (*bedel-i askeriye*), that Armenians paid in lieu of military service. These statistics were made public in the usual way, through the "censuses" and the salnames. In addition, Ottoman palace departments[20] and government ministries also kept summary statements on Armenian population, as a matter of political interest. In the post-1878 period, Armenian nationalism had become an external and internal political threat to the Ottomans. Since population information was a basis for understanding the Armenian situation in the Empire, Abdülhamid's government, known for its intelligence system, kept what it thought to be up-to-date population estimates on the Armenians, or at least attempted to do so.

Published Ottoman population statements on Christian minorities have been strongly criticized by both Europeans and Armenians. At the end of World War I, those in favor of an independent Armenia felt that:

> No scientific census has ever been taken by the government of the Turks and no reliable statistics on anything has ever been prepared by the Turks. The Turkish government has always falsified statistics, with the deliberate purpose of presenting the Armenians as only an insignificant minority in Armenia.[21]

Those who espoused the cause of Armenian independence saw the issue of population size as one of primary importance. They did not accept Ottoman population statements, which they believed to be deliberate falsifications of minority populations. They argued that the Ottomans:[22]

1. Deliberately gerrymandered provincial boundaries so that Armenian population centers would be divided among many provinces, each of which had a Muslim majority.

2. Introduced nonindigenous elements, especially Circassians and Kurds, into Armenian lands, so as to swell the Muslim population.

3. Grouped all Muslims together in population reports, regardless of language, ethnic or sectarian ties (e.g., Turks, Circassians, Yezidis, Kurds), while separating Christians by sect.

4. Overcounted Muslims in official statistics.

5. Undercounted Christians.

These issues are best considered separately.

1. The Ottomans unquestionably did reorganize the traditional province (*eyalet*) of Erzurum, a major center of Armenian population, into a number of smaller provinces, ostensibly as part of the reform and reorganization of provincial governments that came with the Vilâyet Law of 1876. Whether or not the Ottoman government, or individual members of the government, intended to divide up the Armenians by doing so is impossible to answer without documentary evidence, none of which has so far appeared. There is evidence that drawing provincial boundaries in order to minimize the proportion of Armenian population was not a consistent Ottoman policy, if it ever was a policy. If the Ottomans had intended to lower the proportions of Armenians in provinces, why would they, at the same time they divided-up Erzurum Eyaleti, have detached Hakkâri, which was more than 80% Muslim, from the Van Vilâyeti, thus greatly increasing the concentration of Christians in Van?[23] The primary purpose of the division of Erzurum and other eyalets into smaller vilâyets seems actually to have been administrative efficiency.

2. After the 1877–8 war and earlier wars with Russia, migrants from provinces lost to Russia did migrate to Ottoman territories, and migrants were indeed settled in areas inhabited by Armenians. The Ottomans settled immigrants in all areas of the Empire, as they had been doing since the Crimean War.[24] The Armenian area was not itself singled out for colonization. It should also be said, however, that the dynamics of the post-1878 migration in the east did change the balance of Muslims and Christians in the remaining eastern Anatolian provinces. This was not a result of official resettlement,[25] of which there was little in the east, but of Muslims leaving areas newly conquered by Russia for contiguous Ottoman areas and Armenians leaving Ottoman areas for the Russian Empire. The Ottoman government undoubtedly fostered Muslim in-migration, seeing it as a way to ce-

ment its control in the east by increasing the Muslim population and by keeping an embittered anti-Russian element on the border, where they could be counted on to resist Russian advances.

3. The Ottomans did group all Muslims together and separate Christians by sect in most, not all,[26] of their population statistics. This was a result of the millet system and of the theological reluctance to accept differences among Muslims. Though the refusal to divide Muslims by sect and language group did make them appear statistically as a block, this was not done for a nineteenth-century political motive. It was a continuing feature of Ottoman population registration from the fifteenth to the early twentieth centuries.

4. The alleged overcounting of Muslims has been discussed in detail in preceding chapters. The Ottomans actually undercounted, not overcounted, the Muslim population by undercounting Muslim women and children.

5. The final point, undercounting of Armenians, will be considered below in depth. The Ottomans did indeed undercount Armenians, though not to the degree claimed by some critics. In most cases their undercount was part of the same undercounting that affected all segments of the population—undercounting women and children.

One of the main tests of the intended accuracy of population enumerations is consistency. If the Ottoman central government had intended to misrepresent non-Muslim population in its printed records, the records might be expected to have changed dramatically as relations with particular millets changed. That this did not happen with the Greek Orthodox millet is demonstrated below. We will see here that it did not take place with records of the Armenian millet, either.

If they had misrepresented Armenian population intentionally, one would expect to see the numbers of Armenians reported by the Ottomans decreasing as the Ottoman government reacted to increasing claims to Armenian independence or autonomy. The Ottomans would theoretically have attempted to decrease the recorded number of Armenians, in order to demonstrate that there were too few Armenians to create a state. In fact, the opposite took place.

The province of Trabzon provides an example of Ottoman minority registration practices because it was a province in which a significant number of Armenians resided and the only "Armenian" province that had very good

Table 3.7

Gregorian Armenian Population of Trabzon Vilâyeti

| Publication | Publication Date | Population |
|---|---|---|
| 1286 Salname | 1869-70 | 32,798 |
| 1287 Salname | 1870-71 | 35,784 |
| 1288 Salname | 1871-72 | 35,510 |
| 1296 Salname | 1878-79 | 38,958 |
| 1305 Salname | 1887-88 | 40,887 |
| 1311 Salname | 1893-94 | 41,849 |
| 1313 Salname | 1895-96 | 42,349 |
| 1318 Salname | 1900-01 | 49,535 |
| 1319 Salname | 1901-02 | 50,233 |
| 1320 Salname | 1902-03 | 50,678 |
| 1321 Salname | 1903-04 | 51,639 |
| 1322 Salname | 1904-05 | 51,639 |
| 1324 Salname | 1905-06 | 51,483 |
| 1330 Nüfus-i Umumî | 1918 | 64,607 |

Source: According to Ottoman publications.

statistical reporting. Most of the provinces with a significant Armenian population were in areas in which Ottoman central control was weak and population records much poorer than those of Trabzon.

Table 3.7 presents the Gregorian (or Apostolic) Armenian population of Trabzon as it was listed in the Ottoman salnames, and as in the *1330 Nüfus-i Umumî*, at various publication dates from 1869 to 1918. The period was one of gradual, and sometimes rapid, deterioration of Ottoman-Armenian relations, yet the Ottoman statistics show a large and steady rise in the Armenian population of Trabzon. In fact, the *1330 Nüfus-i Umumî* population, the data for which was collected in 1912, shows that the Ottomans had upgraded their figures and actually recorded more Armenians at a time when relations were bad (1912) and published them when relations were abysmal (1918). The Ottoman statistics would seem to have been printed, if in anyone's aid, in aid of the cause of the Armenians. It is hard to believe that the Ottomans would publish such statistics unless they thought them to be accurate representations of the population and thus valuable to the state, no matter what they said about Armenian numbers.

Ottoman records for other provinces are more or less consistent and precise than Trabzon's, as was the case as well with records of Muslim population. Only in Van Vilâyeti and part of Bitlis Vilâyeti were records of Armenians much more poorly kept than those of Muslims. The important point is that there was no wish of the Ottoman government to publish anything but what they considered to be accurate figures on Armenian population.

The one most important factor concerning Ottoman population statistics of minorities was that they were kept as part of an ongoing government intelligence program, not made for polemic use. It was in the interest of the Ottoman state to provide itself with the most accurate statistics possible. While it may have happened that Ottoman officials in some eastern areas, particularly in Van Vilâyeti, may have changed population statistics to fit what they believed their masters in Istanbul wanted to see, it is unlikely that the Ottoman government wanted deliberately to deceive itself. The Ottoman government might rather have been expected to have done all it could to know exactly how many Armenians there were in the Empire, where they lived, and what they were doing, even if the information was kept secret. This is exactly what the Ottomans did.[27] Failures in statistical collection and compilation seem not deliberate, but were the result of untrained officials and of all the problems of counting population in any underdeveloped area, all seen above. The problems were compounded by the fact that much of the Armenian population lived in areas of the Empire in which Ottoman governmental control was weak.

It may be posited that the central Ottoman government might have deliberately published false statistics on the Armenian population, deliberate undercounts, in order to deceive the world, but it is highly unlikely that the Ottomans would have deliberately fooled themselves. Table 3.8 reproduces data from an archival source that was part of the Ottoman Archives' Yıldız Collection,[28] i.e., an unofficial working paper from the palace archives of

Abdülhamid II's government. By all evidence (e.g., sloppy handwriting, smudges, crossed-out sections, and corrections of addition errors) this document was not intended to go beyond the offices of the government. It is simply a list of provincial populations from the *tahrirs* (population registers), as copied and used by an unknown official, and undoubtedly not checked or compiled as accurately as a table intended for publication would have been.

Table 3.8

Armenian Population of the "Six Vilâyets" in Archival and Published Records

| Province | Archival c. 1300 | Published c. 1310 |
|---|---|---|
| Erzurum | 101,119 | 120,147 |
| Bitlis | 101,358 | 108,050 |
| Diyarbakır | 45,291 | 60,281 |
| Sivas | 112,649 | 129,085 |
| Mamuretülaziz | 73,178 | 83,394 |
| Van | 71,582 | 55,051 |
| Total | 505,177 | 556,008 |
| Difference | | 50,831 |
| Rate of Increase per year | | .0096 |

The table was compiled in a period (c. 1300–1882/3) prior to the first of the published "censuses." It is useful to compare this "secret" document's figures with the public figures of the first extensive published list of population, the *1313 İstatistik*, which gave figures compiled in 1310. Some of the differences between figures in table 3.8 resulted from changes in administrative boundaries and the confused borders of this period.[29] It is therefore preferable to compare the total Armenian population of the six provinces in the two schedules. They are remarkably close and their yearly rates of increase are reasonably within the expected range.

Closeness between archival sources only intended for governmental use and published statistics does not prove that the published statements were correct, but it does greatly diminish the possibility of the type of deliberate deception of which the Ottomans were accused.

## European Estimates

European estimates for the population of the Ottoman Armenian community were numerous and often at variance with one another. Some Europeans based their figures on Ottoman population registers, some on the reports of European consuls or personal estimates, and some on reports from members and officials of the Armenian millet. Table 3.9 presents a number of their estimates.

Table 3.9

Some European Estimates of Armenian Population

| Source | Area Estimated | Estimate |
|---|---|---|
| Contenson[1] | "Asiatic Turkey" | 1,150,000 |
| | "European Turkey" | 250,000 |
| Selonoy[2] | "The Nine Vilâyets" | 726,750 |
| Vambery[3] | "The Nine Vilâyets" | 1,131,125 |
| Trotter[4] | "The Nine Vilâyets" | 780,750 |
| Jakmen | "The Nine Vilâyets" | 1,330,000 |
| Cuinet | "The Nine Vilâyets" | 838,125 |
| Zelenof | "The Nine Vilâyets" | 921,000 |
| Lynch | "The Nine Vilâyets" | 1,058,484 |

1. Ludovic de Contenson, Les Reformes en Turquie d'Asie, 2nd ed., Paris, 1913, pp. 10 and 17. The author also quotes Cuinet (p. 12) for an earlier period, but states that the figures here are from "les plus recentes statistiques" (no other reference).
2. Russian general and military advisor in Erzurum, quoted in Esat Uras, Tarihte Ermeniler ve Ermeni Meselesi, Ankara, 1950, p. 133.
3. Deutsche Rundschau, February, 1896.
4. Trotter, Jakmen, Cuinet, Zelenof, and Lynch--as listed in Uras, p. 134.

The question of Armenian numbers became particularly important to European governments after World War I, when the Allies were attempting to divide Anatolia along ethnic lines. The difficulties of the governments in estimating population at that time demonstrate that European authorities had no idea where to turn for accurate population information. European "experts" disagreed among themselves and adopted widely varying estimates of the minority and Muslim populations of the Ottoman Empire, often depending on Armenian, Turkish, Greek, and even Kurdish sources. It is clear that no one at the Versailles Peace Conference had any clear idea what the Ottoman population was or had been.[30]

Much effort could be made and much space devoted here to analyses of European estimates of the Armenian population. It would all be futile. What was established in chapter 1 for Muslim population is true here for Armenian population, as well—only those who were in a position actually to count and record the population could have given an accurate estimate of population numbers. European analysts simply had no way to count the population.

## Armenian Population by Province

The Armenian population of the Ottoman Anatolian provinces is analyzed and corrected below. Two types of problems arise in the analysis. First is the presence of conflicting sets of figures, Ottoman and Armenian. Both must be considered, though the Armenian figures have been demonstrated above to be generally unreliable. Second is the unfortunate fact that the Ottoman population statistics for eastern Anatolia were themselves also imperfect. All Ottoman population records were undercounts of population, but in two eastern vilâyets the level of undercounting of Armenians was considerably larger than that of Muslims.

In analyzing the Armenian population, it has been necessary to use secondary sources that were not necessary for the study of Muslim population. The most important of these is Vital Cuinet's *La Turquie d'Asie*, which, as explained in appendix 2, was actually a somewhat modified Ottoman source. Cuinet has been used sparingly, mainly to see if he also corrected certain Ottoman data that appears to need extensive correction. In this way, Cuinet is especially valuable in corroborating deficiencies in the Ottoman government counts of Armenians in Bitlis Vilâyeti.[31] Other European accounts have also been used, but sparingly. They were uniformly wrong on population, but did give, for example, accurate indications of the large number of Armenian churches and schools in an area such as Siirt Sancağı of Bitlis Vilâyeti that officially listed few Armenians, thus providing an indication that the Armenian population of Siirt was undercounted. The group of Ottoman administrative documents, salnames, and geographers' works used above for Muslim population have of course been used here as well.

Unlike the statistics of Muslim population, Armenian population is listed here for only one year, the year in which data was collected for the 1330 Nüfus-i Umumî, usually 1330 A.H. (1911–12). The year was chosen because the 1330 Nüfus-i Umumî was the best of the published Ottoman population records, and because 1912 was the year listed in the Armenian Patriarchate statistics. The facility of comparison between Ottoman, Armenian, and other population figures makes 1330 A.H. a good choice. (Some confusion may arise over the publication date of the 1330 Nüfus-i Umumî, i.e., 1330 mali or 1913–14, and the dates of collection of the statistics in the volume which, like all dates in tables in this volume, are given in hicra years. Most of the population records on eastern Anatolia listed in the 1330 Nüfus-i Umumî were collected in 1330 A.H. (1911–12), but were compiled together as one set of statistics in 1330 M. (1913–14). The mechanics of this compilation and dates are examined in appendix 4).

No attempt has been made to create a time series of Armenian population from 1878–1914, as was done with Muslim population. For the eastern vilâyets, Ottoman data prior to 1330 was usually more deficient than the 1330 data and would have provided a poor basis for a time series. In addition, the effects of migration, relatively minimal for Muslims, would have been great for Armenians. Both internal migration and out-migration were strong factors affecting the Armenian population in the period. Migrations would have greatly skewed any attempted time series of Armenian population.[32]

A central assumption made below is that the misreporting of age and sex for Armenians was approximately the same as for Muslims. Until extensive archival research has been done, there is no way to prove this assumption. The source on which corrections of age and sex undercounts have been based, the 1313 İstatistik, did not give any age breakdowns by religious group. It did give each religious group by sex and the underregistration of women in each millet was relatively the same.[33] Age group misreporting of Armenians and Muslims has proven to be similar in other situations,[34] and it has been assumed here that it was similar in eastern Anatolia. The process of correction for "normal" undercounting of Armenian population, i.e., the same proportion of undercounting of women and children as found in the total population, is the same as that applied above to the Muslim population (original population × correction factor = corrected population). For two provinces, an additional correction factor for extraordinary undercounting has been applied before arriving at the original population.

For each province below, the statistics of the Armenian Patriarchate have been given for comparison to Ottoman data. Where appropriate, the statistics printed by ex-Patriarch Ormanian have also been included.[35] Ormanian's statistics, published in his volume on the Armenian Church, listed Armenian population by religious subdivision, along with a count of churches and "communes" of Armenians. Though not as well-known as the "Patriarchate Statistics," they, too, are Patriarch's statistics and, in fact, are the only Patriarch's statistics to which one can attach a name. There is no way of knowing if Ormanian consulted any ecclesiastical records for his figures; none are mentioned, but this is true of the "Patriarchate Statistics" also.

## Sivas Vilâyeti

Five of the six provinces in the "Six Vilâyets" were in the area labeled here as eastern Anatolia. This was the area of poorest Ottoman administrative control, poorest statistics, and greatest divergence between Ottoman and Patriarchate statistics. Of the six, the one province that was in central Anatolia, Sivas, while still fairly far removed from the seat of central Ottoman government, was clearly much advanced statistically over Bitlis, Van, or Mamuretülaziz.

Ottoman figures for the Armenian population of Sivas were very close to those of the Armenian Patriarchate, though not those of Ormanian, who listed 300,000.[36] When corrected for age and sex misreporting the 1330 Nüfus-i Umumî figures in fact result in a higher count of Armenian population than the Patriarchate statistics (table 3.10). This accuracy and agreement can be explained completely by the relative proximity of the Sivas Vilâyeti to the center of the Empire and to Ottoman administrative control.

The Armenian Patriarchate was also much closer to and surely more knowledgeable about the Armenians of Sivas and about the accuracy of Ottoman counts in Sivas.

Ottoman population sources uniformly gave the Armenian population of Sivas as approximately 13% of the total population. As Professor Karpat has established, even European and other sources have agreed with the Ottoman figures for Sivas.[37]

When the Ottoman statistics on Sivas Armenians are corrected for undercounting the total is $151,674 \times 1.1836 = 179,521$. The date of the *1330 Nüfus-i Umumî* statistics for Sivas, and thus for the corrected population, was 1330 A.H. (1911–12).

Table 3.10

Armenian Population of Sivas Vilâyeti

| Source | Figure |
|---|---|
| Ottoman | 151,674 |
| Cuinet | 170,433 |
| Patriarchate | 165,000 |

## Mamuretülaziz Vilâyeti

Mamuretülaziz was one of the provinces for which there was considerable difference between the Ottoman and the Patriarchate statistics.

The Ottoman figures from various sources were consistent, allowing for age and sex undercounting, and they seem to have counted Armenians as approximately the same percentage of the population in each case, demonstrating that at least no general policy existed of making the Armenian population look smaller as time, and troubles, advanced. If anything, the Ottoman records, as their collection methods improved, counted Armenians as a greater proportion of the Mamuretülaziz population than they had previously done.

The Ottoman figures for Mamuretülaziz were considerably better than

Table 3.11

Armenian Population of Mamuretülaziz Vilâyeti

| Source | Figure |
|--------|--------|
| Ottoman | 87,864 |
| Patriarchate | 168,000 |
| Ormanian | 111,043 |

those of Cuinet, who made large-scale errors in enumerating the Armenian population of Harput Kazası.

In the final analysis the Ottoman statistics must be used, as corrected, for the Armenian population of Mamuretülaziz Vilâyeti, even though the Ottoman and Patriarchate statistics were extremely different. The decision to use Ottoman statistics is based solely on their proven relative reliability and on the proven unreliability of the Armenian statistics. Intellectually and statistically, this is not a completely satisfactory approach, but, until much

Table 3.12

Percentage of Armenians in Mamuretülaziz

| Source | Percentage |
|--------|-----------|
| 1312 Salname* | 18% |
| 1313 İstatistik | 18% |
| 1330 Nüfus-i Umumî | 20% |

*Comparisons to periods before this time are difficult, due to the addition of Dersim Sancağı to the vilâyet. From the 1305 Mamuretülaziz salname it does appear, however, that the percentage of Armenians in the same area as that of the province in 1912 would be approximately 18%.

more data is available from the Ottoman archives, it is the only approach likely to result in an approximately accurate number of Armenians living in Mamuretülaziz.

The correction factor used for the Mamuretülaziz population assumes that a large proportion of the women and children of the province, both Armenian and Muslim, went unregistered. The *1330 Nüfus-i Umumî* population was 87,864; the correction factor is 1.2638 (see table 3.20).

## Diyarbakır Vilâyeti

The undercounting of Armenian population in Diyarbakır Vilâyeti was approximately the same as that of the Diyarbakır Muslim population. The *1330 Nüfus-i Umumî* was the only reliable record of the Diyarbakır population numbers, but analysis of other Ottoman population records, which are deficient in total population numbers, nevertheless reveals that the percentage of Armenians was recorded as approximately the same in each of them (table 3.13).

It was demonstrated in chapter 2 that the Ottoman registration system for Diyarbakır was not reliable until the *1330 Nüfus-i Umumî*. It appears that

Table 3.13

Percentage of Armenians in Diyarbakır

| Source | Percentage |
|--------|-----------|
| 1313 İstatistik | 15% |
| 1321 salname | 14% |
| Census 1 | 16% |
| 1330 Nüfus-i Umumî* | 15% |

*Viranşehir Kazası, which was added to the vilâyet in 1328, has not been included in these figures.

as the registration of Muslims improved, the registration of Armenians improved as well, leaving them at approximately the same percentage of the population in 1313 (1895–6) as in 1330 (1911–12). No indications appear of a deliberate undercount.

The Armenian population of Diyarbakır, multiplied by the correction factor (1.2172) was 89,131 (see table 3.20). This compares favorably, and surprisingly, with the figures of the Patriarchate (105,000) and Ormanian (81,700).

## Erzurum Vilâyeti

The province of Erzurum was central in the area claimed as an Armenian homeland. It lay between the two centers of Armenian population—Russian

Table 3.14

Armenian Population of Erzurum Vilâyeti

| Source | Figure |
| --- | --- |
| Ottoman | 136,618 |
| Cuinet | 134,967 |
| Patriarchate | 215,000 |

Armenia and eastern Anatolia. The city of Erzurum might have been expected to be the capital of the united Armenia, stretching from the Caucasus to Syria, that was envisaged by Armenian nationalists, had such a state been created. However, the majority of the Erzurum population was Muslim.

The numbers of Armenians in Erzurum seem to have been fairly closely watched by the Ottomans and population registers of Armenians were updated more regularly than those of Muslims.[38] This is not surprising, since the province of Erzurum was on the border with Russia and the Armenians were looked upon as a possible fifth column.

It is certain that the Armenian population of Erzurum was at one time much higher than it was at the end of the nineteenth century. Migration to Russian territory and the effects of numerous wars fought in Erzurum Province may have caused abnormalities in the age and sex distribution of the Armenian population, in addition to lowering its numbers. Therefore, though the same correction factor used previously for the Muslim population is used here for Armenians, it should be kept in mind that the Armenian population of Erzurum in 1330 had been affected by wars and migration and that the correction factor might not be exact. The *1330 Nüfus-i Umumî* population was 136,618; the correction factor is 1.1947 (see table 3.20).

## Van and Bitlis

Researchers are fortunate to have copies of Ottoman household counts for the two most statistically deficient Anatolian provinces—Bitlis and Van. These registers were obtained by a "Russian General Staff Major General (Mayewsky?) who, while on a Foreign Office appointment, properly studied, travelled, and saw nearly every corner of the two provinces in a period of more than five years."[39] The work of this major general was found by the Ottoman War Office, which checked the statistics,[40] translated the book into Ottoman Turkish, and published it, presumably for its own use. Thus Ottoman population registers that have so far not been uncovered in the Ottoman archives have come to light by a circuitous route. In the volume, *Van ve Bitlis Vilâyetleri Askerî İstatistiği*,[41] one-third of the pages were devoted to copies of registers of villages, households, and ethnic-religious groups in Van and Bitlis in 1899.

Use of the house counts in the *Van ve Bitlis Askerî İstatistiği* brings to bear a useful analytic factor in the investigation of the Armenian population of the two provinces, neither one of which has completely reliable Ottoman published statistics. The book is an especially valuable and interesting source of material since it corresponds closely with a detailed list of Armenian villages and houses in Bitlis Vilâyeti, published in Beirut in Armenian and translated by Levon Marashlian.[42] The Armenian Patriarchate estimates for Van and Bitlis were overcounts, but when an Armenian and an Ottoman list of villages and houses agree, the lists can be a valuable guide for correcting Ottoman population statements in an area in which Armenian population was significantly undercounted by the Ottomans.

The use of Ottoman and Armenian house counts, various demographic analyses, and comparisons of various sources of population data can give an estimate of minority populations in Van and Bitlis provinces, but there will always be a great deal of uncertainty about these populations. The Ottomans knew that they had undercounted population in Van and Bitlis, and commented on the fact in published and secret documents.[43] Reports and directives from Istanbul declared that the population registers from these provinces needed improvement and, as will be seen, the registers of Muslims were improved. The registers of non-Muslim population were not significantly improved.

Undercounting of population in Ottoman records is, of course, not a phenomenon restricted to Van and Bitlis. To some extent the Ottomans undercounted the populations in every vilâyet. The undercounts in Van and Bitlis, however, cannot be corrected simply by applying the usual correction factor for underregistration of women and children, because in these two provinces Armenian men were also significantly undercounted. The Ottoman records of minority population in Siirt and Genç sancaks of Bitlis Vilâyeti and in Van Vilâyeti need extensive revision.

### Bitlis Vilâyeti

Probably coincidentally, Armenian and Ottoman population figures for Bitlis Vilâyeti differed less than for other provinces. That this should happen in one of the two provinces in which the Ottomans most undercounted the Armenians is odd.

The Ottoman statistics for most of Bitlis Vilâyeti were as good as those of the rest of the eastern provinces. The Armenian populations of the sancaks of Bitlis and Muş, the largest sancaks, were fairly accurately reported. However, for unknown reasons, the Ottoman statistics for the Armenians of Siirt and Genç sancaks were inaccurate. Cuinet seems to have noticed this and to have adjusted the population accordingly.[44] Other, indirect bits of material indicate that the Armenians in the two sancaks were underrecorded. There were more Armenian schoolchildren listed in Siirt than in Bitlis or Muş,[45] even though the 1330 *Nüfus-i Umumî* listed much larger population numbers in the latter two sancaks. Comparison of the 1330 *Nüfus-i Umumî* population for Siirt and the *Van ve Bitlis Vilâyetleri Askerî İstatis-*

Table 3.15

Armenian Population of Bitlis Vilâyeti

| Source | Figure |
|--------|--------|
| Ottoman | 119,132 |
| Cuinet | 131,390 |
| Patriarchate | 180,000 |

*tiği* house counts yields a very low person per house ratio, one that indicates that the population of Armenians in the two sancaks was undercounted.[46] Siirt and Genç, especially Siirt, according to descriptions of Cuinet and others,[47] were minor centers of Armenian culture, as evidenced by schools, churches, and community organizations, and it seems likely that Cuinet's higher figures for Siirt and Genç were more carefully considered estimates of the Armenian population than were the Ottoman figures. The Cuinet figures have been counted here instead of the *1330 Nüfus-i Umumî* data. It should be born in mind that this is an estimate. As an estimate, it carries much less strength than the more precise population statements available for other provinces.

Using the Cuinet figures for Siirt and Genç sancaks, then, we arrive at a figure of 144,991 before correction for age and sex undercounting. The figure of 144,991 (31.29% of the total population)[48] has the virtue of following the percentage of Armenians in the total Bitlis population established

Table 3.16

Armenian Population in Two Bitlis Sancaks

| Sancaks | Cuinet | 1330 Nüfus |
|---------|--------|------------|
| Siirt | 30,152 | 11,347 |
| Genç | 12,964 | 5,190 |

prior to 1330 by the *1313 İstatistik*, in which 32% of the recorded Bitlis population were Armenians, whereas the *1330 Nüfus-i Umumî* only listed the Armenian population as 27% of the total. Since Bitlis boundaries did not change between 1313 A.H. and 1330 M., it seems unlikely that the percentage of Armenians would have radically changed between the two dates.

When corrected (correction factor: 1.3184), the Armenian population of Bitlis in 1330 was as shown in table 3.20.

## Van Vilâyeti

The *Van ve Bitlis Vilâyetleri Askerî İstatistiği* is a valuable tool for estimating the undercounting of Armenians in Van Vilâyeti. Though its house

Table 3.17

Armenian and Muslim Populations and Households

|          | Households in Registers | Population in Ottoman Records | Population per Household | Armenian Population at 6.69/Household Rate |
|----------|-------------------------|------------------------------|-------------------------|-------------------------------------------|
| Muslim   | 26,830                  | 179,380                      | 6.69                    |                                           |
| Armenian | 13,607                  | 67,792                       | 4.98                    | 91,031                                    |

counts are unquestionably undercounts, comparisons of its household counts for Armenians and Muslims usefully point up deficiencies in the registration of Van Armenians. According to its figures, there were 13,607 Armenian households in Van in 1899 and 26,830 Muslim households.[49] The *1330 Nüfus-i Umumî* listed the population of Van as 179,380 Muslims and 67,792 Armenians. As can be seen in table 3.17, when the two sets of figures are compared, the number of Muslims per household appears to have been much higher than the numbers of Armenians per household. Possible reasons for this are: (1) the number of Armenian households had increased between 1899, when households were counted, and 1912, when the population was registered; (2) there were fewer Armenians per household than

Muslims per household; (3) the Armenian population was undercounted.[50] The third reason must be the answer. In times of troubles, especially those c. 1905–6, the numbers of Armenian households might have contracted, for safety and due to loss of household heads, not greatly increased. Emigration of Armenian males[51] would have meant fewer "new" households to replace those whose heads had died, since the males who would have headed the household had emigrated. Expansion of household numbers is very unlikely. All evidence, furthermore, is that Armenian households were at least as large as Muslim. In the cities they were probably, on the average, larger.[52] The only suitable explanation is the undercounting of Armenians.

Van Vilâyeti officials have been shown above to have had much less grasp on population numbers than did Ottoman officials in other provinces. In terms of central government control, Van was, with the exception of Arabian peninsula provinces and Iraq, the worst of the Ottoman provinces. It is not unusual that minority groups would have been more poorly counted there than in provinces in which the government's control was more effective.

In addition to household counts, other indicators also point to an undercount of Armenians and other Christians in Van (e.g., Cuinet: 79,998 Armenians in Van; 1330 Nüfus-i Umumî: 67,792, an 18% difference). The military exemption tax paid by Van non-Muslims in 1313 indicates a greater non-Muslim population than does the population records.[53] Most significant is the comparison of the percentage of non-Muslims counted in two years, 1313 A.H. and 1330 M. Ottoman statistics indicate that the Ottoman government was gradually improving its counts of Muslims in Van Vilâyeti (table 3.18),[54] but that the enumeration of non-Muslims was improving little. The Muslim population, as recorded, would have had to have been increasing three times faster than the non-Muslim population. This was impossible. No human population could have increased as fast as did the recorded Muslim population (50 per thousand per year, well above the rates of the fastest-growing modern populations). The figures in table 3.18 are completely explained by the increasingly good registration of Muslims, while registration of non-Muslims must have remained at close to its previous level of incompleteness. This interpretation is supported by the other available population sources for Van. For example, "Census 1," though incomplete for Hakkâri Sancağı of Van, listed Armenians as 52% of Van Sancağı, whereas the 1330 Nüfus-i Umumî listed them as 36%. The per-

centages for Van Vilâyeti in "Census 1" would have shown a Muslim majority had Hakkâri Sancağı been included, but the latter-day undercounting
of Armenians in Van is obvious.

If the non-Muslim population of Van were the same percentage of the
1330 *Nüfus-i Umumî* population as of the 1313 *İstatistik* population, then
the non-Muslim population would have been 129,896, of whom 85% would
have been Armenians—110,405.[55] Correspondingly, applying the same persons per household to the Armenian population as was seen in recorded
Muslim population and households, we arrive at 91,031 (as per table 3.17:
13,607 households at 6.69 per household). Both of these figures—91,000

Table 3.18

Recorded Population of Van Vilâyeti, Muslims and Non-Muslims

| Year | Muslims | Non-Muslims |
|------|---------|-------------|
| 1313 | 76,956 (58%) | 55,051 (42%) |
| 1330 | 179,380 (69%) | 79,760 (31%) |

Source: 1330 Nüfus-i Umumî, uncorrected figures.

and 110,000—are strictly comparable to the figures for the Muslim recorded
population as seen in chapter 6, and should be looked upon as sharing the
same factor of undercounting of women and children as the Van Muslim
population (1.3 × listed population = corrected population). When this
correction factor is applied to the two figures above (i.e., 91,000 and 110,000)
we arrive at upper and lower bounds for the Armenian population of Van
in 1330 (table 3.19).

Like the statistics for the Muslim population of Van, the figures for Van
Armenians in table 3.19 cannot be viewed as exact. The demographic perils
of basing a population on household counts ("low" in table 3.19), percentages of population in other enumerations ("high"), or any other calculations
done on very deficient data are numerous. The middle figure is a mean
between high and low estimates; it has been used here as the estimate of

Table 3.19

Estimates of the Armenian Population of Van, 1330

| Estimate | Figure |
|----------|--------|
| High | 143,000 |
| Middle | 130,500 |
| Low | 118,000 |

Van Armenian population that is entered in the general population tables. There may be some hope that possible errors in the high and low estimates may cancel each other out in the middle estimate. A more theoretically reliable position would be that the Armenian population lay between one limit and the other.

The use of a population estimate that considerably increases the numbers of Armenians over the recorded Ottoman figures, while based on little solid statistical ground, is well supported by the fact that each type of analysis

Table 3.20

Armenian Population of Six Eastern Anatolian Vilâyets in 1330 (1911-12)

| Vilâyet | Population |
|---------|-----------|
| Sivas | 179,521 |
| Mamuretülaziz | 111,043 |
| Diyarbakır | 89,131 |
| Erzurum | 163,218 |
| Bitlis | 191,156 |
| Van | 130,500 |

Sources: Van Vilâyeti--medium estimate.
Others--1330 Nüfus-i Umumî, corrected figures.

attempted (e.g., comparisons of household counts, Armenian sources, comparisons to other Ottoman data, European sources) indicates that the Ottoman population records of the *1330 Nüfus-i Umumî* were far too low.

Based on the experience of the surprising accuracy of Ottoman population statistics for other provinces, the assumption made when beginning to analyze the Ottoman data on Van Armenians was that the undercounting of Van Armenians would be of the same magnitude as the undercounting of Muslims. By every experiment and test, this did not prove to be the case.

## Cilicia

Cilicia, as such, was never an Ottoman administrative area. The area known as Cilicia was divided between the Ottoman provinces and Adana

Table 3.21

Populations of Sancaks of Adana, Kozan, Maraş, and Cebelibereket,
According to Ottoman and Armenian Sources

|  | Ottoman | Armenian |
|---|---|---|
| Armenians | 91,855 | 205,000 |
| Muslims | 405,757 | 156,000 |

and Haleb. "Armenian Cilicia" was defined by the Patriarchate as "*Vilayet d'Adana, Vilayet d'Alep (partie septentrionale* [sic] *Aintab, Ourfa, Kiliss, Marache).*"[56] The Armenian delegates to the Versailles Peace Conference considered Cilicia to be the "Sanjaks of Adana, of Maraş, of Khazan, and of Djebel Bereket,"[57] leaving out the Armenians of Urfa. Table 3.21 compares the Ottoman (*1330 Nüfus-i Umumî*) and Armenian (Peace Conference Delegation) figures for the latter boundaries. There is a considerable difference.

One should keep in mind while comparing the statistics in table 3.21 that the Ottoman figures listed undercounted the Muslim population of Adana by more than 20%, so that the actual number of Muslims in the above area was actually more than 500,000. The massive undercounting of Muslims in the Armenian figures follows the pattern seen and analyzed above. The Ottoman data, on the other hand, was much more accurate, if flawed, a part of a steady and consistent system of registration data. While by no means completely accurate, the Ottoman figures can be corrected. Table 3.22 gives the corrected Armenian population of the two Ottoman provinces that contained Cilicia—Haleb and Adana, and the independent sancaks that had been, by 1330 M. (1914–15), detached from them. Totals for the Armenians have been corrected by the same correction factors used for Muslim population, under the assumption that Armenian population experienced the same large underregistration of children.

Table 3.22

Armenian Population of Cilician Vilâyets and Independent Sancaks, 1330

| Location | Population |
|----------|-----------|
| Adana Vilâyeti | 74,490 |
| İçel I.S. | 440 |
| Haleb Vilâyeti | 58,007 |
| Maraş I.S. | 45,051 |
| Urfa I.S. | 21,533 |

## The Other Provinces

Armenian population outside of the "Six Vilâyets" and Armenian Cilicia was not extensively commented on by Armenian sources. The Armenian delegation to the Versailles Peace Conference listed 440,000 Armenians as living "in other parts of Asiatic Turkey"[58] in 1914.

In almost all cases the Armenians in the other parts of Anatolia lived in areas with good population records, at least records much better than those kept in eastern Anatolia. This is aptly demonstrated by the superior age and sex registration in western and northern provinces, shown in chapter 2.

Table 3.23 lists the 1330 Nüfus-i Umumî population data for Armenians in provinces not yet examined and the corrected Armenian populations for

Table 3.23

Armenian Population According to 1330 M. (1913-14)
Provincial Boundaries

| Vilâyets | Original Population | Corrected Population | Registration Year |
|---|---|---|---|
| Hüdavendigâr | 61,191 | 69,134 | 1330 |
| Aydın | 20,766 | 25,231 | 1331 |
| Ankara | 53,957 | 63,605 | 1331 |
| Konya | 13,225 | 16,808 | 1330 |
| Kastamonu | 8,959 | 10,586 | 1332 |
| Trabzon | 40,237 | 41,211 | 1332 |
| Independent sancaks | | | |
| Antalya I.S. | 630 | 800 | 1330 |
| Biga | 2,541 | 2,836 | 1331 |
| Bolu | 2,972 | 3,512 | 1332 |
| Canik | 28,576 | 29,268 | 1332 |
| Eskişehir | 8,807 | 10,161 | 1330 |
| İzmit | 57,789 | 70,659 | 1331 |
| Kayseri | 52,192 | 61,538 | 1331 |
| Kara Hisar (Afyon) | 7,448 | 8,415 | 1330 |
| Karası | 8,704 | 9,834 | 1330 |
| Kütahya | 4,548 | 5,138 | 1330 |
| Mentese | 12 | 15 | 1331 |
| Niğde | 5,705 | 7,250 | 1330 |
| Total | 378,259 | 435,995 | |

each province. Independent Sancaks have been corrected using the correction factors of their "mother" provinces. In the cases of Eskişehir I.S., which was made up of kazas drawn from both Ankara and Hüdavendigâr provinces, the Ankara factor has been applied to the kazas taken from Ankara Vilâyeti (Sivrihisar and Mihalıççık) and the Hüdavendigâr factor applied to the kaza taken from it (Eskişehir). The same system was applied to Kayseri I.S., which took Kayseri, Develi, and İncesu kazas from Ankara Vilâyeti and Bunyan-i Hamid Kazası from Sivas Vilâyeti.

It was in the provinces closest to central authority that Ottoman and Armenian estimates of Armenian population most closely coincided. As a matter of fact, the corrected number of total Armenians listed in table 3.23 435,995, is larger than that estimated by the Patriarchate in 1882, 415,000,[59] and close to the 440,000 estimated by the delegation to the Peace Conference. This correspondence is deceptive, however, since it is only the totals that agree, not figures for individual provinces. For example, the Patriarchate figures for 1882, which closely match later Armenian figures for areas outside the "Six Vilâyets" and Cilicia, gave a population of 120,000 Armenians for Trabzon Vilâyeti (i.e., Trabzon plus Canik I.S. in table 3.23), whereas the Ottomans listed 68,813. For the 1882 province of Hüdavendigar, the Patriarchate gave a population of 60,000 Armenians, whereas the Ottomans listed 61,891.[60] Despite this, the Ottoman and Armenian figures, which are so divergent for the east, do correspond much more closely for western Anatolia.

Those who believe the Ottomans deliberately falsified population statistics must ask themselves why the Ottomans would falsify some data and not others. Could the Ottomans have seriously felt that it was in their interest to state that there were *more* Armenians in certain provinces than the Patriarchate believed to be the case?

There can be no doubt that Ottoman figures on Armenian population in eastern Anatolia were somewhat mistaken, as were Ottoman statistics on eastern Anatolian Muslim population. It must be asserted, however, that the Ottoman errors were errors of underregistration and inadequate system, errors that apply to all developing countries and that, in most cases, applied to all Ottoman communities alike. Ottoman statistics did not selectively discriminate against Armenians.

## NOTES

1. Historians of Armenia have begun to publish analyses of Armenian population and many authors have made explicit or implicit use of population figures in their works on Armenians in the Ottoman Empire. The best of these analyses is that of Richard Hovannisian in *Armenia on the Road to Independence* (Berkeley and Los Angeles, 1967), who states clearly the difficulties of arriving at accurate population

figures and avoids choosing figures for polemic reasons. The worst is exemplified by an article by Sarkis Karayan ("An Inquiry into the Statistics of the Turkish Genocide of the Armenians, 1915–1918," *Armenian Review* 25, 4, 1972, pp. 4–40), which is based on estimates of population size given by Armenian refugees from Turkish Armenia. I have decided that point-by-point refutation of the work of others would generally be out of place here, but feel I should state why the type of analysis used by Dr. Karayan is not found in this study.

Many Armenian refugees from Anatolia wrote books of memoirs that often contained exhaustive descriptions of villages and areas of Armenian population. These studies seem to be a potentially very useful source for the social and economic history of Eastern Anatolia. They cannot, however, be used as sources for total population figures of any but the smallest areas. Demographers have never, for good reason, accepted such "eyewitness" statements on population numbers of large areas as accurate. The reasons for this are numerous, but can be roughly summarized as follows:

1. Very seldom do two observers of population agree on their findings. A good example of this comes from the aforementioned Karayan article, p. 28, fn. 40, in which he quotes three eyewitness accounts for the population of Hajin that differ considerably—24,000, 25,000, and 52,000.

2. There is an innate human interest in stating that the unit of which you are a part is special, e.g., that your village was more populous than others or that more from your village died and your village or area suffered more than others.

3. Memories, especially memories of numbers, are likely to change as time passes between the event and the writing of memoirs.

4. It is not easy to estimate population, even in areas in which one has lived all one's life. Historical demographers of all parts of the world have uniformly found it necessary to discard such estimates because they have so often proved to be wrong when compared to accurate census or registration data. Perhaps the easiest way to demonstrate this to a reader is to ask him to estimate the population numbers of the town or neighborhood in which he grew up. He will find, I believe, that he cannot come up with a reasonable estimate unless he has some knowledge of the census figures on the population.

At best, then, the reports of refugees and other eye-witnesses can only be used to check on the basic accuracy of census and registration reports. For example, a refugee's report that his family and 3,000 other Armenians lived in an area that the Ottoman statistics said had no Armenians would not prove that there were indeed 3,000 Armenians there, but it would indicate that there were probably a good many more in the area than indicated by the Ottomans. As such a check the reports can be valuable, as will be shown below for the province of Van.

2. Hovannisian, *Armenia*, p. 36. Esat Uras, *Tarihte Ermeniler ve Ermeni Meselesi* (Ankara, 1950), pp. 131–133. H. F. B. Lynch, *Armenia, Travels and Studies*, v. 2 (London, 1901), pp. 408–414.

3. See, for example, *The Armenian Question Before The Peace Conference* ("A Memorandum Presented Officially by the Representatives of Armenia to the Peace

Conference at Versailles on February 26th, 1919") pp. 7 and 8. Hereafter referred to as *Armenian Question*.

The Armenians did have a traditionally high birth rate, one of the highest for a Christian population. Frank Lorimer, in *The Population of the Soviet Union* (Geneva, 1946), p. 92, listed a GRR of 3.89, which would of course have been lower in Anatolia in 1878–1912 because of differing conditions.

4. Paris, 1913.

5. Kevork Mesrob, *L'Armenie* (Constantinople, 1919), pp. 67 and 68. Boghos Nubar, *The Pre-war Population of Cilicia* (Paris, 1920), pp. 1 and 2.

6. See the "National Constitution of the Armenians in the Turkish Empire," especially Article 69, in Lynch, *Armenia*, Appendix I.

7. *Population Armenienne de la Turquie Avant la Guerre, Statistiques etablis par le Patriarcat Armenien de Constantinople*, Paris, 1920, hereafter referred to as *Population Armenienne*.

8. A simple equation illustrates the difficulty:

$$\text{Population in } 1912 - \text{Deaths} = \text{Population in } 1922$$

where "Population in 1912" is those Armenians alive in Anatolia in 1912, "Deaths" is those alive in 1912 who died between 1912 and 1922, and "Population in 1922" is those of the 1912 population who survived to 1922. (Notice that births are not included.) If any two factors are known, the other can be calculated, but, in fact, the numbers of Armenians who died between 1912 and 1922 must also be found, so it is not possible to check the accuracy of the 1912 population estimate (i.e., the Patriarchate statistics).

9. See chapter 2.

10. The geographic area of Ottoman Sivas was covered, in 1927, by the Turkish Republic vilâyets of Sivas, Şebin Karahisar, Tokat, and Amasya, the kazas of Havza and Vezirköprü in Samsun Vilâyeti, and the kazas of Bünyan and Pinar Başı in Kayseri Vilâyeti.

11. *Armenian Question*, Annexes 2–4.

12. The difference in dates between the Russian and Armenian figures means that some population increase can be expected to have taken place between the two years, but not enough to account for the discrepancy between the two figures (891,704, increasing at a constant rate of .01 a year between 1897 and 1912 would result in a population of 1,036,012 in 1912). It was not a period of significant migration.

It is difficult to see where exactly the Armenian data divides "Russian Armenia" from the rest of the Caucasus region. The headings in the Armenian table are:

| Province | Area Included |
|---|---|
| Erivan | "The whole of the Province" |
| Gandzak | "The western half" |
| Kars | "Exclusive of the northern part beyond Ardahan" |
| Tiflis | "Southeastern corner only" |

These descriptions are not translatable into Russian Imperial administrative districts. I have chosen the following as approximately matching the Armenian descriptions:

| Province | Area Included |
|---|---|
| Gandzak | Elizavetpol (less Nukhi and Aresh) |
| Kars | Kars (less Ardahan) |
| Tiflis | Akhaltsikh, Akhalkalak, Borchalu |

13. The Russian count of both Muslims and Armenians was surely an underenumeration. Therefore the difference between the the Armenian estimate of Armenians and the actual Armenian population of Russian Armenia must have been smaller than appears here and the difference between the Armenian estimate of Muslims in the same area and the actual number of Muslims larger.

14. See table 3.19.

15.

| Year | | Mortality |
|---|---|---|
| 1894 | Sasun | 12,000 |
| 1895-6 | "Central and Eastern Turkey" | 150,000 |
| 1896 | "Constantinople" | 9,570 |
| | Van | 8,000 |
| | Sasun | 5,640 |
| | Adana | 30,000 |

Source: George Horton, The Blight of Asia, quoted in Garo Chichekian, "The Armenians Since the Treaty of San Stephano: A Politico-Geographic Study of Population," Armenian Review 22, no. 2, Spring, 1968, pp. 42-56.

16. Unfortunately, most remain uncatalogued. Many records of population change (births, deaths, migration) and numerous records of non-Muslims are nevertheless available. See, for example, Kepeci 6491, defters 1 and 2, and Cevdet 12233, 13023, and 13656.

17. Malachia Ormanian, L'Eglise Armenienne, Paris, 1910. Ormanian published figures on Armenian population, by diocese, in an appendix. In a modern translation into English (The Church of Armenia, translated by G. Marcar Gregory, [London, 1955]), the editor, Terenig Poladian, added figures for the population of Armenians in the world by the dioceses of 1954. Both sets of figures have been used here. Those of Poladian are always marked (Poladian) in notes below.

18. 1330 Nüfus-i Umumî, French Version (Tableau . . .), unnumbered page opposite "Avant Propos."

19. "S. Excellence, Salaheddin Bey," Paris, 1867, printed as part of the Ottoman exhibits in the Paris Exposition.

20. See "Archival Population Documents" in the bibliography.

21. *Armenian Question*, p. 21. Armenian authorities also felt that their numbers were deliberately minimized by the Turkish government: "Without modifying materially the total number of the population it [the Ottoman government] reduces, as far as possible, the number of Christians, and adds the difference to that of the Moslems" (*Armenian Question*, p. 21). "There are no accurate Turkish official statistics in existence. All those which have been published by the Ottoman government are certainly erroneous, having been compiled for the purpose of attributing to the Moslem population a majority in all parts of the Empire" (Boghos Nubar, *The Pre-War Population of Cilicia*, p. 1).

22. The charges are repeated in many works on the Armenian question. See, for example, Mesrob, pp. 61–64.

23. See chapter 2.

24. There are many works on the immigrants into the Empire. Many of them are listed in Shaw, *History*, II, p. 448.

25. There were, however, extensive planned settlements in Cilicia, on the Adana plain, including irrigation projects.

26. The French version of the *1330 Nüfus-i Umumî* gives "Armenian" and "Greek" categories, which include uniates and Protestants. Early (pre-1878) population records often give only "Muslim" and "Non-Muslim" or "Muslim," "Christian," and "Jewish" as categories.

27. Numerous archival sources indicate that the Ottomans kept watch over registration data and did what they could to insure accurate reporting. Various sets of regulations are mentioned below and the Ottomans also investigated and punished individuals for inaccurate record-keeping. See Yıldız 18–1872–93–39, İrade Meclis-i Vala 22856, İrade Meclis-i Mahsus 2089, or any of the many other documents that deal with population record-keeping.

28. Yıldız 18–553/49–93–33

29. See chapter 2, "Eastern Anatolia."

30. There is no need to quote at length here from the voluminous correspondance regarding population that was entered into the records of the delegations to the Versailles Peace Conference. After weeks of reading the records of the conference in the Public Records Office in London, I have found nothing in them that can provide a satisfactory basis for population estimates. Those who wish to demonstrate this to themselves should consult F.O. 608, especially classes 78, 84, 85, 88, 95, and 108. Of particular interest is the interplay between those who gave estimates of population, drawn from various sources, and those who disagreed or occasionally (and rightly) questioned and doubted everything. At the time, "sources," whether Europeans or Ottoman citizens, provided population information based on their dedication to one group or another, rather than on good data.

31. Cuinet himself was often in error and he had no understanding of the Ottoman undercount of women and children. His work is no panacea.

32. If a number of points on a time series line were filled with accurate population data, the effects of migration would be seen in the series and the problems

would be small, but when only one or two accurate points are known, a time series would be an inaccurate smoothing of the curve of population increase (i.e., if population is known for every year, then migration is reflected in the data; otherwise, it must be already known to create a proper time series).

33. The correction factors used for the Muslim population in earlier chapters were, of course, actually correction factors for the total population. In applying the factor to subgroups of the population some distortion may result. If, for example, Armenian children were more completely registered than Muslim children, then applying the correction factor to both groups would result in an underestimate of Muslim population and an overestimate of Armenians. Taking Sivas Vilâyeti as an example, if the underregistration of Muslim children were twice as bad as that of Armenian children, Muslim population would be underestimated by approximately .005, Armenian population overestimated by approximately .036.

34. See the 1897 Russian census.

35. See note 17.

36. Ormanian, *L'Eglise Armenienne*, pp. 205 and 206.

37. Kemal Karpat, "Ottoman Population Records and the Census of 1881/2–1893," *IJMES* 9 (2), May, 1978, p. 257.

38. See chapter 2.

39. In translator's opening statement. See notes 40 and 41 below.

40. The book's translator commented that the statistics were out of date, since they were for 1899 and his book was published in 1912. This will not affect the analysis here.

41. Translated by Cavalry Major Mehmed Sadik, Istanbul, Matbua-yi Askeriye, 1330.

42. Garo Sassuni, *Patmutiwn Taroni Ashkhari* (History of the Daron Region) (Beirut, Daron-Duruperan Compatriotic Union, 1956), pp. 331–386. (Source: Levon Marashlian).

It is often difficult to compare villages from one source to the other, because of name differences and changes in villages and households that naturally came over time. The areas I have checked in both seem remarkably close, with none of the great variation that characterizes the Ottoman and Patriarchate statistics of total population. For example, below are villages and *nahiyes* in Hizan for which I could find correspondance in the two lists:

Ottoman and Armenian House Counts

| Villages and Nahiyes | Armenian | Ottoman |
|---|---|---|
| Hizan Nahiyesi | | |
| Horhor (Kharkhots) | 40 | 24 |
| Anabad | 15 | 22 |
| Norşen | 20 | 10 |
| Bahor | 25 | 17 |
| Nam | 8 | 9 |
| Aşağı Karasu | 12 | 18 |

| | | |
|---|---|---|
| Karasu | 40 | 25 |
| Darons (Daronts) | 30 | 38 |
| Andans (Andiants) | 14 | 40 |
| Siyakert (Sbargerd) Nahiyesi | | |
| Han Hayvan (Jajvan) | 40 | 50 |
| Yukarı Konens | 38 | 37 |
| Konens | 13 | 9 |
| Yukarı Kivrik (Hiwruk) | 36 | 40 |
| Kivrik | 20 | 19 |
| Lovar | 14 | 12 |
| Tag | 10 | 8 |
| Geygiz | 11 | 9 |
| Danses | 8 | 8 |
| Dalars | 12 | 15 |
| Hivseb (Hivsb) | 14 | 20 |
| Arancık (Arnchig) | 21 | 20 |
| Davagos (Dvaghus) | 31 | 30 |
| Gran | 8 | 5 |
| Mad | 10 | 20 |
| Tesmen (Tsmen) | 13 | 20 |

43. See the introduction to the *1330 Nüfus-i Umumî*.

44. Vital Cuinet, *La Turquie, d'Asie*, Paris, 1890–94, v. II, p. 527.

45. Ibid., p. 598.

46. E.g., Şirvan kazası, 3.4, Pervari Kazası, 1.8.

47. Cuinet, *La Turquie*, v. II, pp. 596–628. Ormanian, *L'Eglise Armenienne*, p. 206.

48.
$$(P_{ar} + A)/(P_{tot} + A) = .3129$$
where $P_{ar}$ is the recorded Armenian population

$P_{tot}$ is the recorded total population

A is the corrective addition to Armenian population.

No provision has been made in the divisor to allow for potential corrections to Nestorian and Chaldean populations, which might change the .3129 figure slightly downward.

49. 4,252 Turkish, 22,578 Kurdish.

50. Theoretically, overcounting of Armenian houses would also be a possibility, but it is extremely unlikely that the Ottomans would have particularly overcounted Armenian households and a general overcount of all households (also unlikely) would not affect the Armenian population ratio:

$$\frac{(M/H_m) \times K}{(A/H_a) \times K} = \frac{M/H_m}{A/H_a}$$

where M is Muslim population

A is Armenian population

$H_m$ is total Muslim households

$H_a$ is total Armenian households

K is a constant undercounting or overcounting.

In the case where $H_m = H_a$,

$$\frac{M/H_m \times K}{A/H_a} = \frac{M}{A}$$

which is the true ratio of Muslims to Armenians.

51. See Robert Mirak, "Armenian Emigration to the United States to 1915 (I): Leaving the Old Country," *Journal of Armenian Studies* I, no. 1, Autumn, 1975, pp. 5–42, for information on Armenian emigration from Anatolia to the United States.

52. See the *Van ve Bitlis İstatistiği* and the comments of Lynch, *Armenia*, on the Armenians in the cities of the east.

53. This is only meant to serve as an indication of undercounting, since the military exemption tax (*bedel-i askeriye*) was notoriously inexact as a population estimator, primarily because of the methods of its collection, over- and undercollection, and the practice of counting collections arrears in with the collections of another year. The lack of relation between the *Bedel-i askeriye* can be seen in the *İhsaiyat-i Maliye* of 1325 or of 1326, which give figures for population and the tax, or in the *1313 İstatistik*, which also gives both.

54. Table 3.18 uses uncorrected figures. The correction factors are mainly for the sancak of Hakkâri, whereas most of the Armenians lived in Van, and it is unlikely that the *1313 İstatistik* considered Hakkâri, either, so the uncorrected figures are better for comparison.

55. 85% is the percentage of Armenians among the registered non-Muslims of Van in the *1330 Nüfus-i Umumî*.

56. *Population Armenienne*, p. 9.

57. *Armenian Question*, Table No. 2 (Annex).

58. Ibid.

59. *Population Armenienne*, p. 9.

60. In 1882, Hüdavendigâr included the 1330 vilâyet of Hüdavendigâr, plus the sancaks of Kara Hisar, Karası, and Kütahya, which were Independent Sancaks in 1330 M.

# 4.

# *Greek Population*

THE GREEK POPULATION of Anatolia was centered in the coastal areas of the Aegean, Mediterranean, Marmara, and Black Seas. Ottoman Greeks were mainly members of the Greek Orthodox millet, though by the end of the Empire the Ottomans were recording approximately 3.5% of their Greek citizens as Greek Catholic (i.e., uniate).[1] An unknown number of Greek residents of Anatolia were also registered as foreign citizens.[2]

Like the Armenians, the Greeks of Anatolia were the subjects of many conflicting population estimates. The various European estimators of Ottoman population all made estimates of the Greek population of the Empire. As is demonstrated in appendix 2, these European estimates were in no way reliable, simply because the Europeans had no way to count the population. In terms of statistical information, the situation of the Greeks differed greatly from that of the Armenians, because the centers of Greek population were in areas for which the Ottomans possessed good population statistics. The populations of the seacoast provinces were the best recorded in Anatolia and the Greeks lived in these provinces. Therefore, the Ottoman population figures on Greeks are considerably better than those on Armenians, who lived in the most statistically underdeveloped provinces. As will be seen below, Ottoman statistics were the most consistent and reliable records of Anatolian Greek population. The type of detailed province-by-province analysis made above for the Armenian population is obviated here by the quality of the Ottoman data on Greek population. There is also no need for detailed justification of Ottoman population records, analyses of the deficiencies of European estimates of Ottoman population, or descriptions of the techniques used to correct incomplete data, all of which have been considered at length in earlier chapters. Before accepting Ottoman population figures on Anatolian Greeks, the only question is whether or not Greek sources, analogous to the Armenian Patriarchate statistics, should be considered equally with the Ottoman statistics. The Ottomans had the opportunity to count the Greeks accurately and it was in the Ottoman's self-interest to do so. The only ones with a similar, perhaps greater interest in enumerating the Greeks were the Greeks themselves.

If Greek enumerations of Ottoman Greek population had been taken, they might have rivaled the Ottoman counts in accuracy. Were the Greek and Ottoman figures then to disagree, there would naturally be reason to question the Ottoman statistics. Serious consideration must therefore be given to figures on Greek population published by Greeks and philhellenes immediately after World War I. At that time, scholars and politicians, who recognized that credible statements on the Greek population of Anatolia must appear to be drawn from actual enumerations, quoted from two "censuses"—one purportedly taken by the Turks and one by the Greeks—to bolster their claims to land in Anatolia.

The figures of the two "censuses" presented by the Greeks stand in opposition to Ottoman data. They show many more Greek residents in Anatolia than do Ottoman statistics. In the province of Aydın, for example, the Greek statistics listed twice as many Greeks as did the Ottoman statistics for the same period (630,000 to 320,000).[3] This discrepancy is odd, since one of the sources for the Greek figures was avowedly a set of Ottoman official statistics. At the Versailles Peace Conference and in western publications, however, no discrepancy was noticed, since the Greek figures were never compared to actual Ottoman data.

The figures on population presented by the Greek representatives were, in fact, a well-considered deception. This has been demonstrated at length elsewhere,[4] but the findings are summarized below.

The Greek figures consisted of two sets of statistics on Ottoman population. These were referred to as the "Greek Patriarchate Statistics of 1912" and the "Turkish Official Statistics of 1910," the latter supposedly taken from the "Ottoman Census of 1910." The two sets of statistics were broken down by province and ethnic group. Their figures did not agree on Muslim population, but they were in general agreement on Greek population. For example, according to the Greek Patriarchate statistics, there were 1,782,582 Greeks in Anatolia (including the Asiatic shore of Constantinople) in 1912; the "Turkish Official Statistics of 1910" listed 1,777,146 in the same area.

Table 4.1

Greek Population of Anatolia According to
"Greek Patriarchate" and "Turkish Official" Statistics

| Provinces | Greek Patriarchate | Turkish Official |
|---|---|---|
| İstanbul (Asia) | 74,457 | 70,906 |
| İzmit | 73,134 | 78,564 |
| Aydın (İzmir) | 622,810 | 629,002 |
| Bursa | 278,421 | 274,530 |
| Konya | 87,021 | 85,320 |
| Ankara | 45,873 | 54,280 |
| Trabzon | 353,533 | 351,104 |
| Sivas | 99,376 | 98,270 |
| Kastamonu | 24,919 | 18,160 |
| Adana | 90,208 | 88,010 |
| Biga | 32,830 | 29,000 |
| Total | 1,782,582 | 1,777,146 |

The two were in close agreement (table 4.1). This agreement was the best possible proof that the figures were correct, since censuses taken by both the Ottoman government and the Greek Patriarchate listed virtually the same number of Greeks.

The two sets of figures seem to have been first published together in London in 1919 by "Polybius" (D. Kalopothakes) in *Greece Before the Conference*.[5] The Greek Patriarchate statistics had been published a year before by George Soteriadis,[6] also in London. Since 1919, various authors and politicians have used the number of Greeks in the two records as evidence that there were 1.7 to 1.8 million Greeks in Asia Minor before World War I. The British and Greeks used the figures at the Versailles Peace Conference and various authors have quoted them since.[7] They are usually used as part of an equation: original Greek population − refugees = mortality, and as such have been an important factor in shaping the historical picture of Greek losses in the wars in Anatolia.

The "Turkish" and Greek figures were intended to be seen as independent enumerations of the Greek population which supported one another. They are best considered independently.

## The "Ottoman Census of 1910"

There was no official Ottoman census of 1910, though those who read Polybius' book in 1919 and most of those who have used the "1910 Census" figures, having no knowledge of real Ottoman figures, had no way of knowing that. There was, instead, a deliberate deception on the part of Polybius, who must have realized that the Greek Patriarchate statistics would appear unquestionable if they were supported by population data from those most likely to question them, the Ottomans.

For the 1914 edition of the *Almanach de Gotha*,[8] the Ottoman government had provided the editors with population totals drawn from registration data of the Ottoman population. This data was first published under the title *"Notice Statistique. Superficie et Population* (1910)"[9] in the 1914 *Almanach de Gotha* and, with small corrections for boundary changes, was used until the 1923 edition of the *Almanach*.

The *Almanach de Gotha* published only the *total* population of each Ottoman province, not the population by ethnic or religious groups. Polybius took these figures and himself divided them into ethnic groups, always keeping the totals the same as the totals for each province as they appeared in the *Almanach de Gotha*. His ethnic groups reflected roughly the number of Greeks as they appeared in the Greek Patriarchate statistics, not in any Ottoman official statistics. The figures of Greek population in each province were carefully made to be close to, but not exactly the same as, the Patriarchate data. The result was then published under the heading

*"Turkish Official Statistics, 1910:* (See totals in *Almanach de Gotha,* 1915)"[10]

It thus appeared as if Polybius had published the details of what he called the "Turkish Census of 1910," whereas the *Almanach de Gotha* had only published the totals. Polybius had, in effect, made Turks into Greeks, by shifting population numbers from one group to another.

Table 4.2

Greek Population in Anatolian Provinces
in Actual and False Ottoman Statistics

| Provinces | Actual | False |
|-----------|--------|-------|
| İstanbul (Asia) | 45,202 | 70,906 |
| İzmit | 40,048 | 78,564 |
| Aydın | 319,020 | 629,002 |
| Bursa | 183,974 | 274,530 |
| Konya | 95,847 | 85,320 |
| Ankara | 45,760 | 54,280 |
| Trabzon | 260,313 | 351,104 |
| Sivas | 76,394 | 98,270 |
| Kastamonu | 26,109 | 18,160 |
| Adana | 11,481 | 88,010 |
| Biga | 8,550 | 29,000 |
| Total | 1,112,698 | 1,777,146 |

Sources: Polybius, Greece Before the Conference, and
1330 Nüfus-i Umumî.

Note: The figures taken from the 1330 Nüfus-i Umumî
are for the provinces as they were listed in
Polybius, i.e., with the Independent Sancaks
replaced as part of their "mother" provinces.
(e.g., the figure for Trabzon is a combination
of the 1330 figures for Trabzon Vilâyeti and
Canik Independent Sancak, which had been
detached from Trabzon.)

The proof that Polybius' figures were not actually Ottoman official statistics can be seen by comparing the "Turkish Official Statistics of 1910" with actual Ottoman population registration data for any province (table 4.2).

## Patriarchate Statistics

Polybius invented the "1910 Turkish Census" to support a set of previously published statistics from Greek sources, generally known as the Greek Patriarchate statistics.

The Patriarchate figures seem to have first appeared in 1918, published by Professor George Soteriadis, who neither gave a source for the figures nor mentioned the Greek Patriarchate. They were copied exactly, though without citation, in early and influential works by Polybius and by Leon Maccas in *L'Hellenisme de L'Asie Mineure*.[11] While Polybius only listed figures by ethnic group and province, Soteriadis and Maccas offered complete-looking statistics by vilâyet, sancak, and kaza, as well as by ethnic/religious groups. Unlike the usual population estimates of the Ottoman Empire,[12] the Greek Patriarchate statistics were not rounded off to the thousands place, but were detailed population statements, appearing as if they had been taken from actual census or registration data. Neither Soteriadis nor Maccas alluded to the origin of their statistics and neither identified them as Patriarchal, but Polybius stated that they were the result of a "Greek census [that] was carried out because of the general complaint made against the Young Turk Government that in the official census of 1910 the returns of Turks had been enormously exaggerated."[13] Polybius said that the census had been carried out by the Patriarchate, as did E. Venizelos, the Greek prime minister, who stated that the figures were made by the Patriarch for him.[14]

In fact, the census-like appearance of the Patriarchate statistics is illusory. Professor Soteriadis, or another unknown source from which he took his material, created the Patriarchate statistics by altering the population figures of Vital Cuinet.

Cuinet's *La Turquie d'Asie*, though of course almost thirty years out of date by 1918, was the most available source on Ottoman population for those who could not read Ottoman Turkish. The author of the "Patriarchate Statistics" used Cuinet's fingers as his base, then arbitrarily added more Greeks to the figures. This was done kaza by kaza—in some districts only Greek population was added, in other population was taken from Cuinet's Muslim columns and added to the Greek columns. The work was a painstaking reworking of Cuinet's data on Muslims and Greeks. Despite the word of Polybius and Venizelos, the "Patriarchate Statistics" were in no sense a Greek census. They were a deliberate deception, as were the "Turkish Official Statistics of 1910," drawn from the most readily available source of true Ottoman statistics, Vital Cuinet, without citation and altered to fit political purposes. There is, in addition, no evidence that the "Patriarchate Statistics" were ever seen by anyone from the Patriarchate.

The "Patriarchate Statistics" and the "Turkish Official Statistics of 1910" were not the only examples of statistical deception on Greek population. On May 9, 1919 a letter from Chrysanthos, the Greek Metropolitan of Trabzon, reached the British delegation to the Versailles Peace Conference. In his letter the Metropolitan stated that there were more Greeks in the Pontus than there were "real Turks." To prove his point, he quoted from an "official" Ottoman source: "The 'Saalnameh,' or official annual for the vilâyet of Trebizonde for the year 1908, returned the Greek population at 500,000 for the Vilâyet of Trebizonde alone."[15]

The Trabzon salnames were indeed an excellent source of population information, and a listing of a Greek population of 500,000 in Trabzon Province in a 1908 salname would have been strong support for the Metropolitan's position. Unfortunately, there was no 1908 salname. The Trabzon salnames ceased publication in 1905,[16] and no Trabzon salname ever listed a Greek population of more than 200,000. The Metropolitan must have trusted that no one at the conference in 1919 was likely to have a knowledge of, or access to, Trabzon salnames.[17]

There never was a Greek census in the Ottoman Empire. Common sense should indicate to any researcher the unlikelihood of an army of Greek census-takers fanning out across Anatolia and Thrace, counting all the inhabitants, yet that is, in essence, what all those who have accepted the Greek Patriarchate statistics have believed. The "Turkish Official Statistics of 1910," which provided effective support for the Patriarchate statistics, were trusted because no one took the simple step of comparing them to actual Ottoman records.

## Ottoman Statistics on Greek Population

The major centers of Greek population in the Ottoman Empire were all in areas of superior statistical coverage. It is shown in appendix 2 that the Christian population of Aydın province was consistently recorded, despite political changes, as approximately 22% of total population. Table 4.3 further demonstrates the consistency of Ottoman data by listing the proportion of non-Muslims in Hüdavendigâr Vilâyeti in the series of years published in the Hüdavendigâr salnames.

The Ottoman population data for western and northern Anatolia was well-recorded and subject to less undercounting than in central and eastern An-

Table 4.3


Proportion of Non-Muslim Population of Hüdavendigâr Vilâyeti


| Year | Proportion |
|------|------------|
| 1306 | .1545 |
| 1312 | .1520 |
| 1313 | .1541 |
| 1314 | .1526 |
| 1315 | .1514 |
| 1316 | .1537 |
| 1317 | .1521 |
| 1318 | .1540 |
| 1319 | .1551 |
| 1320 | .1563 |
| 1321 | .1531 |
| 1322 | .1551 |
| 1323 | .1497 |
| 1324 | .1542 |
| 1325 | .1541 |


Source:  1325 Hüdavendigâr salname.  Cross-checked for accuracy
         with other salnames.

Note:    All data is by year of publication; no available data
         has been excluded.

atolia. All evidence indicates an attempt on the part of the Ottoman government to collect accurately and publish the population information from these provinces. And, unlike the various Greek sources, no evidence exists to indicate that the Ottoman government deliberately falsified a record of population. Furthermore, published and archival Ottoman population records agree.[18] The figures published by the Ottomans were the ones they also used in their governmental deliberations and which they obviously believed to be the best available.

The most likely way to produce an accurate approximation of the Greek population of Anatolia is to apply to the Greek population, province by province, the correction factor for undercounting used earlier for the Muslim population. The method has one drawback—the Greek population was much more urban than the Muslim or the Armenian.[19] Because of this, the Greeks were probably better counted. In the provinces of Aydın and Hüdavendigâr, especially, the use of the correction factor undoubtedly results in a slight increase in the Greek population and decrease in the Muslim population. In the absence of age-specific data by religion, however, the correction must be applied equally.[20]

Table 4.4 is the Greek population of the Anatolian provinces as recorded in the *1330 Nüfus-i Umumî* and as corrected. The table does not include the Greeks who would have been recorded as alien (*tabii-yi ecnebi*) because they held foreign passports. These should rightfully have been included as Greeks in the table, since they were often full, if not legal, members of the Greek community, but all aliens were listed in a single category and there

Table 4.4

Greek Population According to 1330 M. (1913-14) Provincial Boundaries

| Vilâyets | Recorded | Corrected | Year |
|---|---|---|---|
| Adana | 8,974 | 11,588 | 1330 |
| Aydın | 299,097 | 363,403 | 1331 |
| Haleb | 21,954 | 25,734 | 1331 |
| Ankara | 20,240 | 23,859 | 1331 |
| Bitlis | 0 | 0 | 1330 |
| Hüdavendigâr | 74,927 | 84,653 | 1330 |
| Kastamonu | 20,958 | 24,764 | 1332 |
| Diyarbakır | 1,935 | 2,355 | 1330 |
| Erzurum | 4,864 | 5,811 | 1330 |
| Konya | 25,150 | 31,963 | 1330 |
| Mamuretülaziz | 971 | 1,227 | 1330 |
| Sivas | 75,324 | 89,153 | 1330 |
| Trabzon | 161,574 | 165,484 | 1332 |
| Van | 1 | 1 | 1330 |
| Independent Sancaks | | | |
| Antalya | 12,385 | 15,740 | 1330 |
| Bolu | 5,151 | 6,086 | 1332 |
| Canik | 98,739 | 101,128 | 1332 |
| Eskişehir | 2,613 | 2,952 | 1330 |
| İzmit | 40,048 | 48,967 | 1331 |
| İçel | 2,507 | 3,237 | 1330 |
| Kayseri | 26,590 | 31,349 | 1331 |
| Biga | 8,550 | 9,544 | 1331 |
| Kara Hisar (Afyon) | 632 | 714 | 1330 |
| Karası | 97,497 | 110,152 | 1330 |
| Kütahya | 8,755 | 9,891 | 1330 |
| Maraş | 34 | 40 | 1331 |
| Menteşe | 19,923 | 24,206 | 1331 |
| Niğde | 58,312 | 74,109 | 1330 |
| Urfa | 2 | 2 | 1331 |

is no way to separate Greek "aliens" from French, English, or Armenian aliens.[21]

## NOTES

1. *1330 Nüfus-i Umumî.*
2. Foreign citizens resident in Anatolian provinces in 1313 (1895–6):

| | |
|---|---|
| Aydın | 55,805 |
| Hüdavendigâr | 3,785 |
| Haleb | 2,107 |
| Erzurum | 307 |
| Biga | 252 |
| Trabzon | 232 |
| Sivas | 106 |

All other provinces had less than 100, based on the *1313 İstatistik*. There is no material presently available that distinguishes how many of the above were actually Greeks native to Anatolia but holding foreign passports.

3. The first figure is from the "Greek Patriarchate Statistics," the second from the *1330 Nüfus-i Umumî.*
4. Justin McCarthy, "Greek Statistics on Ottoman Greek Population," *International Journal of Turkish Studies* I, 2, pp. 66–76.
5. London, 1919.
6. *An Ethnological Map Illustrating Hellenism in the Balkan Peninsula and Asia Minor*, London, 1918.
7. For a list of such authors, see McCarthy, "Greek Statistics."
8. Gotha, 1914.
9. P. 1187.
10. Polybius, *Greece Before the Conference*, p. 44.
11. Paris, 1919.
12. Such as the Armenian Patriarchate statistics.
13. Polybius, *Greece Before the Conference*, p. 45.
14. Great Britain, Foreign Office, *Documents on British Foreign Policy, 1919–1939*, 1st series, v. VIII, pp. 64 and 65.
15. F.O. 608.82.342/8/1.
16. 1322 A.H. was the last published. See Justin McCarthy and J. Dennis Hyde, "Ottoman Imperial and Provincial Salnames," *MESA Bulletin*, 1979.
17. I have deliberately not included the analyses of authors such as Botzaris (*Les Hellenes et L'Asie Mineure* [Paris, 1919]) who perform tricks such as listing the Laz people as Greek in their statistical tables and identifying a non-Turkish group called "derviches," etc. There was a type of logic common immediately after World War I that divided the Anatolian Muslims arbitrarily into every known type of division in order to prove that Christian groups were, in fact, the largest single group of many

groups. First Muslims were divided into groups—Sunni, Shii, Yezidi, Alawi, Kizil-baş, even "dervish." Then ethnic differences were called upon—Turks, Kurds, "Gallo-Greeks," Tatars, Yuruks (as a separate ethnic group), Circassians, etc. Once the divisions were made, the Turks were shown to be only one of a large number of ethnic/religious groups and thus, by this logic, it was proper that a large Christian group rule all the individually smaller Muslim groups. That if a plebiscite were held these groups would have identified themselves with a Muslim rather than a Christian government was unmentioned.

18. See appendix 2, "Reliability and Accuracy," and table 3.8.

19. In Aydın Vilâyeti, the largest center of Greek population, 25% of the Greeks lived in the central kaza of İzmir, 73% in the central sancak of İzmir. By contrast, only 8% of Aydın Vilâyeti's Muslims lived in the central kaza (1330 Nüfus-i Umumî).

20. This and other factors may have affected these population estimates slightly. See note 33, chapter 3.

21. Some few Greeks may also have been counted here as Armenians, if they were registered as Protestants, since all Protestants have been counted as Armenians.

# 5.
# Other Population Groups

MUSLIM, GREEK, AND ARMENIAN communities were spread over all of Anatolia. Of all the Anatolian provinces, only Bitlis did not have representatives of each of the three millets. The same was not true of the smaller millets, whose populations often lived in only a few provinces. Depending on where they were settled, the smaller groups had either the best records of population registration, or the worst. Jews, who lived almost exclusively in western Anatolian cities, were well recorded. Bulgars were also well counted. The native Christians of the east, on the other hand, were the most poorly enumerated of any of the Ottoman millets; in fact, there has never been an accurate count of their population in either Ottoman or modern Turkey.

Table 5.1 gives the populations of the smaller minority groups of Ottoman Anatolia, as drawn from the *1330 Nüfus-i Umumî* and corrected by the same correction factors used for the populations of the larger groups. There is one exception—the population of Chaldeans and Nestorians in Van Vilâyeti, which was greatly underenumerated in the *1330 Nüfus-i Umumî*, has been taken from an estimate made by the Ottoman government.[1] Correction factors have not been applied if the number in a millet in a province is very small (under 20). Because of the need for consistency, correction factors have been applied to all groups equally, but it should be remembered that the factors were drawn from *total* population, and that groups such as the Jews, inhabiting cities in more developed and better administered areas, would have been better registered than other groups of the population who lived in rural areas of the same provinces. The correction factor will thus slightly exaggerate the population numbers of the urban groups.

| Vilâyets | Year | Jewish | Bulgar | Yezidi | Gyp |
|---|---|---|---|---|---|
| Hüdavendigâr | 1330 | 4,622 | 0 | 0 | 2,1 |
| Aydın | 1331 | 42,575 | 205 | 0 | 3,3 |
| Kastamonu | 1332 | 8 | 0 | 0 | |
| Trabzon | 1332 | 8 | 0 | 0 | |
| Sivas | 1330 | 407 | 0 | 2,797 | |
| Ankara | 1331 | 1,209 | 8 | 0 | 1,5 |
| Konya | 1330 | 4 | 0 | 0 | |
| Adana | 1330 | 85 | 0 | 0 | |
| Haleb | 1331 | 14,293 | 2,293 | 370 | 1 |
| Bitlis | 1330 | 0 | 0 | 0 | |
| Mamuretülaziz | 1330 | 0 | 0 | 0 | |
| Diyarbakır | 1330 | 2,538 | 0 | 2,891 | |
| Van | 1330 | 1,798 | 0 | 1,776 | |
| Erzurum | 1330 | 10 | 0 | 618 | |
| Independent Sancaks | | | | | |
| Antalya | 1330 | 318 | 48 | 0 | 7 |
| Bolu | 1332 | 24 | 0 | 0 | 1,4 |
| Canik | 1332 | 28 | 0 | 0 | |
| Eskişehir | 1330* | 848 | 0 | 0 | |
| İzmit | 1331 | 523 | 0 | 0 | |
| İçel | 1330 | 13 | 0 | 0 | 3 |
| Kayseri | 1331* | 0 | 0 | 0 | |
| Biga | 1331 | 4,065 | 1,224 | 0 | |
| Karahisar | 1330 | 7 | 0 | 0 | |
| Karası | 1330 | 409 | 6,144 | 0 | 4 |
| Kütahya | 1330 | 0 | 0 | 0 | 2 |
| Maraş | 1331 | 294 | 0 | 0 | |
| Menteşe | 1331 | 1,962 | 8 | 0 | 4 |
| Niğde | 1330 | 0 | 0 | 0 | |
| Urfa | 1331 | 1,014 | 0 | 0 | |

*An independent sancak drawn from more than one province.
°Chaldeans and Nestorians, based on Ottoman estimates.

| Syrian | Old Syrian | Jacobite | Chaldean | Nestorian | Maronite |
|---|---|---|---|---|---|
| 0 | 0 | 0 | 0 | 0 | 0 |
| 2 | 0 | 0 | 11 | 0 | 0 |
| 0 | 0 | 0 | 0 | 0 | 0 |
| 0 | 0 | 0 | 0 | 0 | 0 |
| 3 | 0 | 0 | 0 | 0 | 0 |
| 0 | 0 | 0 | 0 | 0 | 0 |
| 0 | 0 | 0 | 4 | 0 | 0 |
| 603 | 0 | 1,349 | 524 | 0 | 390 |
| 3,465 | 0 | 362 | 428 | 0 | 0 |
| 5,515 | 0 | 0 | 6,017 | 0 | 0 |
| 2,823 | 0 | 0 | 8 | 0 | 0 |
| 46,224 | 5,031 | 0 | 7,296 | 0 | 0 |
| 0 | 0 | 0 | 62,400° | | 0 |
| 105 | 0 | 0 | 13 | 0 | 0 |
| | | | | | |
| 0 | 0 | 0 | 0 | 0 | 0 |
| 0 | 0 | 0 | 0 | 0 | 0 |
| 0 | 0 | 0 | 10 | 0 | 0 |
| 0 | 0 | 0 | 0 | 0 | 0 |
| 0 | 0 | 0 | 8 | 0 | 0 |
| 0 | 0 | 0 | 0 | 0 | 0 |
| 0 | 0 | 0 | 0 | 0 | 0 |
| 0 | 0 | 0 | 0 | 0 | 0 |
| 0 | 0 | 0 | 0 | 0 | 0 |
| 0 | 0 | 0 | 0 | 0 | 0 |
| 0 | 0 | 0 | 0 | 0 | 0 |
| 0 | 0 | 0 | 0 | 0 | 0 |
| 0 | 0 | 0 | 0 | 0 | 0 |
| 0 | 0 | 0 | 0 | 0 | 0 |
| 2,729 | 0 | 0 | 0 | 0 | 0 |

## Jews

Ottoman Jews were generally an urban population. In Aydın Vilâyeti, for example, 70% of the Jewish population of the province lived in the city of İzmir.[2] Less than 1% of Aydın's Jews lived outside of cities or towns (şehir or kasaba). This was true for other provinces as well. Almost 80% of the Jews in Haleb Vilâyeti lived in the city of Aleppo, 85% of the Jews in Hüdavendigâr Vilâyeti lived in Bursa, etc. There was only one exception to this urban pattern. An unexpectedly large number (6.1% of the Jewish population of Anatolia) lived in the southern areas of Van and Diyarbakır provinces. These may have been the northernmost group of the Jews of Iraq, of whom a larger group were in Mosul Vilâyeti, to the south of Diyarbakır and Van. If so, they would have been a very different group than the Jews of western Anatolia, perhaps an Oriental Jewish community that did not survive World War I.[3]

## Bulgars

Bulgars, members of the Bulgarian (Exarchate) Orthodox Church, were found in three kazas near the Sea of Marmara—Balye and Bandırma in Karası Sancağı and Lapseki in Biga Sancağı—part of a small community with members on both sides of the Marmara/Straits waterway. Salnames and other records indicate a high rate of growth in the Bulgar community, for example, an increase of 47% between 1314[4] and 1330 in Karasi Sancağı, which indicates in-migration. The Bulgars of Haleb Vilâyeti lived in the city of Aleppo, were listed by the Haleb population bureau as "Ottoman Citizen Foreigners" (yabancı), and were probably a merchant group.[5]

## Eastern Christians

The smaller Christian sects of eastern Anatolia were of two types—those who were originally Monophysite and those originally Nestorian. Both groups had split into smaller sects along lines of affiliation with Rome.

The Nestorians of Van were a remnant of Iraqi Christianity, literally driven to the mountains. They remained a separate and, to the Greek and Roman churches, heretical church. Others of their number, however, accepted the authority of Rome, while keeping their liturgical autonomy. These "Kaldani" (Chaldeans) were more widely spread throughout the Ottoman Empire than were the Nestorians. Large Chaldean communities existed in the province of Mosul, and there were Chaldeans in Bağdad Vilâyeti, as well as in eastern Anatolia. Both Nestorians and Chaldeans used Aramaic as their liturgical language.

Consideration of the Ottoman Monophysites is somewhat complicated by the presence of two groups who, in addition to the Armenians, kept their Monophysite traditions. The Ottomans called these "Yakubi" (Jacobite) and "Süryani-yi Kadim" (Old Syrian). In Anatolia, the greater part of the latter group had accepted papal authority and were called "Süryani" (Syrian).

To the Ottomans the distinction between the various groups of Eastern Christians was probably more political than religious, and thus they seem to have been more concerned with the welfare, and enumeration, of the uniate groups, who could boast an occasional European sponsor, France. The Eastern Christians were, in any case, an extremely difficult population to record accurately; culturally and linguistically they were closely tied to their Kurdish and Arab Muslim neighbors and they had survived precisely because they lived in the type of areas which were most difficult for the government to control and enumerate.

The precise population numbers of the Nestorians, Syrians, Chaldeans, and Jacobites in the Ottoman Empire will probably never be known. They were very poorly counted by the Ottomans and the records of their populations in the Turkish Republic, from which comparisons might have been made, are almost impossible to analyze. There has never been a listing for any of these groups in the Turkish Republican censuses and what listings are available are confused. In Mardin Province, for example, in 1927, 118 "Orthodox" and 9,521 "Other Religions" were listed in the census. The 1960 census listed, for Mardin, 17,750 "Orthodox" and no members of "Other Religions."[6]

The problem of accurately estimating these groups' numbers seems to be insoluble and no solution has been attempted here. The figures of table 5.1 are those that the Ottomans listed in the *1330 Nüfus-i Umumî*, corrected by the usual factors. For comparison, table 5.2 abstracts the estimates of Vital Cuinet for these populations from his volumes.[7] Cuinet's figures seem

Table 5.2

Cuinet's Estimates of Eastern Christian Populations

| Location | Jacobites | Chaldean Uniates | Syrian Uniates | Nestorians | Non-Uniate Chaldeans |
|----------|-----------|------------------|----------------|------------|----------------------|
| Bitlis | 6,190 | 2,600 | * | * | * |
| Diyarbakır | 22,554 | 16,420 | 4,990 | * | * |
| Haleb | 26,812 | 17,865 | 20,913 | * | 15,300 |
| Mamuretülaziz | * | * | * | * | * |
| Van | * | 6,000 | * | 92,000 | * |

Source: Vital Cuinet, La Turquie d'Asie.

Note: Cuinet includes 20,900 "Syrian Orthodox" in Adana Vilâyeti.

*None listed.

high, and headings such as "Non-Uniate Chaldeans" are confusing, but his figures may be preferable to those of the Ottomans.

The Eastern Christian communities, always excepting the Armenians, were all relatively small, and thus the Ottoman undercount of their numbers has but a small impact on total population numbers.

## Yezidis, Gypsies, and Others

Yezidis are a religious group whose beliefs are a combination of Muslim, Zoroastrian, Christian, and native elements. They are often falsely called devil worshippers due to their sacrifices to the devil to ward off his wrath.[8] Yezidis were almost surely undercounted by the Ottomans, but were usually included in the count of "Muslims," since they were Kurdish-speakers who fit easily into the surrounding population. Even had they been able to separate Yezidis and Muslims, the Ottomans would probably not have done so. They had no wish publicly to accept the presence of the group. Of all the Ottoman censuses, only the 1330 Nüfus-i Umumî even mentions the Yezidis as a separate group.

The Gypsies listed separately by the Ottomans were non-Muslim, eastern Gypsies, probably somewhat undercounted because of their nomadic habits. The bulk of the Anatolian Gypsies were registered as Muslims, though their orthodoxy was in doubt.

Many Muslims in Anatolia were actually members of heterodox religious communities, but were counted under the rubric "Muslim" and are impossible to segregate statistically from the Sunni majority. These groups were generally of Shii orientation. Because of the Ottoman reluctance to record differences within Islam, and the reluctance of members of these groups to be identified, no figures of the groups were kept.

Table 5.3

Proportion Speaking Kurdish in Eastern Provinces
of Turkey in 1927

| Province | Proportion |
|----------|------------|
| Bayazıt | .5825 |
| Bitlis | .7467 |
| Diyarbakır | .6804 |
| Elaziğ | .5262* |
| Erzincan | .4147 |
| Erzurum | .1347 |
| Hakkâri | .6807* |
| Malatya | .4182 |
| Maraş | .1437 |
| Mardin | .5987* |
| Siirt | .7416 |
| Urfa | .4066 |
| Van | .7663 |

*Provinces in which Kurds were greatly undercounted.
Proportions in these provinces are too low.

## Kurds

The largest actual minority group in Anatolia was Kurdish, ethnically and linguistically, but not religiously, separated from the Turkish Muslims. It is not within the scope of this volume to attempt to divide the Ottoman Muslims into Turks and Kurds,[9] but a rough idea of the Kurdish presence in eastern Anatolia can be had by considering the percentage of Kurdish-speakers in the eastern provinces of the Turkish Republic as recorded in the 1927 Turkish census (table 5.3). The census followed a Kurdish civil war against the Turkish government and the nomadic character of many Kurds made them difficult to enumerate properly, so the percentage Kurdish in the provinces was actually higher than that recorded in table 5.3.

## NOTES

1. A small number who were not either Nestorians or Chaldeans were counted in the figure, including a small number of Yezidis, because of the difficulty of knowing what *"Autres Elements"* included and the fact that the estimate was only given in the French version of the *1330 Nüfus-i Umumî* and not the more complete Ottoman version. (*Tableau indiquant le nombre des divers elements de la population dans l'Empire Ottoman au 1er Mars 1330 (14 Mars 1914)*, Constantinople, 1919, p. 4).

2. See *Aydın Vilâyeti Salnamesi, 1317*, p. 132, or any other Aydın salname.

3. Far fewer Jews were listed in the area in the Turkish Republican censuses; e.g., the 1927 census recorded 490 Jews in Mardin Vilâyeti and only 43 in Hakkâri Vilâyeti.

4. *1317 Hüdavendigâr Vilâyeti Salnamesi*, p. 349.

5. See any *Haleb Vilâyeti Salnamesi*, e.g., *1321*, p. 225.

6. Of course, most of the Greek and Slavic churches usually called Orthodox would not accept any of these churches as orthodox, though the Greek Church is listed with Nestorians, Monophysites, etc. in the Turkish censuses as "Orthodox."

7. Cuinet's categories have not been changed in the table, the figures for which have been drawn from various volumes of *La Turquie d'Asie*. Cuinet, however, does appear to have been somewhat confused in his religious distinctions and there is some question as to whether he properly identified the members of the sects.

8. Professor Charles Issawi has accurately styled the Yezidis as devil propitiators, rather than devil worshippers.

9. Those interested in possible ethnic breakdowns of the Muslim population should consult Cuinet and the *Van ve Bitlis Askerî İstatistiği*.

# 6.
# Anatolia in 1912

B Y 1912, Ottoman Anatolia was a developing, ethnically diverse region of 17.5 million inhabitants. Tables 6.1, 6.2, and 6.3 list the population of Anatolia in 1330 (1911–12) by province and religion. The provincial boundaries in tables 6.1 and 6.2 are those of 1330, but to facilitate comparisons with statistics used in other chapters, table 6.3 rearranges the figures in table 6.1 according to the larger boundaries seen in earlier chapters.[1] In table 6.1 the populations of non-Muslim groups are sometimes slightly different than those given in the chapters on Armenians, Greeks, and other groups. This is because the population figures in those chapters are not always for the year 1330. All of the figures in table 6.1 have been projected to the year 1330 (1911–12) so that the populations of each province would be of the same date.[2]

## Population Density

The most dense settlement of population in Anatolia was along the seacoasts of the north and west. These coastal provinces had higher rainfall than the inland provinces, better transportation, more developed economies, and more productive agriculture. It is natural that they were more densely populated.

The relationship of the sea to population density can be best seen in the two most closely settled provinces—Trabzon and İzmit. Both were basically coastal provinces with little hinterland. Their densities are thus higher than Hüdavendigâr or Aydın, which also had dense coastal settlement, but in which large interior regions lowered the province's total population density.

Table 6.1

The Population of Anatolia in 1330 (1911-12)

| Vilâyets | Muslim | Greek | Armenian | Syrian, Chaldean, Nestorian | Jewish | Other | Total |
|---|---|---|---|---|---|---|---|
| Hüdavendigâr | 535,654 | 87,605 | 74,229 | 0 | 4,381 | 2,112 | 704,481 |
| Aydın | 1,734,179 | 384,732 | 25,059 | 13 | 44,206 | 6,230 | 2,194,419 |
| Kastamonu | 846,726 | 24,069 | 10,289 | 0 | 8 | 0 | 881,092 |
| Trabzon | 914,592 | 160,427 | 39,952 | 0 | 8 | 0 | 1,114,979 |
| Sivas | 1,196,300 | 90,419 | 182,912 | 3 | 407 | 2,797 | 1,472,838 |
| Ankara | 1,263,199 | 53,452 | 125,666 | 0 | 1,822 | 0 | 1,444,139 |
| Konya | 1,542,331 | 121,812 | 24,858 | 4 | 323 | 1,060 | 1,690,388 |
| Adana | 573,256 | 14,825 | 74,930 | 2,477 | 85 | 1,005 | 666,578 |
| Haleb | 844,486 | 25,472 | 101,849 | 3,847 | 14,416 | 1,529 | 991,599 |
| Bitlis | 408,703 | 0 | 191,156 | 11,532 | 0 | 0 | 611,391 |
| Mamuretülaziz | 564,164 | 1,227 | 111,043 | 2,833 | 0 | 974 | 680,241 |
| Diyarbakır | 598,985 | 2,355 | 89,131 | 58,551 | 2,538 | 2,891 | 754,451 |
| Van | 313,322 | 1 | 130,500 | 62,400 | 1,798 | 1,776 | 509,797 |
| Erzurum | 804,388 | 5,811 | 163,218 | 121 | 10 | 648 | 974,196 |
| Independent Sancaks | | | | | | | |
| Bolu | 458,553 | 5,915 | 3,413 | 0 | 19 | 1,398 | 469,298 |
| Canik | 264,063 | 98,038 | 28,374 | 10 | 26 | 0 | 390,511 |
| İzmit | 271,751 | 47,973 | 69,225 | 11 | 512 | 18 | 389,490 |
| Biga | 165,508 | 9,441 | 2,805 | 0 | 4,021 | 1,302 | 183,077 |
| Karahisar | 313,699 | 714 | 8,415 | 0 | 7 | 84 | 322,919 |
| Karası | 406,507 | 110,152 | 9,834 | 0 | 409 | 7,460 | 534,362 |
| Kütahya | 342,723 | 9,891 | 5,138 | 0 | 0 | 275 | 358,027 |
| Urfa | 173,053 | 2 | 21,280 | 2,697 | 1,002 | 45 | 198,079 |
| Total | 14,536,142 | 1,254,333 | 1,493,276 | 144,499 | 76,498 | 31,604 | 17,536,352 |

Table 6.2

Proportionate Population in 1330 (1911-12)

| Vilāyets | Muslim | Greek | Armenian | Syrian Chaldean, Nestorian | Jewish | Other |
|---|---|---|---|---|---|---|
| Hüdavendigâr | .7604 | .1244 | .1054 | 0 | .0069 | .0030 |
| Aydın | .7903 | .1753 | .0114 | * | .0201 | .0028 |
| Kastamonu | .9610 | .0273 | .0117 | 0 | * | 0 |
| Trabzon | .8203 | .1439 | .0358 | 0 | * | 0 |
| Sivas | .8122 | .0614 | .1242 | * | .0003 | .0019 |
| Ankara | .8747 | .0370 | .0870 | 0 | .0013 | 0 |
| Konya | .9124 | .0721 | .0147 | * | .0002 | .0006 |
| Adana | .8600 | .0222 | .1124 | .0037 | .0001 | .0015 |
| Haleb | .8516 | .0257 | .1027 | .0039 | .0145 | .0015 |
| Bitlis | .6685 | 0 | .3127 | .0189 | 0 | 0 |
| Mamuretülaziz | .8294 | .0018 | .1632 | .0042 | 0 | .0014 |
| Diyarbakır | .7939 | .0031 | .1181 | .0776 | .0034 | .0038 |
| Van | .6146 | * | .2560 | .1224 | .0035 | .0035 |
| Erzurum | .8257 | .0060 | .1675 | .0001 | * | .0007 |
| Independent Sancaks | | | | | | |
| Bolu | .9771 | .0126 | .0073 | 0 | * | .0030 |
| Canik | .6722 | .2511 | .0727 | * | .0001 | 0 |
| İzmit | .6977 | .1232 | .1777 | * | .0013 | * |
| Biga | .9040 | .0516 | .0153 | 0 | .0220 | .0071 |
| Karahisar | .9714 | .0022 | .0261 | 0 | * | .0003 |
| Karası | .7607 | .0261 | .0184 | 0 | .0008 | .0140 |
| Kütahya | .9573 | .0276 | .0144 | 0 | 0 | .0008 |
| Urfa | .8737 | * | .1074 | .0136 | .0051 | .0002 |
| Total | .8289 | .0715 | .0852 | .0082 | .0044 | .0018 |

*Proportion less than .0001

Note: Totals are the proportion of each religious group to the total Anatolian population.

Table 6.3

Population in 1330 According to Standardized Borders

| Location | Muslim | Greek | Armenian | Other | Total |
|---|---|---|---|---|---|
| Hüdavendigâr | 1,598,583 | 208,362 | 97,616 | 15,228 | 1,919,789 |
| Aydın | 1,734,179 | 384,732 | 25,059 | 50,449 | 2,194,419 |
| Kastamonu | 1,305,279 | 29,984 | 13,702 | 1,425 | 1,350,390 |
| Trabzon | 1,178,655 | 258,465 | 68,326 | 44 | 1,505,490 |
| Sivas | 1,196,300 | 90,419 | 182,912 | 3,207 | 1,472,838 |
| Ankara | 1,263,199 | 53,452 | 125,616 | 1,822 | 1,444,139 |
| Konya | 1,542,331 | 121,812 | 24,858 | 1,387 | 1,690,388 |
| Adana | 573,256 | 14,825 | 74,930 | 3,567 | 666,578 |
| Haleb | 1,017,539 | 25,474 | 123,129 | 23,536 | 1,189,678 |
| Bitlis | 408,703 | 0 | 191,156 | 11,532 | 611,391 |
| Mamuretülaziz | 564,164 | 1,227 | 111,043 | 3,807 | 680,241 |
| Diyarbakır | 598,985 | 2,355 | 89,131 | 63,980 | 754,451 |
| Van | 313,322 | 1 | 130,500 | 65,974 | 509,797 |
| Erzurum | 804,388 | 5,811 | 163,218 | 779 | 974,196 |
| İzmit | 271,751 | 47,973 | 69,225 | 541 | 389,490 |
| Biga | 165,508 | 9,441 | 2,805 | 5,323 | 183,077 |
| Total | 14,536,142 | 1,254,333 | 1,493,276 | 252,601 | 17,536,352 |

Note: All the independent sancaks, except İzmit and Biga, are reunited with their original vilayets for ease of analysis.

Table 6.4

Persons per Square Kilometer in Anatolia in 1330 (1911-12)

| | |
|---|---|
| Trabzon | 48 |
| İzmit | 46 |
| Aydın | 38 |
| Hüdavendigâr | 29 |
| Kastamonu | 28 |
| Sivas | 25 |
| Biga | 24 |
| Mamuretülaziz | 23 |
| Diyarbakır | 21 |
| Haleb | 21 |
| Ankara | 20 |
| Bitlis | 19 |
| Adana | 18 |
| Erzurum | 18 |
| Konya | 16 |
| Van | 14 |

Note: For this table, population has been drawn from Table 6.3, and square kilometers from the 1927 Turkish census (readjusted to fit Ottoman boundaries--see Appendix 5). Anatolia as used here means the greater provinces, i.e., including independent sancaks.

*Area of Haleb that remained in the Turkish Republic.

On the southern coast, unlike the north and west, the relationship between coast and population did not hold. Coastal areas in the provinces of Adana and Konya were as little populated as the interiors of the provinces.

From 1878 to 1912 the western provinces gained in proportionate share of the Muslim population, and probably of the Christian population, as well,[3] at the expense of the eastern provinces. Part of the increase came from the higher rate of natural increase in the west; since the Western populations grew faster than those in the east, they naturally took a greater share of the total population as time went on. Another part of the increase may have come from immigration from east to west, though this is unproven.

Table 6.5

Proportion of Non-Muslim Population, by Regions,
1295 (1878) to 1330 (1911-12)

| Region | 1295 | 1330 |
|--------|------|------|
| North | .1760 | .1709 |
| South | .1196 | .1094 |
| East | .2529 | .1850 |
| West | .1872 | .2594 |
| Central | .2643 | .2753 |

## Christians

There was no one center of Greek population in Anatolia, nor one center of Armenian population. Syrians, Chaldeans, and Nestorians remained in their traditional provinces. As they had throughout Ottoman history, Jews remained city dwellers. Armenians and Greeks, however, were in considerable numbers throughout all the areas of Asia Minor.

Armenian numbers were relatively stronger in traditional Armenia than in other sections of Anatolia. Armenians had spread, though, to the western provinces in great numbers: 74,000 lived in Hüdavendigâr, 70,000 in İzmit, 25,000 in Aydın, 25,000 in Konya, and so on. This Armenian migration may have been one of the reasons, coupled with Armenian migration from Anatolia to Russian Armenia, for the low Armenian numbers in the provinces of the east. Ottoman Armenians had obviously traveled to areas of improved opportunity and greater security.

The Greeks of Anatolia were mainly clustered on the seacoasts, as they had been for centuries. At the end of the nineteenth century, however, Greeks were moving in relatively small numbers into interior regions. Kara Hisar Sancağı of Hüdavendigâr Vilâyeti, for example, had 632 recorded resident Greeks in 1912, but only 100 Greeks twenty years earlier.[4] Records of Greeks in Konya are deficient, but it appears that the Greek population of Konya Vilâyeti was expanding at twice the rate of the population as a whole,[5] indicating in-migration of Greeks.

Table 6.6

Proportion of Non-Muslim in Anatolian Provinces
in 1330 (1911-12)

| Province | Proportion |
|---|---|
| Van | .39 |
| Bitlis | .33 |
| Canik | .33 |
| İzmit | .30 |
| Hüdavendigâr | .24 |
| Aydın | .21 |

Note: All other provinces had less than .20 non-Muslims.

## Muslims

One fact is obvious from table 6.1—all Anatolian provinces had overwhelming Muslim majorities, not simply pluralities (table 6.6). In Anatolia as a whole, only 17% of the population was non-Muslim. In the centuries of Turkish rule Asia Minor had become thoroughly Islamicized.

# NOTES

1. More precisely, in table 6.3 Karahisar, Karası, and Kütahya sancaks have been added to Hüdavendigâr Vilâyeti, Canik to Trabzon Vilâyeti, Bolu to Kastamonu Vilâyeti, and Urfa to Haleb Vilâyeti.

A difficulty arises in this and later chapters with the boundaries of the Haleb Vilâyeti. Strictly speaking, only the northern half of Haleb Vilâyeti was in Anatolia. That section remained in the Turkish Republic. For the sake of comparisons between Ottoman times and the period after the 1912–1922 wars, it has been necessary to consider only the section of Haleb that became part of Turkey. Statistics on 1922 population, wartime mortality, and migration follow the post-1922 borders, so the separation is essential.

The sancaks of Maraş, Urfa (except Rakah), and Anteb remained in Turkey. These comprised 55% of the total Muslim population of Haleb Vilâyeti in 1330 (1911–12).

2. This involves back projections of one, or at most two, years using the rates of increase for each province c. 1330–1332 (1911–12 to 1913–14).

3. Figures for 1878 have been drawn from chapter 2, with the addition of Karası Sancağı, which was not a part of Hüdavendigâr Vilâyeti in 1878, and thus was not included in table 2.7 of chapter 2. Figures for 1912 are from tables 6.1 and 6.3 of this chapter.

4. See "Census 1," which lists 103 Greeks.

5. See the Konya salnames listed in table 2.13 of chapter 2.

# 7.
# *The End of Ottoman Anatolia*

FROM 1878 to 1912, Ottoman Anatolia experienced a steady rate of population growth. The Muslim population increased by almost 50%.[1] The Armenian population may have increased at a slightly slower rate,[2] and the Greeks more quickly,[3] but the Christian population as a whole increased like the Muslim population. The Balkan Wars only slightly altered this rise and only slightly affected the total population, since the wars were not fought on Anatolian soil and any loss of Anatolian soldiery was balanced by gains from immigration of Muslims from conquered territories in Europe.

The rise of Anatolian population was founded on peace, internal peace that the area had not known for centuries. The governments of Abdülhamid II and the Young Turks, utilizing the autocratic, centralized power that had begun to develop in the Tanzimat, had extended government authority into areas that had not been effectively controlled by the Ottoman state since the sixteenth century. As a result, banditry and warfare between local lords were suppressed. New forms of communication such as the railroad and telegraph were introduced.[4] Roads were improved. Where previously bumper crops had rotted in one area while famine reigned in another, grain could now be shipped to needy areas.

To civil calm was added the benefit of relatively healthy times. The last great plague epidemic had been in 1835, the last great cholera epidemic in 1865. Starvation still existed, bandits still attacked from the hills, and civil peace was still imperfect, but, after 1878, all over Anatolia the quality of life improved.[5]

In the absence of the Malthusian checks of civil unrest, war, pestilence, and famine, a population such as that of Anatolia could be expected to have expanded at between .01 and .015 a year. Endemic diseases would have meant the increase could have been no greater. After 1878, the absence of Malthusian checks actually allowed the Anatolian population to grow at an average .011 a year. Very little of this growth was based on medical advances, of which there were few.[6]

In 1914, civil peace and the population growth it fostered ceased. Anatolia was plunged into one of the worst demographic disasters in history. From 1914 to 1923, 20% of the Anatolian people died. In some eastern provinces, one-half of the inhabitants died and a further one-half of the survivors were refugees.

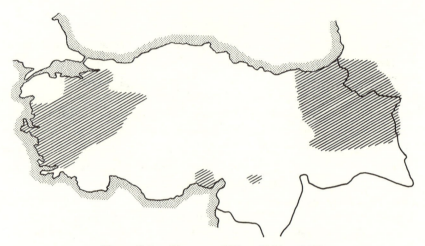

**Figure 7.1.**   Theaters of War, 1914 to 1922

From September 1911 to September 1922, Anatolian soldiers fought in five wars.[7] In those eleven years there were only 22 months of peace. Soldiers from Anatolia died in Europe, Africa, and Asia. Deprivations that accompanied each of the wars affected all regions of Anatolia and each sector of the population. It was, however, the warfare inside Anatolia that most devastated the population.

Inside Anatolia, war was fought in both the east and the west. The political and military history of the times is well known: in eastern Anatolia the war had two dimensions—Russian invasion and civil war.[8] Initial Ottoman defeat on the Russian-Ottoman border (November to December 1914) was followed by the beginning of the insurrection of the Nestorians and Armenians of Van (April 1915) and civil war. Throughout the period, the Kurdish tribes took advantage of the breakdown of order caused by war and raided, especially assaulting the Christian communities.

From the first the civil war and the Ottoman-Russian war were inseparable. Large elements of the Muslim population in the Kars region of the Russian Empire aided the Ottomans whenever possible,[9] and Armenian activities at the rear of the Ottoman army were a factor in Ottoman defeats.[10] Loyalty to the Empire, if it had ever existed, was submerged by religious and ethnic identifications. Though they wanted no war, the Christians and Muslims of the east were forced to take sides. Particularly after the taking of the city of Van by the Ottoman Armenians (April 1915) and the Ottoman deportations of Armenians (beginning in May 1915), neither Muslim nor Christian could conceive of the other as anything but an enemy. For both sides, the war became one of extermination in which the villagers of the other side were annihilated.

At the height of its conquests in the east (spring 1917), the Russian army had taken all of the Erzurum Vilâyeti, the eastern half of Trabzon Vilâyeti, the northern halves of Van and Bitlis vilâyets, and the major cities of Van, Erzurum, Trabzon, Erzincan, Gümüşhane, Bayazit, and, briefly, Bitlis and Muş. As the Russians advanced, the Muslim population retreated to central Anatolia. Then, in 1917–18, when the Turks advanced and recaptured the east, the Christians in turn became refugees, following the Russian army into Trans-Caucasia.

During the three years in which the Turks and Russians battled, the peasants' land was not held long enough for crops to be planted and harvested. Seed grain had, in any case, been eaten and draft animals confiscated or themselves eaten. With each migration the peasants weakened and lost numbers through starvation, hostile armies, and Kurdish raiders. By 1918, even the raiders must have starved, since there could have been little left to steal. Weakened and starving, all were struck by cholera, typhus, influenza, and dysentery. Nevertheless, one more round of battles was fought, between the Turkish Republic and the Armenian Republic, in 1919.

The western Anatolian campaigns began with the occupation of İzmir by the Greek army in May of 1919. Largely in reaction to the Greek occupation, Turkish forces under Mustafa Kemal Paşa battled and eventually defeated the Greeks. From the beginning of the war massacre was followed by counter-massacre. Refugees, first Turks, then Greeks, moved across western Anatolia to avoid both armies and the guns of their fellow citizens. During their journeys and in makeshift refugee camps many who had escaped direct murder died of disease.

The war extended beyond the line of march of the Greek and Turkish armies. Like the war in the east, the Greco-Turkish War was also a civil war between two Ottoman communities, in this case the Muslims and the Greeks. Much of the murder and destruction in the war came from groups of Ottoman civilians, intent on avenging real and imagined injuries—some recent, some centuries old. Rules of war did not apply.

**Figure 7.2.**     Percentage Widows in 1927

NOTE: Widows/Females 20+. Eastern Anatolia not included.

Figure 7.2 shows the horrors of the war through a simple index: widowhood among the survivors, as shown in the Turkish census of 1927. The line of provinces in which widowhood was over 30% could also describe the Greek line of march and the civil war in western and Central anatolia. In each of the provinces marked in figure 7.2, widows were more than twice the normal percentage of the population.[11]

The mortality in the west was less than in the east. This can be attributed to the relative shortness of the war (May 1919 to September 1922), two full years less than the war in the east and the better agricultural land and living conditions in the west.

No other country suffered in the period of World War I as did Anatolia. The "lost generation" in England, France, and Germany was a real and terrible loss. Yet the total populations of the United Kingdom and Germany actually rose between 1911 and 1912, while that of France only declined by one percent.[12] The Anatolian population fell by more than 30%—10% were emigrants, 20% died.[13]

Much of the mortality in Anatolia was the result of intercommunal war. Whether or not individuals intended it, they stood or fell with their religious group, and lived, died, and migrated as Greeks, Armenians, or Muslims. For that reason, the following analyses of mortality and migration are done separately for each of the three groups. The mortality listed for each group is not actually a count of deaths, but of the difference in population numbers between 1912 and 1922. The number of persons within Anatolia in 1922, minus migrants into Anatolia, plus migrants who had left Anatolia, leaves the number of survivors. The number of survivors is subtracted from the 1912 population of Anatolia. The result is deaths, or losses of population. Population loss is a more strictly accurate term, but deaths is the properly descriptive term for the results of the events in Anatolia.

## The Armenians

Of the one and a half million Armenians who had lived in Anatolia before World War I, only about 70,000[14] remained in the Turkish Republic in 1923. Most of them had gone to Istanbul as refugees, and many of these soon left for the Caucasus, America, or Europe. In many provinces of what had been Ottoman Armenia few who would call themselves Armenians could be found. The 1927 Turkish census registered not one person of the Gregorian Armenian faith in Van, only one in Bayazit, and twelve in Erzurum.[15] A people who had lived in eastern Anatolia since before recorded history were simply gone.

A great number of Armenians were refugees after the world war and the Turkish War of Independence, and a great number died in the wars. To find the wartime mortality, one must first estimate the number of Armenian refugees. The problems of counting them precisely are great, perhaps insurmountable. When the Armenians left Anatolia, they found refuge in Transcaucasia, the Arab world, Persia, the United States, Western Europe, and Latin America. Few of the areas to which they migrated kept accurate immigration records on Armenians and even those that did so did not list Armenian migrants by place of first origin or birthplace. Thus, for example, in a country whose census registered 10,000 more Armenians after than before World War I, it is impossible to know whether the new Armenian inhabitants originally came from Anatolia, Persia, Russia, or elsewhere. Furthermore, in the main area of Armenian in-migration, the Caucasus, it is impossible to know how many of the survivors of the wars were natives and how many migrants.

Numbering the survivors of the Armenians of Anatolia is a process of estimation, not exact analysis. When estimating refugee numbers, care must be taken to avoid multiple counting of refugees. An Armenian refugee might, for example, have left Anatolia, remained for a while in Allied-held Istanbul, left for Greece by way of Bulgaria, and finally migrated to the United States or to the Armenian Republic. With the possibility of multiple entries in mind, estimates of Armenian refugee numbers must be compared, when possible, to census or registration statistics taken four or more years after the main Armenian migrations from Anatolia ended in 1922.[16] By that time earlier estimates of refugee numbers, which were in the heat of that emotional moment exaggerated, had been succeeded by calmer estimates and census enumerations.

## Those Who Remained

The only statistical record of Armenians in Anatolia after the wars is the 1927 Turkish census which, unfortunately, did not list Armenians by ethnic group. Instead it identified Armenians by language (i.e., Armenian as mother tongue) and religion. Since the mother tongue of many Armenians was Turkish, not Armenian, language is no guide to total Armenian population.[17] Under religion, the census listed "Gregorians," "Protestants," and "Catholics." While all of the first group were obviously Armenians, not all of the second two were Armenians. In addition, as the director of the census admitted,[18] Christians were not always enumerated in the proper sect. There was in 1927 a suspiciously large number listed as Christians (24,307) in Turkey, without description of sect; some of these must also have been Armenians.

A certain number of Armenians remaining in Anatolia must not have been counted in the 1927 census. Some would have misidentified themselves, while others would simply have been uncounted as part of the gen-

eral undercount of women and children in the 1927 census.[19] Many others
would have migrated from Istanbul and other regions between the end of
hostilities in 1922 and the census in 1927. It is probable that approximately
140,000 Armenians remained in the Turkish Republic immediately after the
end of the war in 1922. This estimate allows for an expected amount of out-
migration of Armenians from Turkey between 1922 and 1927 and takes into
consideration both Turkish and Armenian population figures. The estimate

Table 7.1

Gregorian, Protestant, and Catholic Population

As Recorded in the 1927 Turkish Census

| Religion | In Turkey | In İstanbul Vilâyeti |
|----------|-----------|----------------------|
| Gregorian* | 77,433 | 53,129 |
| Protestant | 6,658 | 4,421 |
| Catholic | 39,511 | 23,930 |

Source:  Turkish census of 1927, vol. 1, pp. liv
         and lx.

*Listed as "Ermeni" religion.  Pro, stant and
 Catholic groups include some who ar. not Armenian.

assumes, based on information from the Ottoman censuses, that a large
number of the Catholics living in Turkey in 1927 were Armenian. In the
*1330 Nüfus-i Umumî*, 88% of Catholics (i.e., those listed as Roman Catholics or uniates) in the geographic area of modern Turkey were Armenian
Catholic.[20] It has also been assumed that most of the Protestants were Armenians. The 140,000 figure is compatible with estimates of the Armenian
Apostolic Church on the number of Armenians living in Turkey after 1927.[21]
    Of the 140,000, probably 70,000 were Armenians who had lived in An-
atolia before World War I, many of whom were living in Istanbul by 1922.
The remaining 70,000 were Armenians born in İstanbul Vilâyeti or in European Turkey (table 7.2). This is a median estimate based on the number

Table 7.2

Armenians in European Turkey Before World War I

| Location | Armenian Gregorian | Armenian Catholic | Protestant* |
|----------|-------------------|-------------------|-------------|
| İstanbul Vilâyeti | 72,962 | 9,918 | 1,213 |
| Edirne Vilâyeti | 19,725 | 48 | 115 |
| Çatalca Sancağı | 842 | 0 | 0 |
| Total | 93,529 | 9,996 | 1,328 |

Note:   Uncorrected population, c. 1911-12, boundaries of 1914.

*Not entirely Armenian.

of Armenians in European Turkey in 1914 who could have been expected to remain there until 1922. It is admittedly an informed guess, one that generally conforms to the statistics of Armenian population in European Turkey as recorded by the government in 1912 and 1927.[22]

## Armenian Refugees

Armenian refugees scattered to all continents. There were four main areas of settlement—the Caucasus, the Arab world, France, and North America—and many minor refuges.

The largest number of Armenian refugees to Western Europe went to France. The French census of 1931[23] listed 29,227 Armenian aliens, 612 naturalized citizens born in "Armenia," and 5,114 naturalized citizens born in "Turkey." Since the pre-war censuses listed few Armenians in France,[24] one can assume that 30,000 were refugees from Anatolia. (The other 5,000 were either refugees from European Turkey or came to France from other refuges, in which they are counted below.)

As recorded by the Canadian government, 1,244 Armenians migrated to Canada between 1912 and 1924.[25] The United States, in the same period, accepted 34,136 migrants from Armenia. All of these North American immigrants were from Anatolia, according to immigration records.[26]

Though a large number passed through its borders and are counted elsewhere, Greece accepted as refugees 34,000 Armenians from Turkey. This figure is taken from a comparison of the number of Armenians listed in the 1920 and in the 1928 Greek censuses.[27] A number of Armenians also came to Greece temporarily. These were eventually "repatriated" to the Caucasus or migrated to Western Europe or North America. The addition of these transient refugees brings the number of Armenian refugees to Greece to 45,000, the number estimated by the League of Nations Refugee Commission.[28]

Almost all of the Armenian migrants to Bulgaria came after the Greek loss to the Turks and the Allied evacuation of Turkey. The Bulgarian census of 1920 listed 10,848 "Armeno-Gregorians" and that of 1926 listed 25,402. On that basis, one can assume that 15,000 Armenian refugees from Turkey migrated to Bulgaria and remained until 1926.[29] (Armenian Catholics or Protestants were not present in any number in Bulgaria.)[30] The League of Nations estimated a further 5,000 Armenian refugees to Bulgaria, and it is reasonable to assume that refugees from Turkey before the 1920 census (and possibly census underenumeration) accounted for the extra 5,000[31] refugees, leaving the League figure of 20,000 as the correct number of Armenian refugees to Bulgaria.

The League of Nations estimated 2,500 Armenian refugees in Cyprus. The figure corresponds with the recorded increase in Armenians shown in three Cyprus censuses: 1911—588 Gregorians; 1921—1,197 Gregorians; 1931—3,375 Gregorians (Armenian Catholics and Protestants were not counted separately from other Catholics and Protestants.)[32]

For the number of Armenian migrants to the Arab world, I have accepted the estimates of Professor Richard Hovannisian (table 7.3). No data better than his rough estimates has been discovered. Census figures, of varying accuracy, do list the Armenian population of some Arabic-speaking countries, but the figures were usually taken long after the initial migration of Armenians and thus further migration, births, and deaths have clouded the picture. Nevertheless, available census statistics support Hovanissian's estimates (table 7.4).

The League of Nations Refugee Commission estimated that 400,000–420,000 Armenian refugees had migrated "from Turkey to Russia during

Table 7.3


Armenian Refugees to the Arab World and Iran


| Country | Number |
|---|---|
| Syria | 100,000 |
| Lebanon | 50,000 |
| Palestine & Jordan | 10,000 |
| Egypt | 40,000 |
| Iraq | 25,000 |
| Iran | 50,000 |


Source:   Richard G. Hovannisian, "The Ebb and
          Flow of the Armenian Minority in the
          Arab Middle East," Middle East Journal
          28, no. 1, Winter, 1974, p. 20.

the Great War."[33] Though this figure was, at best, an educated guess, it seems to be an accurate approximation of the number of Armenian refugees from Anatolia to Russia who survived the war.

In evaluating the number of Armenian refugees to Russia one must consider the entire Armenian population of Russia, not only the Caucasus regions, since their national disaster resulted in the spread of Armenians to all parts of the Soviet Union. There were 400,000 more Armenians registered in the Soviet Union in 1926 than in the Russian Empire (excluding Poland) in 1897 (table 7.5), according to the censuses taken in those years. The count of Armenians in 1897 included the Armenians in the northeastern Anatolian area later returned to Turkey, but the survivors of this group were by 1926 living in the Soviet Union, so there is no problem in comparing the disparate areas of the 1897 and 1926 censuses.

By analyzing the rates of growth observed in eastern Anatolia and the population as recorded in the 1897 Russian census, one can assume that the pre-war Armenian population of the Russian Empire rose at approximately .012 a year. Natural increase would have effectively ceased with the

Table 7.4

Armenian Population of Arab Countries,

According to Government Figures

| Country | Population | Year |
|---------|-----------|------|
| Syria [a] | 125,550 | 1945 |
| Lebanon [b] | 72,797 | 1944 |
| Palestine[c] | 3,802 | 1931 |
| Egypt [d] | 19,596 | 1937 |
| Iraq | not available | |

Note: Figures on how many Protestants were Armenians were not available. In establishing the number of Armenian Protestants, the estimates of Poladian have been followed.
a. 104,331 Gregorian, 16,979 Catholic (Syrian Republic, Ministry of National Economy, Directorate of Statistics, Statistical Abstract of Syria 1953, p. 21); 4,240 Protestants (Poladian).
b. 59,749 Gregorian, 10,048 Catholic (quoted in A.H. Hourani, Syria and Lebanon, 3rd edition, London, 1954); 3,000 Protestant (Poladian).
c. 3,167 Gregorian, 330 Catholic (Palestine, Superintendent of the Census, Census of Palestine 1931, vol. 1, p. 98); 305 Protestants (Poladian).
d. 15,877 Gregorian, 3,169 Catholic (Egypt, Ministry of Finance, Statistical and Census Department, Population Census of Egypt 1937, Cairo, 1942, p. 344); Protestant, 550 (Poladian).

coming of wartime conditions and the calling-up of Armenian soldiers. With an increase of .012 a year, the Armenian population of Russia would have grown to 1,432,000 by 1914 and then remained relatively stable until 1918. In 1918 it dropped drastically.

From 1918 to 1921 the Armenian population of the former Russian Empire was buffeted by invasion from the Ottoman Empire, wars with Turks, Georgians, Tatars, and Soviet Russians, and epidemics of both cholera (1918) and typhus (1919). While estimates of mass mortality are always difficult, it is known that hundreds of thousands died during the period. In one episode in 1918, 30,000 of 80,000 refugees from Akhalkalak died.[34] 200,000

Table 7.5

Armenians in the Russian Empire and the USSR in 1897 and 1926

| Year | In the Empire | In the Caucasus° | Percent in the Caucasus |
|------|---------------|------------------|-------------------------|
| 1897 | 1,167,962* | 1,161,909 | 99.5% |
| 1926 | 1,567,568 | 1,332,593 | 85.0% |

*Poland excluded.
°Geographic areas are slightly different. The Kars and Ardahan area is included in the 1897 figures, but not the 1926 figures. The effect is negligible.

were estimated to have died from the typhus epidemic and starvation of 1919. Areas controlled by Russia and the Armenian Republic, such as Kars, were held, lost to the Ottomans, held, then lost again. Some 50,000 Armenian refugees returned to Kars in 1919,[35] only to be routed again by Turkish victory in 1920.[36] With each exchange, refugees migrated, losing more of their numbers to war, disease, and famine with each migration.

Because of the terrible suffering of the Armenian population of Russia, it does not seem possible that the number of Armenians had not, by 1922, dropped below the 1897 numbers. If one assumes that the League of Nations estimates of Armenian emigration from Anatolia were correct, a coherent picture of the Armenian population of Russia from 1914 to 1922 emerges. The 1926 Soviet census listed 1,567,568[37] Armenians in the Soviet Union. Projecting this figure back to 1922 and allowing for in-migration of Armenian refugees who first migrated to other areas but came to the USSR before 1926, the Armenian population of the USSR in 1922 was 1.45 to 1.5 million.[38] This figure includes the approximately 400,000 Armenians who migrated from Ottoman Anatolia to Russian Armenia. When the 400,000 Anatolians are subtracted from the total, 1.05 to 1.10 million Armenians is the resulting figure, i.e., approximately 1.1 million Armenians lived in the USSR in 1922, not counting refugees—a loss of 25%

Table 7.6

Armenian Refugees from Anatolia

| Country | Numbers |
|---|---|
| USSR | 400,000 |
| Greece | 45,000 |
| France | 30,000 |
| Bulgaria | 20,000 |
| Cyprus | 2,500 |
| Other European* | 2,000 |
| North America | 35,380 |
| Syria | 100,000 |
| Lebanon | 50,000 |
| Iraq | 25,000 |
| Palestine and Jordan | 10,000 |
| Egypt | 40,000 |
| Iran | 50,000 |
| Others° | 1,000 |
| Total Refugees | 810,880 |
| Remaining in Turkey | 70,000 |
| Total Survivors | 880,880 (59%) |

*For "Other European" are included (in the League figures):
Austria (270), Czechoslovakia (200), Hungary (15),
Yugoslavia (543), Switzerland (250), Italy (603), which
totals 1881. The extra 119 are assumed to be refugees to
England and possibly other European countries that did not
report refugees to the League.

°Including Japan, China, India, Latin America. See League
of Nations A.33.1927 and A.27.1926.viii, and Ferenczi.
It is impossible, due to lack of records that specify
religion or ethnicity, to trace original Armenian immigrants
to Latin America. However, most Armenian refugees to Latin
America came from an intermediary refugee country and many
are thus counted here as refugees to that intermediary
country.

from the 1.4 million Armenian population of Russia in 1914. A loss of 25%
of the 1914 population seems, in the light of the high mortality mentioned
above, to be a reasonable figure. This 25% mortality was less than that
experienced by the Armenians of Anatolia, as will be seen below, but this

Table 7.7


Anatolian Armenians, 1912-22


| Year | Population |
|------|------------|
| 1912 | 1,465,148* |
| 1922 | 880,880 |
| Loss | 584,268 |


*Not including 28,128 in southern
Haleb Vilâyeti.


is to be expected, since the Anatolians' condition was relatively worse. Thus, statistics on the Armenian population of Russia and the USSR make plausible the League estimate of 400,000 Armenian refugees from Anatolia to the Caucasus.

The figure of 400,000 Armenian refugees to Russian Armenia is further supported by official Russian population estimates of 1916 and 1917, which listed 1.78 million Armenians in the Caucasus. This is the expected figure for the number of Armenians in the Caucasus in 1914, plus 400,000 refugees.[39]

Some 81,000 Armenians fled from Anatolia; 70,000 remained in Turkey. Approximately 880,000 Anatolian Armenians had survived the wars. Almost 600,000, 40% of their population, had died.


## The Greeks

Few Greeks left Turkey before the beginning of World War I. Stephen Ladas contends that in 1914 85,000 Greeks were deported from eastern Thrace "to the interior of Asia Minor"[40] and that "150,000 Greeks were driven from the coast region of Western Anatolia and came to the shores of Greece".[41] Ladas offers no sources, however, and his figures are questionable. In any case, most of the early Greek refugees from Anatolia seem to have returned in 1918–19.[42]

The main period of Greek emigration came after the Greek loss (1922) in the Greco-Turkish War. Most of the Greeks of western Asia Minor left before or with the evacuated Greek troops. The Greeks of the Pontus and eastern Thrace soon followed and those who remained were forcibly taken to Greece, in exchange for Greek Muslims, under the terms of the Lausanne Treaty of 1923.

The Greek census of 1928 recorded the number of Greek refugees from Turkey living in Greece at that time (table 7.8). These census figures are the only accurate statistics on Greek migration from Turkey to Greece. They must be adjusted, however, for the presence of Armenian refugees in the totals, deaths of refugees between 1922 and 1928 (the census date), and Anatolian refugees who migrated elsewhere between 1923 and 1928 after first coming to Greece.

The number of refugees from Asia Minor and Pontus reported in 1928 was 809,123. Of these, 35,000 were Armenians, leaving 774,123 Greeks. These Greeks were all over seven years of age by 1928, and they were the survivors of a larger number who had come to Greece in 1922. Of those who had died between 1922 and 1928, approximately 75,000[43] were the

Table 7.8

Refugees from Turkey Residing in Greece in 1928

| Origin* | Number |
|---------|--------|
| Asia Minor | 626,954 |
| Eastern Thrace | 256,635 |
| Pontus | 182,169 |
| Constantinople | 38,458 |

Source: Greek Census of 1928.

*Titles of areas are as they appear in the census. Exact geographical references are unknown.

result of the natural mortality that would have applied to them whether or not they were refugees. These 75,000 must be added to the recorded refugees numbers of 1928 to total 850,000 refugees from Anatolia to Greece between 1912 and 1928. More than 75,000 refugees must actually have died between 1922 and 1928, but these deaths were a result of their refugee status (i.e., they would not have died had they not been refugees) and they must be considered as war casualties.

The figure of 850,000 refugees who remained in Greece until 1928 is actually the lowest possible estimate. It does not take into account the almost certain undercount of refugees as part of the general undercount in the Greek census.[44] At the time of the refugees' arrival in Greece, various

Table 7.9


Anatolian Greeks, 1912-22


| Year | Population |
|------|-----------|
| 1912 | 1,229,491 |
| 1922 | 916,000 |
| Loss | 313,491 |

authorities of the relief commission, the League of Nations, and the Greek government listed higher numbers of refugees, some considerably higher.[45]

A number of Greek refugees from Anatolia did not go to Greece or, if they initially fled to Greece, soon remigrated to Europe, the United States, or Egypt. Ladas suggests that 50,000 who had initially migrated to Greece had left again before the 1928 census was taken.[46] The United States listed 94,137 "Immigrant Aliens" to America from "Turkey in Asia" in the years 1922 to 1928. Of these, approximately 30,000 were Anatolian Greeks[47] who had come directly from Anatolia to America. An additional 10,000 Greeks reached America from Anatolia after first stopping in areas other than Greece.[48] These figures are known with some certainty. What is not known is the number of Greeks who first migrated from Anatolia to Greece and then went on to America. They were recorded by the American immigration authorities as coming from Greece.[49] To enumerate these one must have recourse to Ladas's rough estimate of 50,000. Ladas stated that his figure included Armenians as well as Greeks, reducing the figure of Greeks by 11,000[50] to 39,000. This estimate of remigration is consistent with figures on the numbers of Greek migrants to America, France, and Egypt.[51] If Anatolians were the same proportion of remigrating Greeks as they were of the refugee population who remained in Greece, they were two-thirds (.6622) of the total remigrants, or 26,000. This figure, added to the 40,000 who reached America without stopping in Greece, brings the total number of Anatolian Greeks who migrated to countries other than Greece to 66,000.

Approximately 850,000 Anatolian Greek refugees came to Greece; 66,000 went elsewhere. The 916,000 refugees were the remains of the Anatolian Greek community, which had numbered 1,229,491 in 1912 (not including 24,842 Greeks in the Southern, Syrian, sections of Haleb Vilâyeti); 313,491, or 25%, had been lost.

## The Muslims

Two and a half million Muslims died in Anatolia in the period of World War I and the Turkish War of Independence, or 18% of the total Muslim population. The figure of 18%, however, does not properly elucidate the mortality of Anatolia's Muslims. Death rates were actually much higher in the theaters of war.

The area of greatest mortality was the east. Not since the Black Death has there been mortality as great as that of the Muslims of Bitlis, Van, and Erzurum. In those three provinces the zones of war coincided with areas of population concentration, but such great mortality can only be explained as a product of starvation, disease, and a civil war of extermination, as well as the Russian-Ottoman war.

In the rest of Anatolia, the picture of wartime deaths is confused by postwar migration. It is doubtful that provinces such as Trabzon and İzmit, which were at least peripheral war zones, would have escaped with relatively minor death rates, while others such as Konya registered great loss. The problem lies in the effect of migration on the figures in table 7.10.

To find the losses in each province, the 1927 Muslim population, as shown in the 1927 Turkish census and corrected for underenumeration and international migration,[52] has been projected back to find the population of

Table 7.10

Muslim Deaths  1912-22

| Province | Loss* | Proportion of 1912 Muslim Population |
|----------|-------|--------------------------------------|
| Adana | 42,511 | .07 |
| Ankara | 104,823 | .08 |
| Aydın | 333,230 | .19 |
| Biga | 24,793 | .15 |
| Bitlis | 169,748 | .42 |
| Diyarbakır | 158,043 | .26 |
| Erzurum | 248,695 | .31 |
| Haleb° | 50,838 | .09 |
| Hüdavendigâr | 160,612 | .10 |
| İzmit | 12,039 | .04 |
| Kastamonu | 224,679 | .17 |
| Konya | 418,442 | .27 |
| Mamuretülaziz | 89,310 | .16 |
| Sivas | 180,413 | .15 |
| Trabzon | 49,907 | .04 |
| Van | 194,167 | .62 |
| Total† | 2,462,250 | .18 |

*Actually, population decrease.  More than this
number died, but births and in-migration replaced
them in the population.

°The section of Haleb Vilâyeti within the borders
of the Turkish Republic.

†Population loss in the part of Ottoman Anatolia
that remained in the Turkish Republic and the
proportion of that loss to the total population
of that area.

the area of each Ottoman province in 1922. Each province's 1922 population was then subtracted from its 1912 population. The results are the Muslim losses in each province, as they appear in table 7.10. Provinces that
received large numbers of migrants from other provinces between 1922 and
1927 appear to have had lower wartime mortality than they actually had.

Provinces that sent out many migrants appear to have had a greater mortality. ("Deaths," or population loss, are found by subtracting the population in 1922 from the population in the same area in 1912. If the 1922 population has been swelled by in-migration, then the deaths appear to be less than they actually were. Correspondingly, in the province that sent the migrants, the 1922 population appears smaller and the deaths greater.)

The beneficiaries of the great internal migrations of the early Turkish Republic were the fertile and more developed provinces whose populations had been greatly reduced in the wars—Aydın, Hüdavendigar, and Trab-

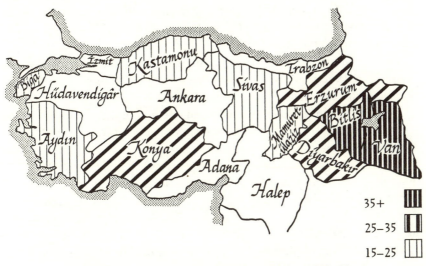

**Figure 7.3.** Percentage of Muslim Deaths, 1912–22

zon—and Ankara, the capital of the new Turkish Republic. The provinces that donated population were primarily Kastamonu and Konya. There were economic opportunities in many of the provinces ravaged by the wars. Trabzon, Hüdavendigâr, and Aydın were centers of trade and contained the best agricultural land in Anatolia. Poor men naturally migrated to lands that had been opened by deaths of Muslims and deaths and migrations of Christians. The total population of the area of the Ottoman Aydın province, for example, had dropped by almost one million persons, 45% of the population, leaving much fertile land and opportunity for migrants from poorer provinces.

The provinces of the east did not experience this great in-migration, probably because they offered little to entice the immigrant.

Muslim mortality was of three sorts. The first type was seen in all the belligerent countries of World War I, deaths of young male soldiers. The magnitude of this loss on Anatolian Muslim numbers can be seen in the first Turkish census. In both theoretical and recorded populations,[53] the number of females and males in the 20–45 age group of a normal population should be approximately equal, but the 1927 Turkish census showed 830,000 more women aged 20–45 than men.[54] These can be considered battlefield casualties of World War I, the civil wars, and the Greco-Turkish War, though the majority of the dead combatants were not enrolled in the regular army. The proportion of these battlefield dead was by far the worst of any country in the World War I period.[55]

Soldiers, in and out of uniform, accounted for less than one-third of the deaths. The largest mortality came in the second group of victims—civilian deaths in the war zones. This is most obvious in the eastern provinces, where half the Muslim men, women, and children in the provinces of Russian invasion died. The effects of intercommunal war can be seen, though, in provinces such as Sivas, where no foreign army entered but mortality was high. Sivas had a large number of Armenians—183,000, more than any other province—and many Sivas Muslims and Armenians must have died in the civil war between the two groups. Migration, of course, accounts for part of the high mortality in Sivas in table 7.10; some of the mortality listed for Sivas actually took place in Trabzon.

The third group of Muslim dead were not direct victims of the wars. They rather died due to wartime conditions of scarcity, famine, and disease. These losses were great. Indeed, the loss of four, seven, or eight percent of a province's population appears small only in relation to the massive losses of the other provinces. The situation in even the provinces that escaped actual warfare is shown in table 7.11. In this table, the populations of the Anatolian provinces have been projected forward to what they would have been in 1922, had they been allowed to grow as they had from 1878 to 1912.[56] They are then compared to what the 1922 populations actually were. Many of those in the difference column were deaths, many children never born. The figures make it obvious that no part of the Anatolian Muslim community was spared.

Table 7.11

Projected and Actual Muslim Populations, 1922,
Showing the Effect of the Wars

| Province | Population in 1912 | Projected Population in 1922 (Without War) | Actual Population in 1922 | Difference |
|---|---|---|---|---|
| Adana | 573,256 | 629,158 | 530,745 | 98,413 |
| Ankara | 1,263,199 | 1,404,174 | 1,158,376 | 245,798 |
| Aydın | 1,734,179 | 1,900,129 | 1,400,949 | 499,180 |
| Biga | 165,508 | 186,237 | 140,715 | 45,522 |
| Bitlis | 408,703 | 483,353 | 238,955 | 244,398 |
| Diyarbakır | 598,985 | 654,607 | 440,942 | 213,665 |
| Erzurum | 804,388 | 909,315 | 555,693 | 353,622 |
| Haleb* | 562,197 | 632,632 | 511,359 | 121,273 |
| Hüdavendigâr | 1,598,583 | 1,732,305 | 1,437,971 | 294,334 |
| İzmit | 271,751 | 335,206 | 259,712 | 75,494 |
| Kastamonu | 1,305,279 | 1,430,653 | 1,080,600 | 350,053 |
| Konya | 1,542,331 | 1,782,015 | 1,123,889 | 658,126 |
| Mamuretülaziz | 564,164 | 613,420 | 474,854 | 138,566 |
| Sivas | 1,196,300 | 1,346,176 | 1,015,887 | 330,289 |
| Trabzon | 1,178,655 | 1,332,878 | 1,128,748 | 204,130 |
| Van | 313,322 | 340,197 | 119,155 | 221,042 |
| Total | 14,080,800 | 15,712,455 | 11,618,550 | 4,093,905 |

*The portions of the vilâyet that remained in the Turkish Republic.

## Conclusions

The pattern of mortality in Anatolia was both geographic and ethnic. Those in the regions of Anatolia with a high proportion of Christian inhabitants were very likely to have died. This was true regardless of the religious or ethnic group of the inhabitant. While Christian–Muslim warfare was, with foreign invasion, at the root of the Anatolian mortality, it is an error to speak of Greek deaths, Muslim deaths, or Armenian deaths as if each somehow had a separate existence. To mention the sufferings of one group and avoid those of another gives a false picture of what was a human, not simply an ethnic, disaster.

Table 7.12

Armenian Population and Muslim Deaths in the "Six Vilâyets"

| Vilâyet | Armenian Population | Proportion Armenian | Muslim Deaths* | Proportion of Muslims Dead |
|---|---|---|---|---|
| Van | 130,500 | .26 | 194,167 | .62 |
| Bitlis | 191,156 | .31 | 169,748 | .42 |
| Erzurum | 163,218 | .17 | 248,695 | .31 |
| Diyarbakır | 89,131 | .12 | 158,043 | .26 |
| Mamuretülaziz | 111,043 | .16 | 89,310 | .16 |
| Sivas | 182,912 | .12 | 180,413 | .15 |

*Population loss.

In the east, the areas of Muslim deaths and Armenian deaths were almost perfectly correlated. From all evidence, the "Six Vilâyets" of the Armenian homeland were the area of the greatest number of Armenian deaths. Some 40% of the total Armenian population of Anatolia died, but the percentage must have been higher in the "Six Vilâyets." In the same area, the Muslims suffered their worst mortality. In numbers, the Muslims lost many more persons than did the Armenians; in percentage of total population, less. The great mortality of both Muslims and Armenians does not fit into any theory that posits one group of murderers, another group murdered. Both Muslims and Christians were killers, both Muslims and Christians were killed.

In the west it was much the same. The number of Muslim deaths was greater and the percentage of Christian deaths was higher, though figures for both Christians and Muslims are greatly affected by the need to consider large areas of Anatolia in the figures of table 7.13. Because of the effect of post-war migration and lack of knowledge of the home provinces of Greek refugees, a very large geographic area, including many relatively tranquil provinces, was selected for table 7.13. Actual mortality in war areas such as Aydın Province must have been much higher for both groups.

The events of 1914 to 1922 permanently changed Anatolia. By 1922, 3.5 million Anatolian Muslims, Greeks, and Armenians, and uncounted Nestorians, Chaldeans, and others, had lost their lives—more than one-fifth of the population. Another 1.8 million had emigrated to other lands. In Anatolia, the rulers were new men with new visions and new political philosophies. The form of government had changed and soon even the sultan-caliph himself would be banished. The deepest changes, however, were in the population. Centuries of Anatolian Christianity had come to an end, though Armenians and Greeks have to this day kept their love of Anatolia

Table 7.13

Greek and Muslim Deaths

|  | Deaths* | Proportion of Population |
|---|---|---|
| Greeks | 285,910 | .27 |
| Muslims | 1,223,702 | .16 |

*Population loss in the provinces of Kastamonu, Trabzon, İzmit, Hüdavendigâr, Biga, Aydın, Konya.

and generations of children who have never seen Anatolia have been raised with a strong irredentism. Turkey, though a secular state, was for the first time almost completely Muslim. Most of the old entreprenurial class was gone, making way for Atatürk's state capitalism and a new class of Muslim merchants. Agricultural and city lands, once held by those who had died or migrated, were now open to new farmers and landlords, who made opportunities and new lives out of disaster. The Turkish Republic grew and eventually flourished.

Turkey has been called a phoenix that rose from the ashes of the Empire, but the analogy is not really proper. When it rose from the flames, the phoenix was renewed, but remained the same creature. The Turkish Republic was in very few senses the same as Ottoman Anatolia. When 20% of its people died, Ottoman Anatolia had died as well. The Turkish Republic was its successor.

# NOTES

1. From 9,820,560 to 14,510,145, a .4877 increase.
2. Due to the lower rate of increase in the eastern provinces and the troubles of 1895–6 and 1908–9.
3. See chapter 4.
4. The following railroads were constructed after 1878:

| Line | Kilometers |
|------|------------|
| Haydar Paşa to İzmit | 578 |
| Eskişehir to Konya | 445 |
| Konya to Ereğli | 200 |
| İzmir to Kasaba | 266 |
| Alaşehir to Afyon Karahisar | 251 |

Source: McCarthy, Statistics, Table XI.1.

5. In this period, production of silk cocoons tripled and export of tobacco leaf tripled. Mineral production rose 69% between 1902 and 1907 alone. (McCarthy, Statistics, Tables XII.1, XIV.21, and XIV.2.)
6. In 1895, there were only 1,615 hospital beds for the sick in all of Anatolia, of which 969 were in Aydın province—one bed for every 8,000 persons. Only 88 physicians worked in hospitals (42 of them in Aydın) or one physician for every 150,000 persons. (McCarthy, Statistics, Table IV.1.)
7. Tripolitanian, First Balkan, Second Balkan, World War I, War of Independence.
8. The best accounts of the wars themselves is in W. E. D. Allen and Paul Muratoff, Caucasian Battlefields, Cambridge, 1953, especially Book IV.
9. Caucasian Battlefields, p. 293.
10. Caucasian Battlefields, pp. 297–302; M. Larcher, La Guerre Turque dans la Guerre Mondiale (Paris, 1926), p. 395; Armenian Question, pp. 4, 6, and 7.
11. In both the Turkish Demographic Survey and the 1965 Turkish census, widowhood in these provinces averaged approximately 15%. In 1927, when polygamy was a much stronger force than in 1965 (almost forty years after it had been outlawed), the normal (i.e., without the effects of war mortality) number of widows should have been less than 15%.
12. B. R. Mitchell, European Historical Statistics, 1750–1970 (N.Y.: Columbia University Press, 1975), and D. V. Glass and E. Grebenik, "World Population, 1800–1950," in The Cambridge Economic History of Europe, vol. VI (Cambridge: Cambridge University Press, 1965).
13. See tables 7.7 to 7.10.
14. See table 7.1.

15. Listed under "Ermeni" religion category in the census.

16. The Greek census of 1928, Turkish census of 1927, Russian census of 1926, French census of 1931, etc.

17. Only 64,745 inhabitants of Turkey listed Armenian as their mother tongue in 1927. It is possible that some Armenians were listed as foreign citizens in the census (see Book I, p. lxxxviii).

18. 1927 census, v. III, p. 32.

19. See appendix 1.

20. Greek Catholics         1.8%
    Armenian Catholics     87.7%
    Latin Rite (Roman)     10.5%

21. This statement is based on the fact that the 1927 census figures were taken in the middle of a period of continuing out-migration of Armenians from Turkey. The 1935 Turkish census listed far fewer Armenians in Turkey than the 1927 census. Since categories changed, exact comparison is impossible, but the 1935 figure for Gregorians, compared to the 1927 figure for Ermeni religion, yields: 1927, 77,433; 1935, 44,526; a loss of 42%. The figure of 140,000 total Armenians (including Catholics, Protestants, and unrecorded) in 1927 fits well into the general picture of Armenian emigration from Turkey. (Many of the migrants would have come into the United States from the Turkish Republic under the category "Southeastern Europe," which included "Turkey in Europe" and thus are impossible to trace.)

Armenian sources give estimates of Armenian population in Turkey that indicate a greater number than the Turkish censuses have recorded, e.g., 100,000 in 1945 (Leon Arpee, A *History of Armenian Christianity*, New York, 1946, pp. 3–7). They include a large number of Armenians who were unregistered as such in the censuses. While 100,000 in 1945 is an exaggeration, the higher figures do generally support the estimate of 140,000 in 1922.

22. In 1927, 53,273 Gregorian ("Ermeni"), 24,183 Catholics, and 4,682 Protestant were listed in the provinces of Istanbul, Kırklareli, Edirne, and Tekirdağ. The percentage of Armenians in the latter two religious groups is unknown.

23. V. I, pp. 102 and 103.

24. The 1906 census listed only 27,000 total non-Europeans under "*Lieu de Naissance.*" Armenians were not separately listed, but could not have made up many of the 27,000.

25. Others, less than 200, may have come also, listed within the category "Turkish, not specified." See Imre Ferenczi, *International Migrations*, v. I (New York, 1929), p. 891.

26. For Armenian migration to the United States I have accepted the work of Robert Mirak ("Armenian Emigration to the United States to 1915 (I): Leaving the Old Country," *Journal of Armenian Studies* I, no. 1, Autumn, 1975, pp. 5–42). For 1912–14 I have taken his figures (22,362) and I have applied his multiplier (.4 of all the migrants from "Turkey in Asia" were Armenian) to the United States immigration statistics from 1915 to 1924. (United States Department of Commerce,

*Historical Statistics of the United States,* Part I [Washington, 1975], p. 107—"Immigrants, Turkey in Asia.")

The United States Commissioner General of Immigration listed 49,901 Armenian immigrant aliens entering the United States from all points of origin from 1912 to 1928 (United States Department of Labor, Bureau of Immigration, *Annual Report of the Commissioner General of Immigration,* 1928 [Washington, 1928], pp. 201 and 202.

27. A. A. Pallis, "The Greek Census of 1928," *The Geographical Journal* LXXIII, no. 6, June, 1928, pp. 545 and 546.

28. See League of Nations, International Labor Organization, *Report by Dr. Fridtjof Nansen,* A41.1925 (Annex) and the many other League publications on refugees, many of which repeat the same statistics. The League recorded 42,200 Armenian refugees in Greece in 1926 and 1927 (A29.1926.viii and A33.1927), which brings either the Greek census figures or those of the League into question. The answer probably lies in Greek undercounting of women and children and in the general confusion of the refugee situation.

29. Bulgaria, *Annuaire Statistique du Royaume de Bulgarie 1931* (Sofia, 1931), p. 35.

30. Ormanian, p. 206; Poladian in Ormanian, p. 211.

31. A.29,1926.viii: 20,000; A.33.1927: 22.000.

32. Republic of Cyprus, Ministry of Finance, Statistics and Research Department, *Statistical Abstracts 1968,* p. 23.

33. *Report by Dr. Fridtjof Nansen,* p. 2.

34. Richard G. Hovannisian, *The Republic of Armenia,* v. I (Berkeley and Los Angeles, 1971), p. 68.

35. Ibid., p. 222.

36. Stanford J. Shaw and Ezel Kural Shaw, *History of the Ottoman Empire and Modern Turkey,* vol. II, Cambridge: Cambridge University Press, 1977, pp. 356 and 357.

37. 13,539 Armenian refugees to the Armenian SSR were recorded from 1921 to 1925 (*Report by Dr. Fridtjof Nansen*); this number would have increased slightly by the time of the 1926 census. A natural increase rate of .010 would explain the rest of the difference.

38. The scenario of Armenian immigration into what would become the USSR could change, based on greater number of deaths in the Caucasus or greater number of migrants. Where $P_1$ = the initial population, $P_2$ the final population, D the deaths, and M in-migration, $P_1 - D + M = P_2$. Increasing D must cause a decrease in M and vice versa.

39. How the estimates of Armenian numbers were compiled is not known, but they were surely not census statistics. (The wartime statistical abstracts published by the Russian central government merely republished general figures from the war.) The estimates are quoted by Hovannisian, *Armenian on the Road to Independence,* pp. 13–15.

40. Stephen P. Ladas, *The Exchange of Minorities,* New York, 1932, p. 16.

41. Ibid.

42. Ladas (p. 16) contends that 100,000 returned. In the 1928 census, the Greek government listed 55,256 refugees as having come from Asia Minor and Pontus before 1922 and staying in Greece.

43. The mortality rate has been derived from a stable model (Coale and Demeny, West − 9, GRR = 3.0) based on the mortality experience of the Greek population in 1879 and between 1926 and 1930 (Kingdom of Greece, National Statistical Service, *Life Tables for Greece* [Athens, 1964]). The annual mortality of the cohort of refugees would, of course, have decreased as the cohort grew older and left the high mortality years of early childhood behind. Because of this, the mortality for each year has been adjusted (based on the model stable population) as follows:

| | |
|---|---|
| 1922–23 | .026 |
| 1923–24 | .016 |
| 1924–25 | .015 |
| 1925–26 | .013 |
| 1926–27 | .012 |
| 1927–28 | .011 |

It is assumed that the above approximates the mortality actually experienced by the cohort, not counting the extra deaths resulting from their refugee status.

44. All of the Greek censuses from 1920 to 1940 show significant undercounts of children.

45. See Dimitri Pentzopoulos, *The Balkan Exchange of Minorities and Its Impact Upon Greece*, Paris, 1962, pp. 98–100, who quotes the figures of McCartney, Howland, Eddy, the League, etc.

46. Ladas, *Exchange of Minorities*, p. 644.

47. Under the category "Races and People" the immigration service registered 254,338 Greeks. They also listed 204,502 as coming from Greece. Assuming that almost all of those who came from Greece were Greeks, at least 50,078 Greeks came to the United States in these years from other lands. Most of these must have come from Istanbul and Asiatic Turkey, since virtually the entire Greek population of Turkish Thrace was recorded as having migrated to Greece in the 1928 Greek Census. (Migrants: 256,635, a figure which does not include those who died between migration and 1928; Greeks in Thrace in 1912: 261,477, as registered in the *1330 Nüfus-i Umumî*, a slight undercount.)

48. Assuming that 10,000 of the 50,000 Greeks who migrated to the United States from outside of Greece were from Russia, the Balkans, etc. This is, if anything, an overcount of those who did not come from Anatolia. The numbers of migrants from Bulgaria, Rumania, etc. to the United States recorded by the immigration service is very small (see the Commissioner General's *Reports* for the years 1912 to 1928).

49. There is also some question about the large number of Greek "non-immigrant aliens" who came to the United States. For example, in 1926, 2,852 Greek non-immigrant aliens came into the country, but only 1,457 left. Those who remained have not been counted here in the expectation that their numbers would roughly

balance those of immigrants from Anatolia to the United States who remigrated from America, usually returning to Greece.

50. See table 7.6.

51. Ladas, p. 644.

52. See appendix 1.

53. See any of the Coale and Demeny or other stable models for theoretical populations. The Turkish census of 1970 showed .4979 female and .5021 male proportions in the 20–45 age group.

The 20–45 age group, which includes the age 45, is an odd grouping, but the 1927 Turkish census only lists population by the age groups $-1$, $1+2$, 3–6, 7–12, 13–19, 20–45, 46–60, 61–70, 71+. The 46–60 age group also shows a significant excess of males.

54. 2,151,604 males and 2,983,138 females, a difference of 831,534. Female population has been increased by 1.0662 to allow for undercounting. The figures as recorded were 2,151,604 males and 2,797,916 females, a difference of 646,312. No matter what the actual undercount, the point would be the same.

55. B. Urlanis, in *Wars and Population* (Moscow, 1971), pp. 201–210, estimates that the proportion of wartime deaths to total population in the Ottoman Empire was second to that of Serbia and Montenegro. Urlanis only counts uniformed casualties, however, and counts the entire population of the Ottoman Empire (including Arabs and Kurds) as the population. The actual mortality of Anatolian Muslims was many times that of Serbia-Montenegro, even when civilian deaths are not included.

56. The rates have been calculated as if the population had been steadily increasing at the same rate from 1878 to 1912. Boundary changes have been included in the calculations.

# Appendix 1.
## Turkey in 1927 and 1922

ON OCTOBER 29, 1923 the Turkish Republic was established in Anatolia and Thrace. With the exception of major southern sections of Haleb Vilâyeti and small sections of Van and Diyarbakır vilâyets, the Anatolian provinces of the Ottoman Empire were included in the new Republic. To them were added the areas of Kars and Ardahan lost to the Russians in 1878.[1] (Figure A1.1 shows the relation of old and new boundaries and figure A1.2 the new Turkish provinces.)

In the 1920s the Turkish Republic began to initiate social and economic changes that necessitated an exact knowledge of the demographic situation of the country. After trial enumerations and partial censuses of various areas, a census was taken in October of 1927.[2]

The 1927 census, coming soon after the great upheavals of the Balkan Wars, World War I, and the Turkish War of Independence, is a major source of information on the effects of these wars and the state of Turkey at the beginning of its history as a republic, yet the census has not been seriously studied. Its demographic defects have kept researchers from mining its valuable information. These defects can be corrected, however, and this chapter analyzes the 1927 census for the total population of Turkey and the population of each province.

### Population in the 1927 Census

Comparison with the other censuses of Republican Turkey demonstrates that the census of 1927 undercounts the Turkish population. Table A1.1 gives the comparative population increases (rate of increase per year) for the

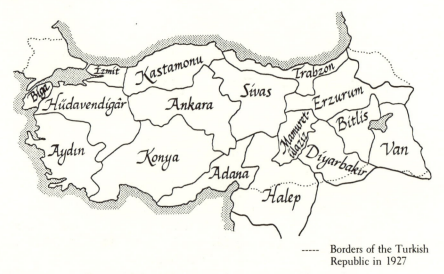

----- Borders of the Turkish
Republic in 1927

**Figure A1.1.**   Ottoman and Turkish Republic Borders

censuses from 1927 to 1970. It is unreasonable that the rate of increase between 1927 and 1935 should be of the same magnitude as post-World War II rates. As will be seen below, fertility levels c. 1927 were lower than those of 1950 and mortality higher. In addition, a drop in the rate of increase from 1927–35 to 1935–40 would indicate an economic or medical decline in the later period, and no such decline took place until the 1940–45 period. Thus the 1927–35 rate of increase must be in error, either through

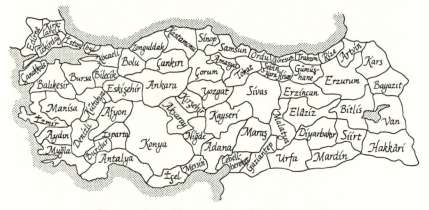

**Figure A1.2**   The Republic of Turkey in 1927

Table A1.1

Increase between Censuses

| Census Years | Rates/Year |
|---|---|
| 1927-35 | .0214 |
| 1935-40 | .0170* |
| 1940-45 | .0106 |
| 1945-50 | .0217 |
| 1950-55 | .0277 |
| 1955-60 | .0285 |
| 1960-65 | .0246 |
| 1965-70 | .0252 |

*This figure probably indicates a higher rate of increase per year than .0170 from 1935 to 1938 and a decreased rate in 1939 and 1940, when wartime mobilization and economic pressure had an effect.

an understatement of the 1927 population or an overstatement of that of 1935. All indications are that the 1927 census undercounted the population.

The 1927 census of the Turkish Republic lies between the Ottoman and modern Turkish census traditions. It intends to be a modern census, but fails in various ways. In the basic enumeration of the population, the census follows in the tradition of the Ottoman censuses. Women and children are undercounted and there are deficiencies in the enumeration of the eastern provinces. In form, the census is relatively modern, incorporating census categories not found in Ottoman censuses, such as "Married, Widowed, and Divorced," "Population by Place of Birth," and "Population by Mother Tongue." These categories are a valuable feature of modern censuses. More valuable, and more in the modern census tradition, is the presentation of population by age groups. Only one Ottoman population document did this, the *1313 İstatistik*. The 1927 age groups, though, are not the five-year age groups used in modern censuses (0–4, 5–9, 10–14, etc.), but are odd groupings—1, 1 + 2, 3–6, 7–12, 13–19, 21–45, 46–60, 61–70, and 71+.

The 1927 census is more complete than any Ottoman population document. It gives male, female, and total populations for each of several categories, including literacy, and for each vilâyet, sancak, and kaza in the country. The census's listing of the area of each administrative subdivision in square kilometers facilitates comparisons to other Turkish censuses for changes in district size, and thus population.

Unfortunately, the modern categories and tables of the 1927 census have often not proved useful to either demographers or historians, because the information in them is often incorrect. Tables of population by age are very inaccurate and some provinces record considerable errors in their statements on total population. Females are systematically undercounted. Due to these deficiencies, the 1927 census figures are never used by the Turkish State Institute of Statistics. All of their comparative tables begin with the census of 1935.

In analyzing the Turkish population in late Ottoman and early Republican times, one cannot, unlike the Turkish State Institute of Statistics, afford to ignore the 1927 census. Coming as it does soon after the 1911 to 1922 period of wars, it reflects the demographic effects of that catastrophic period much better than the more accurate 1935 census, taken eight years later. The 1927 population can be adjusted and its errors corrected. It must be used for the picture it gives of the population of the early Turkish Republic.


Age Groups

The custom in population tables, followed by all modern censuses, is to enumerate the population by both single years and five-year age groups. Single years allow an analysis of errors in age registration and five-year age groups are convenient groupings for cohort analysis—i.e., following a group of population members through their lives by comparing the numbers in their age group in successive censuses. For example, the age group aged 0–4 in the 1935 census will be 5–9 in the 1940 census, 10–14 in the 1945 census, etc. Using cohort analysis, researchers can derive the actual mortality experience of a population.

The 1927 Turkish census divides its population into neither one-year nor five-year age groups. Its strange age groups (0, 1 + 2, 3–6, 7–12, etc.) make

Table A1.2

Cohorts 1927-1935

| | 1927 | | 1935 | | Survivors | |
|---|---|---|---|---|---|---|
| Age | Population by Cohort | Age | Population by Cohort | Recorded | Expected |
| 0 | 647,073 | 8 | 570,118 | .8811 | .7908 |
| 1+2 | 1,075,227 | 9+10 | 799,175 | .7433 | .8920 |
| 3-6 | 1,444,465 | 11-14 | 1,074,056 | .7436 | .9316 |
| 7-12 | 1,349,884 | 15-20 | 1,566,951 | 1.1608 | .9546 |
| 13-19 | 2,081,932 | 21-27 | 1,907,972 | .9164 | .9317 |
| 20-45 | 4,962,766 | 28-53 | 4,489,236 | .9046 | .9023 |
| 46-60 | 1,364,352 | 54-68 | 1,067,479 | .7824 | .5269 |
| 61+ | 722,571 | 69+ | 433,685 | .6002 | .4483 |
| Age | Cumulative Population | Age | Cumulative Population | | |
| 0-2 | 1,722,300 | 8-10 | 1,369,293 | .7950 | .8156 |
| 0-6 | 3,166,765 | 8-14 | 2,443,349 | .7716 | .8775 |
| 0-12 | 4,516,649 | 8-20 | 4,010,300 | .8979 | .9111 |
| 0-19 | 6,598,581 | 8-27 | 5,918,272 | .8969 | .9176 |
| 0-45 | 11,561,347 | 8-53 | 10,407,508 | .9002 | .9098 |
| 0-60 | 12,925,699 | 8-68 | 11,474,987 | .8878 | .8856 |
| Total | 13,648,270 | 8+ | 11,908,672 | .8725 | .8419 |

many types of analysis very difficult. There is, in addition, no way to divide the odd 1927 age groups into more traditional five-year age groups. The ages are so misstated and, due to the effects of war, the general age structure so unusual (table A1.2) that no method of age redistribution works. The methods of Brass[3] and of the United Nations[4] are inapplicable, as is the fitting of a polynomial.[5] It is both impossible to redivide the 1927 age groups into five-year age groups and impossible to readjust them for age misreporting. They must be used as they are published, if they are to be used at all.

It should still be possible to analyze the 1927 census by comparing the 1927 census cohorts with the same groups as they appear in the Turkish census of 1935. The group that is 0–6 in 1927, for example, can be compared to the group 8–14 in 1935. Both groups should be made up of the same individuals, less those who died in the eight years between 1927 and 1935. Assuming the 1935 census to be relatively correct,[6] one can compare the census experience of each cohort in 1927 and in 1935. Mortality in the cohort could then be compared to standard tables. Those cohorts that show unreasonably low mortality would be those in which the population was underregistered in 1927.

The data in table A1.2 indicates the age groups that were under- and overenumerated. The "Recorded" column is the proportion of the age cohort that survived between 1927 and 1935, as recorded in the respective censuses. "Expected" is the proportion that should have survived. It is drawn from the $L_x$ values of Brass Model Life Table 40 ($e_0^0 = 40$) and represents the mortality experience of the 1927 to 1935 Turkish population very closely.[7]

In looking at table A1.2, two facts are immediately evident. First, the recorded census figures are very close to those expected. The "Total" row has a difference of only .03 between the recorded and expected proportions. Second, the age misreporting is fairly extensive. This is due to under- and overenumerations in both the 1927 and 1935 censuses. For 1927, only age groups are recorded, but for the 1935 census, in which single years of age are recorded, the effects of misreporting of age are evident. The cohort 7–12/15–20, for example, is affected by overenumeration of ages 15 and 20 in 1935: age 19—138,571; age 20—515,469; age 21—172,858. Similar errors must have been incorporated in the 1927 census's age groups. For the sake of analysis of the total population, much of the difficulty can be eased by the use of cumulative figures.

Cumulative figures indicate more strikingly the closeness of the census mortality experience to the expected mortality. As more and older age groups are included the effect of misenumeration is lessened and the "Recorded" more closely approaches the "Expected." It becomes evident that many individuals in the population overstated their ages, a phenomenon present in modern Turkish censuses, as well as those of 1927 and 1935.[8] Because of this, the slight underenumeration of the 1927 population does not appear until the "0–60" and "Total" rows when, in fact, the undercounting must have taken place at earlier ages.[9] The main effect is that the 0–2 age group in 1927, which is surely undercounted, does not appear to be so, due to the corresponding overcounting of the 8–10 age group in 1935, to which it is compared.

The discrepancy between the recorded and expected rates in table A1.2 is not great. It might perhaps be considered a minor deviation in the statistics and let stand, did we not know from previous analysis that the 1927 census population is too low (table A1.1). Applying the "Expected" rates as more accurate than the recorded, the 1927 population can be adjusted upward to 14,144,996, an increase of 3.5 per cent, before allowance for underenumeration of females. A correction of this magnitude is supported by study of fertility and mortality levels of Turkey in 1927.

## Fertility and Mortality

One of the best ways to discover the numbers of population of an area or to evaluate the accuracy of a census is to use the fertility and mortality conditions in an area to construct population projections. If both birth rate and death rate are known and migration is regligible, a projection back in time from a known population will give the population at a given year. Thus a projection of the 1935 census can give the population in 1927.

In order to ascertain the rate of increase for a country, representative fertility and mortality must be known. For an area in which births and deaths are not well registered, such as Turkey in 1927 to 1935, it is necessary to have recourse to standard tables. To use these tables, one must estimate, in this case, the expectation of life at birth and a measure of fertility, the Gross Reproduction Rate.

It is reasonable to assume that the mortality rate in Turkey from 1927 to 1935 was slightly greater than that of 1935–40. Lingering social disruption from the wars of 1911 to 1922 and the effects in the southeast of the Kurdish revolts would ensure some higher mortality, but, in the absence of plague or famine, one must assume that mortality from 1927 to 1935 was not far from that of the later period. One can assume, therefore, based on the work of Bulutoğlu,[10] that the expectation of life ($e_0^0$) was approximately forty years, correspondingly to a 1935 to 1940 expectation of life at birth of 44 to 45 years.

One cannot, however, assume that the Gross Reproduction Rate in 1927 is comparable to that of earlier and later years, assumed to be approximately 3.0.[11] A Gross Reproduction Rate of 3.0 seems to have been the norm for Turkish populations when age groups were relatively complete and almost all women of childbearing age were married. The decrease in the male population of Turkey due to war and the great number of widows force one to assume a reduction in the Gross Reproduction Rate. This does not, of course, mean that the women who were bearing children were experiencing

Table A1.3

Proportion of Married Females, 1935 and 1968

| Ages | 1935 | 1968 |
|------|------|------|
| 15+ | .65 | .73 |
| 20+ | .70 | .81 |
| 25+ | .68 | .81 |

Note:  The 1968 totals are from the Turkish Demographic
       Survey (rural Turkey) and include those listed as
       "separated" since there was no "separated" category
       in the 1935 census and those women must have been
       listed as married.

decreased fertility. Quite the contrary. The greater amount of arable land per family, the coming of peace, and the rise in health and economic standards following long wars all traditionally lead to an increase of fertility in a society. The Gross Reproduction Rate, however, does not reflect the fertility of the childbearing women, but the fertility of the society, i.e., of all women, and widows and unmarried women (both due to the death of eligible partners) bring down the rate.[12] Direct material on fertility in 1927 is unavailable, but by comparing the marital status of females in 1935, the first year in which the Turkish census listed marital status by age, with modern data, we can see that gross fertility in the 1927 and 1935 populations must have been lower than in more recent times (table A1.3). The data on female marital status in 1927 and 1935 are comparable; in both years 41 to 42% of all women were married.

It is true that illegal and thus unrecorded polygamy might have affected the 1935 results.[13] In 1935, .009 of the females over 15 were recorded as having unknown marital status, whereas in 1968 only .0003 were so listed. None of those listed in 1935 as "marital status—unknown" were under 15 and many of them probably were polygamously married. There are also a larger than expected number of unmarried females in the early marriage ages, and some of these may in fact have been illegally married.[14] If, however, half of the "unknowns" and the extra unmarried women are added to the number married in 1935, the proportion of married females over 15 would only change from .65 to .67.[15] In a society such as Turkey's, in which there is no significant extramarital fertility, a drop in the rate of married females must signify lower fertility for the society as a whole. Table A1.3 demonstrates that Turkish fertility, as judged by marital rate, must have been lower in 1935, and by analogy lower in 1927, than in 1968. Without more detailed information on fertility, it is impossible to estimate the exact rate of reproduction. The 1968 female population in table A1.3 had a Gross Reproduction Rate of 3.0; the Gross Reproduction Rate for 1927, given the difference in married females, must have been somewhat lower. I have chosen a Gross Reproduction Rate of 2.7 as most likely. This rate is obviously an estimate, based on the general assumption that the marital fertility rate in 1927 would be very similar to that of 1968, but that the lower percentage of married women would bring down the Gross Reproduction Rage.

Knowing both the Gross Reproduction Rate and mortality level (in this case, expectation of life at birth—$e_0^0$) allows the selection of a population model from which a rate of increase can be drawn. In this case a life expectancy at birth of 40 and Gross Reproduction Rate of 2.7 indicate a population that increased at between .017 and .018 per year.[16] It is best to take the lower rate of increase, .017 or 17 per thousand per year, as representative of the 1927 to 1935 Turkish population increase, since the population in question was not actually stable and fertility was adversely affected by the war time experience of the population.[17]

A growth rate of 17 per thousand per year is an estimate and subject to a certain amount of error. It is supported, though, by the previous analysis of

Table A1.4

Marital Status in Turkey, 1935

|  | Males | Females |
|---|---|---|
| Never Married | 4,611,363 | 3,785,929 |
| Married | 3,160,567 | 3,305,967 |
| Widow/Widower | 110,412 | 1,049,837 |
| Divorced | 13,173 | 35,735 |
| Unknown | 41,197 | 43,470 |
| Total | 7,936,512 | 8,220,938 |

Source: Turkish Census of 1935, vol. 60, p. 128.

Note: These are uncorrected figures. Females are somewhat underenumerated.

1927 and 1935 age groups, which yielded a similar figure (16.9 per thousand per year) and by the fact that the increase (table A1.1) from 1935 to 1940 is the same. The figure for the 1927 population arrived at above, 14,144,996, thus appears even more likely to be correct.

## Female Population

To the 1927 population, already corrected above, must be added a correction for the underenumeration of young females. No comparison of the 1927 and 1935 census figures can bring out this underenumeration, since the 1935 census undercounted young females to the same degree as in 1927. Indeed, this undercounting has been a constant feature of Turkish Republic censuses (table A1.5).

In correcting the underenumeration of females 0–19 in the 1927 census it is not possible to assume simply that the male and female populations were equal in size, since this is not true for the younger age groups in which most underenumeration occurs. Analysis of modern Turkish data suggests that females 0–19 made up 49% (table A1.6) of the 0–19 total population. Yücetürk's study of births in Turkish hospitals between 1956 and 1966 indicates that 107.7 Turkish males were born for every 100 females, seemingly a very high rate, but one derived from actual recorded births.[18]

One can apply to these figures survivorship figures drawn from the Turkish Demographic Survey[19] (survivorship rates give the proportion of the population that survives between the first and last ages in an age group. The survivorship rate for the age group 1–4, for example, tells the number who survive from the beginning of their first year to the end of their fourth.) In table A1.6 the number of male births and female births are multiplied by survivorship ratios. The results show how many of the original

Table A1.5

Percentage Female in Turkish Censuses:  1927, 1935, and 1965

| Ages | 1927 | 1935 | 1965 |
|------|------|------|------|
| 0-19 | 47.4 | 47.4 | 47.9 |
| Under 1 | 45.7 | 46.4 | 48.4 |

group survive at the end of age 1, and at the end of age 4, 9, 14, and 19. This is done in the following manner, for example, for males: 107.7 (the number of males born) is multiplied by the survivorship ratio for the years 0–1 (approximately .801). The result is the number of males alive at the end of age 0. This figure, in turn, is multiplied by the survivorship ratio for ages 1 to 4, and this results in the number of males surviving at the end of age 4. This is done for each group until age 19. These totals are then summed to obtain the final figures, which are, strictly speaking, the sum of males who are ending their 0, 4, 9, 14, and 19th years. The "Total 0–19" figures give us an approximation of the proportion of males and females in the 0–20 age group, 48.9% females. (The numbers in table A1.6 would be slightly more comparable to census data were the $L_x$ (survivors in the age interval in the stationary life table population) values for single years used instead of the survivorship rates for five-year age groups. Single-year life tables were, however, not available and the difference would have been minor, in any case. Using the $L_x$ values for 0–1, the percent female is 48.6 instead of 48.8.)

Though the absolute numbers of total survivors would change if a greater mortality schedule, such as that of 1927, were applied, the proportion female would remain approximately the same. The percentage female in the

Table A1.6

|  | Male | Female |
|---|---|---|
| Births | 107.7 | 100.0 |
| Survivors |  |  |
| 0-1 | 86.31 | 82.19 |
| 1-4 | 80.50 | 76.91 |
| 5-9 | 79.25 | 75.74 |
| 10-14 | 78.67 | 75.10 |
| 15-19 | 77.82 | 74.20 |
| 1+4+9+14+19 | 402.55 | 384.14 |
| Percentage Female |  |  |
| 0-19 |  | 48.9 |
| 0-1 |  | 48.8 |

Note: "Survivors" indicates the number who survive at the end of the age group, i.e., for 0-4, the number remaining at the end of age 4.

age group 0–19 in 1927 should have been 49%.[20] The 1927 census shows a 0–19 female population of 47.4% and must be corrected.

## The Population of Turkey in 1927

The foregoing analysis indicates that between 1927 and 1935 the population of Turkey increased at approximately the same rate as between 1935 and 1940. The figure arrived at, without correcting for the undercounting of females, is 14,144,996. To this must be added the correction factor for females—plus .0314,[21] leaving a total population in 1927 of 14,589,149.[22]

The enumerated population of Turkey in the 1927 census was too low by approximately seven percent. Considering the unsettled conditions in Anatolia and the difficulties experienced by the new Turkish government, the relative accuracy of the 1927 census is remarkable. The censuses of many countries in the 1970s did not approach the degree of accuracy of the first census of the Turkish Republic.

Table A1.7

Female Population, 1927 and 1935

| Year | Female Population |
|------|-------------------|
| 1935 aged 8+ | 6,199,616 |
| 1927 Recorded | 7,084,391 |
| 1927 Expected | 7,363,839 |
| Total Females* | 7,851,325 |

*Correction factor of 1.0662 applied to the 1927 expected population.

Methods used in arriving at the actual 1927 population were based on total population, not population by sex. It is important, however, to find the male and female populations in 1927. In studying matters such as the effects of the 1911 to 1922 wars, figures for population by sex provide valuable insights.[23]

Using techniques mentioned previously,[24] it is possible to compare the 1935 and 1927 Turkish population cohorts (table A1.7) and to adjust the 1927 census figures for females. In table A1.7, the "1927 Expected" population is derived by dividing the 1935 population by the survivorship rate .8419.[25] Further adjustment for underreporting of females (.0662 underenumeration) yields a final female population of 7,851,325 and a total population of 14,589,149 (table A1.8).

Table A1.8

The Population of Turkey in 1927*

|         | Population   | Proportion |
|---------|--------------|------------|
| Males   | 6,737,824    | .4618      |
| Females | 7,851,325    | .5382      |
|         |              |            |
| Total   | 14,589,149   |            |

*Frederic Shorter, using a different type of analysis, has arrived at somewhat different figures for the population of Turkey in 1927. I have unfortunately not been able to see his article ("The Population of Turkey after the War of Independence," Regional Papers, West Asia and North Africa Region, Population Council, Giza, Egypt, 1983.).

## The Muslim Population of Anatolia in 1922

Assuming the same correction factor[26] used above for the total population, the Muslim population of Turkey in 1927 was 14,184,381.

For the calculations in chapter 7, it has been necessary to compute the Muslim population of 1922 by Ottoman provincial boundaries.[27] The computation has included the following steps:

1. Finding the Muslim population of Each Turkish province in 1927. After extensive analysis and statistical manipulations, simply dividing the Muslim population of 1927 so that each province had the same percentage of the total population as in 1935 proved to be the best way of allowing for the errors of the 1927 census. Much more complicated analyses produced no better results.

2. Subtracting refugees. Officially registered in-migrants to each province from 1922 to 1927 were subtracted from each province's total Muslim population. (These were international refugees into Turkey. Internal migration statistics are not available and out-migration of Muslims was practically nonexistent.[28]

Table A1.9

The Muslim Population of Anatolia in 1922

| Location | Population |
|----------|-----------|
| Adana | 530,745 |
| Ankara | 1,158,376 |
| Aydın | 1,400,949 |
| Biga | 140,715 |
| Bitlis | 238,995 |
| Diyarbakır | 440,942 |
| Erzurum | 555,693 |
| Haleb | 511,359 |
| Hüdavendigâr | 1,437,971 |
| İzmit | 259,712 |
| Kastamonu | 1,080,600 |
| Konya | 1,123,889 |
| Mamuretülaziz | 474,854 |
| Sivas | 1,015,887 |
| Trabzon | 1,128,748 |
| Van | 119,155 |
| Total | 11,618,550 |

3. Correcting the populations for undercounting, using the same correction factor as derived for the total population.

4. Combining the Muslim populations from the Anatolian Turkish provinces into the boundaries of the larger Ottoman vilâyets.[29]

5. Projecting the populations back to 1922, assuming the same rates applied as from 1927 to 1935.[30]

The vilâyet of Kastamonu serves as an example of the process. The area of Ottoman Kastamonu was made up of the 1927 Republican provinces of Kastamonu, Sinop, Çankırı, Bolu, and Zonguldak. In 1927, these had a combined (minus refugees) corrected population of 1,157,792. When projected back to 1922, the Muslim population of the area of Ottoman Kastamonu was 1,080,600. Table A1.9 gives the results of such calculations for each Ottoman province. It should be noted that the Haleb Vilâyeti in table A1.9 does not include the southern sections of Ottoman Haleb, which were not included in the Turkish Republic.

## NOTES

1. The Turkish Republic provinces of Artvin (except Yusufeli), Kars, and part of Erzurum.

2. Censuses of Istanbul were taken soon after the creation of the Republic.

3. See Norman Carrier and John Hobcraft, *Demographic Estimation for Developing Societies* (London: Population Investigation Committee, London School of Economics, 1971).

4. United Nations, Department of Economic and Social Affairs, Population Studies No. 42, *Methods of Estimating Basic Measures From Incomplete Data* (New York, 1967).

5. Third- and fourth-degree polynomials distort the middle and upper ages and greater degrees do not adjust the younger populations to a great enough extent.

6. As does the Turkish State Institute of Statistics, which lists it as the first fairly accurate census, ignoring the 1927 census.

7. Carrier and Hobcraft, *Demographic Estimation*, pp. 70–84. See the section on methodology for the method of estimation of the rates and the table of $L_x$ values.

8. See Sağlik ve Sosyal Yardım Bakanlığı. *Vital Statistics from the Turkish Demographic Survey, 1965–1966*, Ankara, 1967, pp. 13–15.

9. Children are given a few extra months of age. Adults may take many years. The model is thus skewed away from the earlier years, in which much of the underreporting takes place, toward later years, only appearing in the final years. An example illustrating this could be:

|  | *Loss* | *Gain* |
|---|---|---|
| P(0–4) | −20000 | 0 |
| P(5–9) | −20000 | +20000 |
| P(10–14) | −20000 | +20000 |
| P(15–19) | −20000 | +20000 |
| . . . | | |
| P(55–59) | −20000 | +20000 |
| P(60+) | 0 | +20000 |

where P(x − y) = the population for each age group and in which each group's gains (from persons overstating their ages) are offset by the losses (from understating) in all age groups but 0–4 and 60+. Population numbers are, in effect, shifted from the youngest to the oldest age groups. The reality is, of course, much more complex.

10. Yakut Bulutoğlu, *La Structure par age et la mortalite de la Population de la Turquie*, Paris, 1970, pp. 132 and 134, in which different methods of analysis yield the following $e_0^0$:

| Masculine | Feminine | Total |
|-----------|----------|-------|
| 42.3 | 47.5 | 44.9 |
| 44.0 | 46.0 | 45.0 |

11. See chapter 2.

12. The Gross Reproduction Rate is the sum of children born in one period divided by the number of women in the population between the ages of 15 and 45, times the percentage of female births, times a constant (here 1,000).

13. Illegal polygamy is still a factor in modern Turkey. See the T.D.S. and Serim Timur, *Türkiye 'de Aile Yapısı*, Ankara: Hacettepe University Press, 1972, especially pp. 93 and 94.

14. If the proportion of unmarried females in the 15–34 ages in 1935 were the same as that in the TDS, 124,782 married females would be added. (Unmarried females, 15–34: TDS—.25; 1935 Census—.22.)

15. [(124,782 + 43,470) / 2 + 3,305,967] / 8,220,938.

16. This result comes from both the Brass Model Life Table, Level = 45, and the Coale and Demeny East, Level = 9.

17. In a stable population it is assumed that the population has experienced the same conditions of fertility and mortality over a long period. This is obviously not the case with the 1927 Turkish population. It had just emerged from a low fertility period of war, civil war, and war-caused disease and famine. In this period, those in the high fertility ages were hard hit.

18. Alper Yücetürk, "Sex Ratios at Birth and Monthly Distribution of Births," in *Turkish Demography, Proceedings of a Conference*, Frederic G. Shorter and Bozkurt Güvenç, eds. (Ankara: Institute of Population Studies, Hacettepe University, 1969), pp. 167–174.

19. Aysel Alpay, "Abridged Life Tables for Three Metropolitan Cities and Selected Regions of Turkey by Sex, (Table I, Region I, Rural)," in *Turkish Demography*, pp. 83–108.

20. This is a conservative estimate. The Turkish Demographic Survey reported for "Number of Live Births" 49% female births. If this figure is assumed to be correct, the correction factor for female underenumeration would be greater. Yücetürk's study, however, unlike the Turkish Demographic Survey, was based on actual observation of births, while the TDS counted births reported by mothers. The TDS data also contained some surprising findings. For example, TDS counted 53% female births in the Urban area of western Turkey, a questionable finding that contradicts known biological evidence. What appears to be undercounting of male or overcounting of female births obviously affects the TDS birth figures. Because of this, Yücetürk's figures were chosen.

21. Males/.526 = Old Population; Males/.51 = New Population; e.g., old: 526 males/.526 = 1000; new: 526/.510 = 1031.4. Increase =.0314.

22. Exact numbers are used here because they reflect the process used and its results and should facilitate critical analysis. I felt it best to leave these numbers as they are, rather than round them, but it should be emphasized that these are estimates.

23. See, for example, figure 7.2.           1935:        1927:

24. See appendix 4. Correction Factor = $\sum_{80+}^{8}L_x / \sum_{80+}^{0}L_x$

25. The population factor is the same as that used above as a correction for female underenumeration. The proportion here is larger, because it is applied to only the females, not the total population.

26. Approximately 1.069. All the multipliers given in this section have been rounded off to the thousandths place, since there is no need to give eight-place precision here.

27. Boundary changes between the 1927 and 1935 censuses are considered in the calculations.

28. It was, in any case, more than balanced by unrecorded in-migration of Muslims. See appendix 3.

29. The boundaries used are those of the Greater Provinces, the independent sancaks included. Since the boundaries of the Republican provinces often do not fit exactly into the Ottoman boundaries, extensive mathematical manipulation is involved. See appendix 5 for the Ottoman and Republican boundaries.

30. .0138 per year.

# Appendix 2.
## Sources and Evaluation

IN THE FINAL half-century of the Empire the Ottoman government had reason to be concerned about population. Population information was needed for military recruitment planning, refugee settlement, placement of railroad and telegraph lines, and many of the new economic and social activities that the government was increasingly directing from Istanbul. Beginning with the Tanzimat and coming to full force under Abdülhamid II, the Ottoman government realized that it must know its own population in order to plan. In addition, rising nationalism and European pressures made it necessary for the Ottomans to know as accurately as possible the minority populations of the Empire. Though the Empire had never taken a modern census, the Ottoman government of the late nineteenth century could draw on a long tradition of population registration. From the fifteenth century the Ottomans had kept population registers by household and in the nineteenth century had created a system of registration for, at least theoretically, every male in the Empire. Each male was to be registered by household, his place in the household (i.e., head, son of head, grandson, etc.), and age. Imams, Christian religious leaders and, later, "population officials" (*nüfus memurları*) were charged with updating the registers for births, marriages, and deaths. With the coming of the Tanzimat, copies of local registers were regularly collected in Istanbul and used to compile population tables for the Empire.[1] These tables were at first only for internal governmental use, but were eventually published.

As the control of the provinces of the Empire by the central government improved, registration records improved as well and became a basis for taxation.[2] Laws of registration were passed enjoining strict procedures for population registration and updating of records and infractions of the regulations

were made the affair of the most important bodies of the central government.[3] To a remarkable degree, these rules were followed, as will be seen
below.

The administrative mechanics of the Ottoman population bureaus are not
the province of this study. Two articles[4] have thoroughly considered the
registration laws and the makeup and techniques of the population registers.
It must be noted, however, that, although certain detailed population records are commonly called "censuses," there never was a true census taken
in the Ottoman Empire. A census is by definition taken of all inhabitants
of a country at one time[5] and is usually far superior to a registration system,
in which persons are registered at various times. The Ottoman Empire had
a registration system. The first census in Anatolia was taken by the Turkish
Republic in 1927.

There are three types of accessible nineteenth-century Ottoman population statements—the so-called "censuses," salnames, and archival population registration records. The censuses were actually statements of empire-
wide population that were drawn from registration records. Salname population material appeared in yearbooks issued by individual Ottoman provinces. With very rare exceptions, the population figures given in the provincial salnames were for that province alone.

Both censuses and salnames drew on Ottoman government documents
that have rarely come to light. Both drew their population figures from figures registered by *nüfus memurları* and recorded in each province. Thus the
population statements in the censuses and in the salnames came from the
same source and, barring clerical error, should have been equally representative of the population of a province.

## Censuses

Ottoman "censuses" were written or printed for internal bureaucratic use,
in some cases being presented to the sultan. While some of them were lists
of the population of every, or almost every, vilâyet (province), sancak (sub-
province), and kaza (district) in the empire, others simply listed the population of each province. Two of them, the censuses of 1831 and 1844,
occurred before the beginning year of this study; the others are listed below.

*1302 Senesinde 1307 de Türkiye Vilayatında Bulunan Mebani, Arazi, ve*

*Nüfusun Tezayüd ve Tenakasunu Gösterini İstatistik* ("Statistics which show the increase and decrease of buildings, land, and population that are found in the Vilâyets of Turkey in 1302 and 1307," entered in the tables in this study as "Ist. U. Register").[6] Population statistics were given in this source as part of a presentation volume of statistics on the Ottoman Empire. Total numbers of Muslims, non-Muslims, and households were given for each province at two dates, ostensibly 1302 (1884–5) and 1307 (1889–90), but actually for various years over a wide time span. The presentation of two years' figures and household numbers are valuable features not found in the other general compendia of Ottoman population.

*The Census of 1311* (in tables, "Census 1"). One of the most complete of Ottoman censuses. Two seemingly identical copies have been found, one in the Istanbul University Library by Professor Stanford J. Shaw,[7] and another in the Baş Bakanlık Arşivi (Prime Minister's Archives) in Istanbul by Professor Kemal Karpat. The census divides the population by vilâyet, sancak, and Kaza, and by sex and millet, for each administrative subdivision. Through internal evidence, Professor Shaw[8] has dated the census as representing the year 1882, while Professor Karpat's copy of the census indicates a presentation date of 1893. The actual dates for the populations of various provinces in the census fall at many different years. The 1311 census is by far the most accessible of the censuses, having been published, with exhaustive and valuable comment, by Professor Karpat.[9]

*Devlet-i Aliye-i Osmaniye'nin 1313 Senesine Mahsus İstatistik-i Umumisi* ("General statistics for the Ottoman Empire in 1313").[10] As part of this volume, the Ottoman Ministry of Commerce and Construction gave the population of each province. No data was given for the smaller administrative sub-divisions, but in other ways the population material is very complete. Information appears on population by sexes and age groups, religion, citizenship, and other criteria. The listing by age groups is especially important, since none of the other Ottoman empire-wide population lists gives this essential information.

*The Census of 1324* (in tables, "Census 2").[11] An internal bureaucratic document that contained very detailed information. In 73 pages, this "census" gives data on sex and religion by vilâyet and sancak. It includes figures for gypsies and foreign citizens in each sancak. The only known copy was found by Professor Stanford J. Shaw in the Istanbul University Library.

*1326 [1908–09] İhsaiyat-i Maliye* ("Enumerations of the Ottoman Finance Ministry for 1326 M.," in tables, *Census 3"*).[12] In this, the second volume of the *İhsaiyat-i Maliye* series, the Ministry, of Finance included male, female, and total population for each province. This information was printed as part of an introductory summary sheet that also included the provinces' income and expenditures, square kilometers, etc. The population data did not go beyond the provincial level. In 1327, the third volume of the *İhsaiyat-i Maliye* repeated the 1326 figures for Anatolia.

*Memalik-i Osmaniye'nin 1330 Senesi Nüfus İstatistiği* ("Statistics of the Ottoman Empire for the year 1330 M.").[13] The 1330 "Census" has been known from a French language edition published in Istanbul in 1919.[14] This French version, published to acquaint the Allied victors at the Paris Peace Conference with Ottoman population figures, is an abridged form of the original report. It gave complete populations for each vilâyet, sancak, and kaza, but truncated the information on millets to *"Mussulmans," "Grecs," "Armeniens,"* and *"Autres Elements."* I have found the original, more complete census, printed in Ottoman Turkish, in the Istanbul Archeological Museum Library. It goes into much greater detail, listing 22 religious and linguistic groups. Unfortunately, the *1330 İstatistik* only gives total population, not a male-female breakdown.

In addition to the above, the Imperial salnames (*Salname-i Devlet-i Aliye-yi Osmaniye*) of 1294 (1877–8) and 1295 (1878–9) give some summary population data for each province in the Empire. After 1299 (1882–3) the imperial salnames became little more than lists of governmental officials and gave no population information.[15]

## Provincial Salnames

Taken as a whole, the salnames issued by the Ottoman provincial authorities are the most valuable printed sources for the study of late Ottoman Empire population. They often provided information on male and female population down to the kaza level, data on migration, numbers of households, births and deaths in urban areas, population by millet, and city and even village size, though the depth and quality of information varied by geographic area.

Only the salnames of the Anatolian provinces will be considered here. Of these, the most informative and complete are those issued by the Hüdavendigâr (capital: Bursa) and Aydın (capital: İzmir) vilâyets. Both give long time series of population change, Hüdavendigâr issuing 34 salnames from 1287 (1870–71) to 1325 (1907–08) and Aydın 26 salnames from 1296 (1879–80) to 1327 (1909–10). Kastamonu and Konya salnames also printed important material on population and household size.

The quality and completeness of demographic materials in the salnames varies widely. At their worst, the yearbooks presented only summary statements of population, i.e., the total or male population of the vilâyet and its sancaks. Most gave more detailed information. The presentation of this data falls into specific types:

1. Summary Tables. The standard salname population table contains male, female, and total population for each kaza in the province and for religious groups. These religious groups are either broad categories, usually "Muslim," "Christian," and "Jewish," or particular religions, e.g., Jewish, Greek, Armenian Gregorian, Protestant. In addition, tables often listed *ta-bii-yi ecnebi* or foreign citizens and *yabancı* or Ottoman subjects who were living in the area, but were not natives. Certain vilâyets, especially Aydın, listed in their tables the officially recorded births and deaths for that year. Numbers of households (*hanes*) may also have been given, though usually only as totals, not in all the sub-divisions mentioned above.

2. In Texts. Some salnames gave population for each administrative sub-division, not in tables, but as part of written-out texts that describe statistical, social, geographic, and economic features of the areas. These texts may include markets, baths, mosques and churches, houses, population, post offices, etc., all written as part of a narrative description.

3. Detailed Household–Population Tables. A few salnames devoted hundreds of pages to lists of the population and number of households in each village of the province. Though they often contained male and female populations, such lists seldom gave population by millet.

The great benefit of salnames is that their large number allows a long-term view of population change over time.

## Archival Population Materials

Potentially, the most valuable source of population data on the Ottoman Empire is the Ottoman Archives. Though there are other archives, in practice population materials for the period after 1878 are only to be found in the Baş Bakanlık Arşivi (Prime Minister's Archives) in Istanbul. Unfortunately, the Ottoman Archives' catalogued population data for the post-1878 period has many deficiencies. It is strongest in an area where the salnames are most weak—summary statements of the populations of eastern Anatolian provinces, undoubtedly prepared to allow Ottoman bureaucrats to keep a close watch on minority population in these provinces. It is very weak, though, in areas extremely important to demographers—raw data from censuses and registration, records of births and deaths, and age-specific data. We know from earlier, pre-1878, records and other evidence that these records were kept. Thousands of volumes of statistics were compiled as the bases of the various censuses compiled between 1831 and 1914. They may be in the collection of the Prime Minister's Archives, as yet uncatalogued, or in the records of various ministries, particularly the Dahiliye Nezâreti (Interior Ministry, today the İç İşleri Bakanlığı), that have never been opened to investigators.

The summary tables of population that are presently available in the archives are almost all internal administrative documents intended to give Ottoman bureaucrats a picture of the population situation in areas of governmental concern. As such, they can be considered as "working papers" such as are used by any bureaucracy.

The most common type of archival population data for this period comes in tables very similar to those found in the salnames. In them the population is divided by province and millet, or is given by province for one millet, usually Armenian. A few list *yerli* (natives of the area) and *yabancı* (Ottoman citizens normally resident in other provinces) and some give more complete breakdowns by administrative sub-divisions. The Archives also contain tables of household and population totals.[16]

## Reliability and Accuracy

In analyzing Ottoman population statistics one must look for both consistency and conformity to demographic rules. Consistency, even if this sometimes means consistent errors, indicates that the Ottomans intended to publish correct data and that they did not change their data capriciously. For example, we can see that, if the registers show 25,000 persons to be in one area in 1878, 14,000 in 1879, and 25,000 in 1881, the inconsistency probably indicates random error. If errors of this type appear frequently, the whole body of Ottoman demographic data must be called into question. Consistency also allows an analyst to find what the deficiencies in the data are and apply correctives, knowing that errors are constant and that the correctives will thus apply to all population statements for an area. Thus one can, if the population statements are consistent, apply knowledge gathered from one census to other censuses as well. This is especially important for corrections for age and sex misreporting.

Conformity to demographic rules is a basis for analysis of both the intention to produce accurate statistics and of whether or not accurate statistics were actually produced. The Ottomans did not know the rules that govern human populations. No one at the time did. They did not know, for example, that their empire's population could not have increased by 3% a year.[17] Therefore, if we find that their data indicates such an increase, we know that they were in error. If such impossible rates of increase often occur, one must, once again, question the use of any Ottoman data. By comparing the age and sex structures of Ottoman population statements with demographic rules, one can see the types of errors into which Ottoman population registers fell. Should these errors be of a type normally found in censuses of developing countries, it indicates that the Ottomans probably intended to produce accurate data, but were stymied by misinformation on ages, undercounting of women and children, and other mistakes common to censuses in statistically underdeveloped countries. The knowledge gained from this analysis can be used to see exactly in what way and to what degree Ottoman statistics were deficient and to use this information to correct them.

One problem that must be considered before any demographic research can begin is migration. International migration is a factor that compounds the difficulty of demographic analysis, since migration affects both rates of increase and total population. Fortunately, the period of this study for which year-by-year population statements are desirable, 1878–1914, fell between two periods of great in-migration, but was not itself greatly affected by the migration. From 1880 to 1895 the average in-migration of Muslims to Anatolia was a fairly constant ten to fifteen thousand a year[18] and these numbers have been calculated as part of the normal rates of increase for each province. In 1877–8 and after 1914 in-migration was much greater.

Each of the Ottoman Anatolian provinces collected population data separately,[19] each had different conditions, and each must be considered separately. For a general analysis of Ottoman published governmental statistics, however, I have selected one province, Aydın. The Aydın Vilâyeti serves as a good illustration of the best Ottoman population data since it (1) was one of the most statistically developed provinces and (2) had only minor changes in its borders from 1878 to 1912, facilitating comparisons over time.

Table A2.1 contains figures on Aydın population from each of the censuses and seven representative salnames.

Table A2.1

Aydın Vilâyeti Census and Salname Population Figures

| Year | Census | Salname |
|------|--------|---------|
| 1884-85 | 1,147,172 | |
| 1887-88 | | 1,391,497 |
| 1889-90 | 1,322,796 | |
| 1892-93 | | 1,495,482 |
| 1893-94 | 1,410,424 | |
| 1995-96 | 1,534,229 | 1,507,525 |
| 1897-98 | | 1,532,701 |
| 1898-99 | | 1,561,968 |
| 1899-1900 | | 1,586,845 |
| 1902-03 | | 1,634,048 |
| 1906-07 | 1,727,317 | |
| 1908-09 | 1,702,911 | |
| 1914 | 1,797,658 | |
| 1927 | 1,532,997 | |
| 1935 | 1,765,299 | |

Note:   For rates of increase between 1884 and 1914, see
        Chapter 2.

The 1914 figure has been adjusted to include the Menteşe Sancağı, which was detached from Aydın Vilâyeti between 1908 and 1914. The years 1927 and 1935 in the table are not the populations of the Turkish Republican province of Aydın in 1927 and 1935, but the recorded populations of the same area as that of the Ottoman province of Aydın, much larger than its modern Turkish counterpart.

In table A2.1 the censuses and salnames appear, at a glance, to be internally consistent. In each the population steadily rises throughout the period. When the two lists are compared, however, serious discrepancies are evident. If both salname and census populations are correct, the population of Aydın must have gone up in 1892–3, down in 1893–4, up in 1985–6, down again in 1897–8, etc. Such activity is unlikely, yet comparisons of censuses and salnames for each Antolian province indicate the same phenomena.

The problem is one of dates, and, unique among the provincial salnames, the Aydın yearbooks offer a solution to the difficulty. In all the other provinces' salnames, population figures were simply entered without dates, and one naturally supposes that the figures were those for the year of the salname. This is not the case. Ottoman population data was gathered by officials at the local level, compiled, sent to the district level, compiled, sent to the provincial level, and so on until the data was finally entered in the salnames and censuses. We know this because, unlike the authors of the other salnames, the Aydın provincial government did not simply publish their statistics; they also stated the year in which they were collected. The Aydın salnames indicated that the population data entered in them generally had taken three years to come from the first collection to publication in the book. For example, the Aydın salname of 1320 listed its population as being that of the year 1317, while those of the 1317 salname were for 1314.

Since the actual dates for the Aydın salnames' populations are known, they can be used to place properly the dates of the population figures for Aydın in the censuses, as well.

The difficulty of dating is more severe in the censuses than in the salnames. It was by no means unusual for a census to be ordered ten years before it was completed, as other studies have shown.[20] This cannot be seen as unusual, if one considers that data on the provincial level for one of the most statistically advanced provinces, Aydın, took three years to compile and print. One might also consider that the modern Turkish census bureau, benefiting from vastly better collection and tabulation methods as well as modern communications, does not print final census results until four years after the census date. Ottoman province such as Aydın or Hüdavendigâr, provinces benefiting from strong governmental authority and good communications, might, upon receipt of an order to take a census, have sent the results to Istanbul in two years. Before the census could be published, however, these results might well have waited eight more years for the results from less statistically developed areas to be added to them. When the census was finally published, the figures for certain provinces would be long out of date. This would be true of special "censuses," i.e., registrations specifically ordered and carried out as a separate and special event. It would not necessarily be true of censuses that were in reality simply compilations of population materials already on hand in the provinces. These latter might wait slightly longer than did the data in provincial salnames for publication, but not eight to ten years. We cannot, then, tell the exact date for the populations in any of the Ottoman censuses from the compilation dates of the censuses themselves.

The only way to date the census populations accurately is by comparing them to populations whose dates we know—those given in the salnames. Table A2.2 indicates the combining of the census and salname populations of Aydın, their dates corrected. Dates of census populations have been changed so that their populations fit into the pattern set in the salnames.

When the dates of Ottoman population statistics are properly set, one can see that they, as represented by figures from the Aydın Province, do fit the first criteria for reliability—consistency. From 1878 to 1914, the Ottoman statistics for Aydin show a consistent pattern of population increase, not the pattern of inconsistencies that would have resulted from capriciousness or deliberate falsification of data.

Analysis of the second criteria, conformity to demographic models, is more complex. Ottoman population must be considered in the light of various demographic rules and theories. If it conforms to these models, we go a long way toward establishing the accuracy of the data. If, however, it does not conform to demographic models, other considerations arise. The greatest barrier to accurate population analysis is the deliberate falsification of population records. If errors in population statements were accidental, arising out of misstatements of age, undercounting of children, etc., the errors were constant and were reflected in all population statements, since they

Table A2.2

Population of Aydın Vilâyeti   (Corrected Dates)

| Date | Population | Increase |
|------|-----------|----------|
| 1878-79 | 1,147,172 | |
| 1882-83 | 1,322,796 | .0285* |
| 1884-85 | 1,390,497 | .0253 |
| 1886-87 | 1,410,424 | .0068 |
| 1891-92 | 1,495,482 | .0117 |
| 1892-93 | 1,507,515 | .0080 |
| 1894-95 | 1,532,701 | .0083 |
| 1894-95 | 1,534,229 | ° |
| 1895-96 | 1,561,968 | .0179 |
| 1896-97 | 1,586,845 | .0158 |
| 1899-1900 | 1,634,048 | .0098 |
| 1903-04 | 1,702,911 | .0103 |
| 1904-05 | 1,727,317 | .0142 |
| 1914 | 1,797,658 | .0044 |

*High rates of increase in this uncorrected data are
the result of changes in administrative sub-divisions.
°Compilation of registration statistics at different
times of the year sometimes results in two different
populations being presented for the same year.

arose from the conditions under which the count of population was taken, not deliberate falsification. These errors can be allowed for and the population statements corrected accordingly. If, however, errors were deliberate, such as the undercounting of one group for political purposes, then they are much more difficult to allow for and correct, because the errors did not come from an observable social trait, such as age misstatement, but rather from the minds of a few political men.

While deliberate errors are often impossible to correct, they are luckily fairly easy to observe and avoid. By examining how closely population estimates conform to certain demographic criteria, one can see whether the compilers of population data intended it to be correct or if they intended to deceive. Ottoman population data can be examined in this way and, once examined, is generally found to fall into the former category. Its compilers aimed at accuracy, not deception. An examination of Ottoman population data demonstrates this fact. (This does not mean, of course, that those enumerated by the census takers did not give false information. They often did so, and corrections for the resulting problem are examined in the following appendixes.)

First to be considered is the rate of increase. Given the relative high fertility of Anatolian peasants and the relative lack of war, epidemic disease, or extensive out-migration, the population of Anatolia can be expected to have increased in this period.[21] It cannot, however, have increased beyond certain limits decided by the mortality structure of the area. Before the advent of modern medicine and, perhaps more important, modern sanitation, a population's natural growth was limited by its environment.

This demographic limit can be used in evaluating the accuracy of population statements. If, however, the rates of increase demanded by a series of Ottoman figures fall within the possible demographic limits, one can usually assume that they approach accuracy. We know that a population such as that of nineteenth-century Anatolia must, during periods of peace, have increased. The population dynamics of such a society must have provided an excess of births over deaths from normal causes, because deaths due to conditions of war, civil unrest, famine due to poor distribution of food, etc., would also have taken lives. The excess of births would be needed in bad times simply to keep the population numbers stable. In times of peace and civil order, this excess would cause population increase. A population estimate that shows population decrease in a time of peace and civil calm is almost surely in error. From 1878 to 1914, the Ottoman population figures for Aydın increased by .0124 a year. This is a bit higher than one might expect, but much of this is explained by in-migration to Anatolia. In any case, the figure of .0124 and the rates of increase in table A2.2 are well within the possible range of rates of population increase. A figure for the period of under .0100 would have been questionable, one of over .0200 impossible.[22]

It should be noted that some discrepancies in the rates of table A2.2 are because they were drawn by years, not by years and months; this can affect the rates greatly when the years of the populations are close together. Populations labeled as being one year apart (e.g., 1317 A.H. and 1318 A.H.) may in reality have been almost two years apart, if the enumerations were taken at the beginning of the first year and at the end of the second. The rates also reflected small inaccuracies in the Ottoman registers and should be regarded as approximate.

The next demographic criteria to consider are the age and sex structure of the population. In these criteria, Ottoman population data was by no means precise. The errors, though, are what should be expected from a nation that was newly developing its enumeration system. They reflect a system of age and sex misreporting which is still common in the Middle East today. For example, the Turkish Republican censuses have consistently shown a considerable excess of males over females. This excess has decreased, however, as census taking methods improved and the Turkish census became more accurate. The 1927 census showed that males were 54% of the population aged 0 to 2; the 1950 census showed 52%, and the 1965 census 51%, indicating a gradual improvement in enumeration techniques. The number of young females recorded in the census has always been lower than their actual numbers.

Research into age discrepancies in Ottoman statistics cannot be done with most Ottoman population statements. Only one salname, the Hüdavendigâr salname of 1303 A.H., gives age-specific data. The other salnames and all of the censuses but one are the same; they offer only total population tables, ignoring ages. This is not because the Ottomans did not keep age-specific population records. Ottoman regulations of various years all required that the person's age be recorded and archival documents demonstrate that local population registrars did keep this information.[23] For some reason, the Ottomans simply did not include ages in their general tables of population.

The 1313 İstatistik-i Umumî is the one exception. It gave the population of each Ottoman province by five-year age group and sex. Since the 1313 İstatistik-i Umumî's population figures, as shown above for Aydın, fit into the pattern of the other Ottoman population statements, it is reasonable to think that age and sex discrepancies, i.e., undercounting of certain ages or of females, in the enumerating of the 1313 figures were present in the other Ottoman population statistics, as well, especially since the types of underreporting found in the 1313 figures are those that one would expect to find in any Middle Eastern census.

The *1313 İstatistik* population statements on provinces, considered in appendix 4, demonstrate the type of undercounting and age misrepresentation that was common in nineteenth-century Ottoman population statistics. The populations of both developed and underdeveloped areas of provinces in both eastern and western Anatolia all exhibited the same characteristics. Children were very much undercounted. The underregistration of children is also frequently seen in modern Turkish statistics, though not to the degree seen in Ottoman figures.[24]

Adult ages were also falsely recorded, but in terms of total population,

Table A2.3

Proportion Male and Female in Anatolian Provinces as Recorded

| Province | Males | Females |
|----------|-------|---------|
| Konya | .503 | .497 |
| Haleb | .503 | .497 |
| Aydın | .504 | .496 |
| Hüdavendigâr | .504 | .496 |
| Adana | .507 | .493 |
| Ankara | .507 | .493 |
| Kastamonu | .508 | .492 |
| Trabzon | .508 | .492 |
| Sivas | .514 | .486 |
| Biga | .518 | .482 |
| Mamuretülaziz | .520 | .480 |
| İzmit | .527 | .473 |
| Erzurum | .533 | .467 |
| Diyarbakır | .536 | .464 |
| Van | .541 | .459 |
| Bitlis | .560 | .440 |

the age misreporting of adults has little effect. Adults were still counted in the totals, no matter what age they gave. The underregistration of young children, however, causes a serious numerical deficiency. In the case of Aydın, the 1313 İstatistik figures for total males were wrong by 20% due to underregistration of children. Figures for eastern provinces were even more in error.

Women were undercounted, as well. In each Ottoman province (1313 İstatistik—table A2.3) the numbers of women were recorded as being much less than those of men. This is not possible. In a society such as that of Ottoman Anatolia, women must have been at least as numerous as men, and very likely were more numerous, since the male population was diminished by

Table A2.4

Population of Aydın in 1313

|  | Original | Corrected |
|---|---|---|
| Males | 745,614 | 898,124 |
| Females | 732,790 | 898,124 |
| Total | 1,478,404 | 1,796,248 |

military mortality. There may have been up to 7% more males than females born in such a society, but by age 2 women were in a majority, male children dying at a greater rate than female. By age 29, 50% of the males were dead; the comparative age for women was 34. When male mortality in war is included, women should have had a fairly large majority. Certain factors such as better care and feeding of male children may affect this, but not to such a degree as to put women in a minority. Numerical equality of the sexes is a conservative assumption, since women may actually have been in the majority, yet all of the Ottoman vilâyets in 1313 registered an excess of men. As might be expected, the worst underregistration of women was in the least developed area—eastern Anatolia. This, once again, is consistent with the misreporting pattern found in modern Turkish censuses.[25]

Luckily, age and sex misreporting is correctable. To obtain approximately the proper male population, we must fill in the number of underregistered males, correcting the age structure to that of the model,[26] taking into account age groups that, due to migration, death in the military, or other causes, cannot be made to fit the model. This figure is then doubled, with any necessary modifications (e.g., corrections for the lack of military death among women), thus correcting for underregistration among women. This has been done for the Aydın province in table A2.4.

The above method is used throughout this study to correct deficient data and arrive at more accurate statements of Ottoman population.


## Minorities

In considering the accuracy of population statistics, it is useful to consider the recording of minority population as part of the general description of Ottoman statistics. If the Ottoman statistics of minority population are found to be consistent, it would help to demonstrate not only the reliability of Ottoman data on minority population, but also the quality of the statistical practices of the Ottoman registrars and whether or not they allowed political motivations to affect their counts. Consistency does not prove that the Ottomans were not undercounting minorities, but it does show that they were not deliberately doing so. Table A2.5 demonstrates that, for the minorities in the Aydın province, mainly Greeks, the Ottoman records were consistent.

Ottoman governmental population statistics were, in fact, remarkably consistent. Moreover, when they were in error, their errors are amenable to correction. They are unquestionably the prime source for the study of the Anatolian population.


## Ottoman Nongovernmental Population Sources

In the latter half of the nineteenth century, with the increase in the literate and interested public, Ottomans began to publish geographical handbooks of the Empire. These were called atlases, geographies, or geographical dictionaries and were intended to be both educational tools and source books for soldiers, bureaucrats, students, and the literate public. The number of

Table A2.5


Minority Population in Aydın


| Year | Proportion |
| --- | --- |
| 1884–85 | .22 |
| 1886–87 | .21 |
| 1891–92 | .21 |
| 1892–93 | .21 |
| 1893–94 | .22 |
| 1894–95 | .22 |
| 1895–96 | .22 |
| 1896–97 | .22 |
| 1899–1900 | .21 |
| 1903–04 | .24 |
| 1914 | .22 |


Notes: Dates are for the salnames
and censuses in tables A2.1
and A2.2.

these publications was not large and only a few contained fairly accurate population figures. Five of them have been selected here (table A2.6).[27]

The columns in table A2.6 are roughly in chronological order of publication. Ali Cevat's *Coğrafya Lugatı* was published in two volumes, one in 1895–96 (1313 A.H.) and the other the following year. Şemseddin Sami published six large volumes of the *Kamusülalam*, the most valuable of the Ottoman geographic works, from 1889 to 1899; the publication year in which a province's population is given in *Kamusülalam* is written in parentheses in table A2.6.

Some of the obvious discrepancies in the list arise out of border changes that affected the area of the population estimate, but most come from the

Table A2.6

Ottoman Non-Governmental Population Estimates

| Location | Ali Cevat, 1895-7 | Ali Saib, 1886-7 | İbrahim Hilmi, 1905 | Şemsüddin Sami, Various | Ahmed Cemal, 1894 |
|---|---|---|---|---|---|
| Adana | 403,439 | 349,000 | 422,400 | 350,000 (1889) | 399,000 |
| Ankara | 892,900 | 688,000 | 1,038,010 | 850,000 (1889) | not given |
| Aydın | 1,408,387 | 1,005,000 | 1,666,568 | 1,251,629 (1889) | 874,000 |
| Bitlis | 300,000 | 300,000 | 398,625 | 300,000 (1899) | 352,000 |
| Diyarbakır | 482,940 | 420,000 | 471,462 | 471,462 (1891) | 470,000 |
| Erzurum | 645,702 | 582,000 | 645,000 | 581,753 (1899) | 555,000 |
| Halep | 995,758 | not given | 995,800 | 776,652 (1891) | 784,000 |
| Hüdavendigâr | 1,366,807 | 925,000 | 1,691,277 | 1,500,000 (1891) | 925,000 |
| Kastamonu | 1,018,912 | not given | 1,025,000 | 980,024 (1896) | 922,000 |
| Konya | 1,088,000 | 885,000 | 1,088,000 | 1,588,000 (1896) | 750,000 |
| Mamuretülaziz | 284,000 | 284,000 | 575,314 | 575,314 (1898) | 430,000 |
| Sivas | 1,086,015 | 894,000 | 1,860,000 | 1,086,455 (1894) | 950,000 |
| Trabzon | 1,477,000 | 920,000* | 1,281,786 | 1,071,477 (1894) | 757,000 |
| Van | 430,000 | 447,000 | 430,000 | 430,000 (1898) | 450,000 |

*Males given (doubled here).

authors' cavalier attitude toward the dates of their sources. For their data, the better of the geographic works went to Ottoman governmental sources. The same figures appeared in their works as appeared in Ottoman salnames and censuses, though the authors of the geographic volumes appear to have used whatever governmental material was on hand, regardless of date. For example, Ali Cevat's figure for the Hüdavendigâr province seems to have been taken from the 1311 *Hüdavendigâr Vilâyeti Salnamesi,* while his figure for Haleb seems to have been taken from the *Haleb Vilâyeti Salnamesi* of 1300, eleven years earlier. İbrahim Hilmi used data from provincial salnames from 1300 and 1317 and from the census of 1324, a 24-year span. Ali Cevat, İbrahim Hilmi, and Şemseddin Sami all seem to have borrowed data from the best European source, Vital Cuinet's *La Turquie d'Asie,*[28] or used the same sources as Cuinet, who, in turn, used Ottoman governmental sources.

In the geographic works, the Ottoman authors were content to use various bits of population information from various governmental sources. Because of this, the population they gave for one province can be for a date ten years or more from the date of the population they gave for another province. None of the population estimates was dated, so one naturally assumes, while reading the population tables, that the estimates for each province were for the same year. The best in this regard was Şemseddin Sami, but even his population figures varied over three to four years. It is far better to base analyses of Ottoman population on Ottoman governmental documents than on Ottoman secondary sources. Şemseddin Sami's work, because of its comparative accuracy and completeness, may be used to provide information where governmental statistics are missing. The others are not usable as population sources.

## Non-Ottoman Population Sources

European sources for Ottoman population are numerous. Every nineteenth-century traveler seems to have assumed he could accurately estimate population size, either from his own experiences or from "informed sources." Nikola Michoff[29] published five large volumes full of short entries, sometimes only bibliographic citations, on Bulgarian and Turkish population, and many sources were not included. European consular reports frequently gave population estimates. Nineteenth-century Germans published volumes of world population in which the population of the Ottoman Empire was prominently featured.

Some, especially those who have used European estimates of population, will say that European sources have been incompletely considered here. They would feel that an extensive review of the European material, followed by examples of the estimates, is desirable. This would involve an extensive search of the literature, and such a search has been made. Very little evidence of the search will appear here, however, because the search resulted in little that was of any use. Of the hundreds of travelers' journals seen, none produced demographic material of acceptable quality or completeness. This is not true of all consular reports, which are often valuable sources for the population of small areas and for various phenomena that affect population—epidemics, uprisings, and mass migrations. Unfortunately, little of this type of consular material fits into the scope of this work.

The critical problem with European population estimates is unsurmountable—to know population numbers you must first count the population. Europeans in or out of the Ottoman Empire never were able to do this, except on a very small scale (i.e., villages and small towns). Because of this, there were actually only two types of European statements on Ottoman population: those that reproduced Ottoman registration statistics and those that were wrong. The only European who would have been able, from his own resources, to give an accurate statement on the population of an Ottoman province would have been an European who went to every house in the province and counted the inhabitants. To my knowledge, no European traveler or consul ever did so.

The best nineteenth-century European population estimates summarized or reproduced Ottoman data. The best example of the presentation of Ottoman data is an article printed by M. Ubicini in *L'Economiste Française*,[30] in which he translated the complete population tables of the Imperial salname of 1295 and published them with minor comments on boundaries and ethnic groups.

With the exception of Ubicini's articles and Cuinet's books, the best contemporary European sources on Ottoman population are in German. Of these, the most complete are *Die Bevolkerung der Erde*, mentioned below, and A. Ritter's *Die Volker des osmanischen Reiches*.[31] The latter gave population for 1872, prior to the period of this study, and before the best Ottoman sources were available. It is valuable, though, because, unlike many other works, it detailed the sources from which it drew its estimates and because Ritter considered administrative boundaries fairly carefully and gave maps. The book can serve as a good introduction to what the best-informed European sources thought of the Ottoman population.

The series known as *Die Bevolkerung der Erde*, in various years the work of Ernst Behn, Hermann Wagner, and Alexander Supan, was published in supplements to the German geographic magazine, *Petermanns Mitteilungen*. It was an admirable effort to collect various population estimates for all the areas of the world into one usable volume. Material on the Ottoman Empire in the tables varied from brief tables[32] to fairly complete analyses, tables, and comments on conflicting sources.[33] The eleventh volume[34] contained twenty pages of statistics on the Ottoman Empire, accompanied by a map and discussions on minorities and administrative boundaries.

*Die Bevolkerung der Erde*, unfortunately, was only as good as its sources. It made use of every conceivable European article and book that considered Turkish population, including the Ritter volume mentioned above, a much-quoted but inaccurate article by Ravenstein,[35] and hundreds of other traveler's accounts, articles in geographic journals, etc. These sources shared the difficulties of all European estimates. Nevertheless, *Die Bevolkerung der Erde*, even more than Ritter, is a valuable compendium of what Europeans thought of Ottoman population.

Without doubt, the best European source on Ottoman population is the four volume work by Vital Cuinet, *La Turquie d'Asie*.[36] In it, population is presented as one of many statistical and descriptive passages on each separate province, along with maps and tables of administrative boundaries. Population is given for vilâyets, sancaks, kazas, and often towns, all in their geographic and economic setting. Cuinet's volumes are monumental studies, extremely valuable books that could only have been compiled by one intimately familiar with published and unpublished Ottoman statistics.

It is the use of Ottoman statistics that makes *La Turquie d'Asie* the best European source on Ottoman population. Cuinet used Ottoman population data, sometimes stating that he had received it from government "officials," and he realized that Ottoman data had deficiencies. He attempted to correct these deficiencies, and thus his published statistics are always different than those given in their Ottoman sources. A comparison between Cuinet's figures and those in the hundreds of Ottoman population sources used in this study has revealed not one instance in which Cuinet's figures match those in an Ottoman document. Every one of his population figures was probably corrected or changed, subtly or greatly, from the original. His figures were usually close to those in the Ottoman sources, though, and his corrections were often slight,[37] but, because he never gave the information, one cannot find upon what Ottoman figures Cuinet based his own. Without this knowledge, it is impossible to evaluate the accuracy of Cuinet's corrections. He never gave the exact source of his data, nor even the Ottoman government office which gave it to him.

Other major problems with Cuinet's figures are his lack of dating and errors in administrative boundaries. His volumes were published from 1891 to 1894 and he collected his figures in the years preceding publication. He never stated, however, which years his population statements were meant to represent. He did give dates for some economic data, but not for population, perhaps because he underestimated the amount of yearly population change and expected that his figures would still be accurate in the years to come. The administrative boundaries that Cuinet gave for eastern Anatolian provinces were sometimes incorrect, or at least not the boundaries and administrative sub-divisions that Ottoman publications gave for the same areas.[38]

Collectively, these problems make it impossible to use Cuinet as an accurate population source. One never knows if he accurately corrected the Ottoman figures or what years his data represented. It is far better to go back to Cuinet's source, Ottoman population records, and to use Cuinet for his economic, social, and descriptive materials.

Like the printed European works, Consular sources were best when they gave data from Ottoman registers.[39] Even those consular reports that did so often have out-of-date information.[40] After searching through consular reports one can see that consuls only had two ways to obtain statistics on Ottoman population—personal observation, for small areas, and reports from Ottoman governors and officials or printed works such as salnames. Indeed consular reports on population were often preceded by words such as "from a publication by Ahmed Pasha, Governor."

The ultimate dependence on Ottoman data is also true of the diplomatic documents of the Paris Peace Conference, in many ways the most interesting European archival documents. Since the conference was extremely concerned about the numbers of the various confessional groups in Anatolia, many different estimates of population were considered. When they are examined, however, the only population statistics that in any way reflect the actual population situation are, once again, those taken from Ottoman records.[41] The guesses presented by others, predicated on the "obvious" falseness or nonexistence of Ottoman records, so undercounted the Muslim population as to be ludicrous.[42]

## NOTES

1. Ziya Karamürsel, *Osmanli Malî Tarihi Hakkında Tetkikler* (Ankara: Turk Tarih Kurumu, 1940), p. 206; Enver Ziya Karal, *Osmanlı İmparatorluğunda İlk Nüfus Sayımı, 1831* (Ankara: 1943), pp. 6–10.

2. Stanford J. Shaw, "The Nineteenth Century Ottoman Tax Reforms and Revenue Systems," *IJMES*, 6 (4), October, 1975, pp. 426 and 427.

3. Collections of registration rules, called *sicil-i nüfus nizamnameleri* ("regulations for population registers") were first sent out as internal government documents and later published. See the following: Dahiliye Nezareti, Sicil-i Nüfus İdare-i Umumiyesi Müdüriyeti, *Sicil-i Nüfus Nizamnamesi*, Istanbul, 1300 (1882–3); İrade Dahiliye 22856 (1280); İrade Mahsus 2089 (1290); Yıldız 113–47–52 (1318).

The Ottoman Archives possess numerous documents that show the Ottoman government's interest in population statistics. Examples of the types of documents: records kept of the numbers of defters (compiled population registers) and their quality (Cevdet 12545); new defters ordered for recent immigrants (İrade Dahiliye 23167 (1281)); orders sent out to correct errors in defters and do a better job of registration (Cevdet Maliye 1313, 4198, 7995, 8153, İrade Vala 23357).

4. Stanford J. Shaw, "The Ottoman Census System and Population," *IJMES* 9 (3), August, 1978; Kemal Karpat, "Ottoman Population Records and the Census of 1881/2–1893," *IJMES* 9 (2), May, 1978.

5. Henry S. Shryock, Jacob S. Siegel, and associates, *The Methods and Materials of Demography* (Washington, DC: U.S. Department of Commerce, 1973), I, pp. 15 and 16.

6. *1302 Senesinde (unreadable) 1307 de Türkiye Vilayatında Bulunan Mebani, Arazi, ve Nüfusun Tezayüd ve Tenakasunu Gösterini İstatistik*. Istanbul University, No. 80872. This volume gives no indication who the book was presented to, but it is bound with the type of weighted red leather covers used for presentation volumes given to the sultan or ministers. Since it comes from the Yıldız Library collection, it is possible that the book was presented to Abdülhamit II.

7. Istanbul University, TY 4807.

8. Stanford J. Shaw and Ezel Kural Shaw, *The History of the Ottoman Empire and Modern Turkey*, vol. II (New York: Cambridge University Press, 1977), p. 117.

9. Karpat, "Ottoman Population Records."

10. Nezaret-i Umur-i Ticaret ve Nafia, *Devlet-i Aliye-i Osmaniye'nin 1313 Senesine Mahsus İstatistik-i Umumisi*, Istanbul, 1315.

11. Istanbul University, MS TY 947.

12. Maliye Nezareti, *İhsaiyat-i Maliye*, 1326, Istanbul, 1329, pp. 2 and 3.

13. Dahiliye Nezareti, Sicil-i Nüfus İdare-i Umumiyesi Müdüriyeti, *Memalik-i Osmaniye'nin 1330 Senesi Nüfus İstatistiği*, Istanbul, 1330m.

14. *Tableau indiquant le nombre des divers elements de la population dans l'Empire Ottoman au 1er Mars 1330 (14 Mars 1914)* "Constantinople," 1919.

15. Justin McCarthy and J. Dennis Hyde, "Ottoman Imperial and Provincial Salnames," *IJMES*, 1978.

16. Some of this material is in the İrade-Dahiliye collection of the Baş Bakanlık Arşivi, but most of the data mentioned here was found in the Yıldız Collection of the same archives. The Bab-i Ali Evrak Odası documents were not available to me and thus have not been examined.

17. The modern Turkish population grew at the following rates, according to the 1965 Turkish Republic Census: 1950–55—.0277; 1955–60—.0285; 1960–65—.0246.

18. *1313 İstatistik-i Umumî*.

19. See Karpat, "Ottoman Population Records."

20. See Karpat, "Ottoman Population Records."

21. A GRR of 3.00 is probably very close to accurate, from the evidence of the TDS and from the populations in chapter 2.

22. See the model rates of increase given for each Anatolian province in chapter 2.

23. See *nizamnameleri* in note 3 above.

24. See appendix 1.

25. See appendix 1.

26. See appendix 4.

27. For information on geographical texts, see especially Selçuk Trak, *Turkiye Ait Coğrafî Eserler Genel Biblioğrafyası, I* (Ankara, 1942).

Brief descriptions of Şemseddin Sami and Ali Cevat are in Bursalı Mehmed Tahir, *Osmanlı Müellifleri* (haz. İsmail Özen), (Istanbul: Meral Yayınevi, 1975).

28. See note 36 below.

29. Nikola Michoff, *La Population de la Turquie et de la Bulgarie au XVIIIe et XIXe s.: recherches bibliographico-statistiques* (Sofia: 1915–1935).

30. July 28, 1877.

31. Gotha: Justus Perthes, various years.

32. For example: I, 1872, p. 26; II, 1894, p. 36.

33. For example: V, 1878, pp. 25–28; VII, 1891, pp. 118–126.

34. 1901, pp. 3–23.

35. E. G. Ravenstein, "The Populations of Russia and Turkey," *Journal of the Royal Geographic Society*, September, 1877.

36. Paris, 4 vols., I (1892), II (1891), III (1894), IV (1894).

37. These statements are intended to describe Cuinet's figures on Muslim population. His estimates on Christian populations present special difficulties.

38. Cuinet's maps for the southeastern provinces, especially Diyarbakır and Van, were in error as well. The first really accurate maps of the eastern provinces were

the Ottoman maps of the World War I period (see the bibliography) and even these sometimes seem to have been based on Russian and Austrian originals.

39. This section is based on British consular reports, as found in the Public Record Office in London. French records have not been seen.

40. See, for example, F.O. 195, 1238, in which the British consul at Trabzon gave detailed tables of government and expenditures and population. The population is as accurate as any other Ottoman data, which it in reality is, but is for c. 1875, not, as dated, 1879. (Biliotti to Layard, May 29, 1879, no. 62).

41. See Great Britain, Foreign Office, Historical Section, No. 59, *Anatolia*, H.M. Stationery Office, London, 1920, p. 8. Compare statistics here to those of chapter 2. See also F.O. Class 608, the diplomatic documents of the Paris Peace Conference, which is full of population claims and counter-claims.

42. For example, the Armenian Patriarch's figures, presented to the Peace Conference, stated that there were 403,000 Muslims in Erzurum Vilâyeti in 1912, less than one-half of the actual Muslim population. Patriarcat Armenien de Constantinople, *Population Armenienne de la Turquie Avant la Guerre* (Paris, 1920).

# Appendix 3.
## Migration

THE FOLLOWING is a list of migration into the Turkish Republic from 1921 to 1927. It is drawn from the first statistical yearbook of the Turkish Republic and obviously represents only officially recorded in-migration.[1] A certain amount of migration may not have been recorded, especially in the eastern provinces.

These figures have been used as part of the formula for computing deaths among the Muslim population from 1912 to 1922. If unrecorded in-migration were estimated and added to the recorded figures, the effect would be to slightly increase the estimated Muslim mortality (as calculated in chapter 7). This has not been done because no estimate for unrecorded migration exists.

### NOTE

1. Turkey, *Annuaire Statistique de la Turquie III* (Ankara, 1930).

APPENDIX 3

Table A3.1

Migration into the Turkish Republic, 1921-27

| Province | Migrants |
|----------|---------:|
| Adana | 7,628 |
| Afyon | 1,045 |
| Aksaray | 3,286 |
| Amasya | 3,673 |
| Ankara | 1,779 |
| Antalya | 4,702 |
| Artvin | 46 |
| Aydın | 6,484 |
| Balıkesir | 37,088 |
| Bayazıt | 2,856 |
| Bilecik | 4,126 |
| Bitlis | 2,329 |
| Bolu | 194 |
| Burdur | 432 |
| Bursa | 34,148 |
| Cebelibereket | 2,718 |
| Çanakkale | 10,856 |
| Çankırı | 0 |
| Çorum | 1,575 |
| Denizli | 2,459 |
| Diyarbakır | 298 |
| Edirne | 49,336 |
| Elaziz | 1,452 |
| Erzincan | 97 |
| Erzurum | 1,095 |
| Eskişehir | 2,441 |
| Giresun | 596 |
| Gümüşhane | 596 |
| Gaziantep | 811 |
| Hakkâri | 145 |
| İçel | 1,000 |
| İzmir | 30,095 |
| Isparta | 1,096 |
| İstanbul | 35,487 |
| Kars | 2,512 |
| Kastamonu | 769 |
| Kayseri | 6,703 |
| Kırklareli | 27,254 |
| Kırşehir | 193 |

Table A3.1 (continued)


| | |
|---|---:|
| Kocaeli | 20,470 |
| Konya | 5,020 |
| Kütahya | 1,855 |
| Malatya | 76 |
| Manisa | 13,829 |
| Mardin | 0 |
| Maraş | 1,132 |
| Mersin | 3,330 |
| Muğla | 4,045 |
| Niğde | 15,671 |
| Ordu | 1,123 |
| Rize | 0 |
| Samsun | 22,579 |
| Siirt | 0 |
| Sinop | 1,189 |
| Sivas | 4,892 |
| Şebinkarahisar | 5,779 |
| Tekirdağ | 30,243 |
| Trabzon | 404 |
| Tokat | 8,209 |
| Urfa | 1 |
| Van | 275 |
| Yozgat | 32 |
| Zonguldak | 1,241 |

# Appendix 4.
## *Methodology*

### Rate of Increase

ALL YEARLY RATES of increase computed in this study use the formula

$$P_2 = P_1 \times e^{rt}$$

where $P_1$ is the original population, r the rate of annual change, t the time (before 1914, in hicra years, which give a slightly lower rate of change than the Gregorian years used after 1914), and $P_2$ the resulting population.

Rates used in the construction of the yearly population by province tables in the chapters 2 to 6 use the above formula, modified:

$$\ln(P_2/P_1)/t = r$$

where for example, $P_2$ is the population of a province in 1310 and $P_1$ the population of the same province in 1300. The rate (r) is applied to each year between 1300 and 1310 to obtain population (e.g., 1300 population $\times e^{rt}$ = 1301 population; 1301 population $\times e^{rt}$ − 1302 population . . . 1320 population). That is, the yearly population was found by interpolation between the two dates.

Changes in administrative boundaries complicate the procedure. If, in the above example, a new kaza had been added in 1305, the rates would have to be calculated in a different fashion. The least complicated method would be: (1) Take the population in 1300 and find the rate between it and the 1310 population minus the added kaza. This rate is then used to project the yearly population between 1300 and 1304. (2) Find the rate from the 1310 population to the 1300 population plus the added kaza and project the 1310 population back to 1305, the date at which the kaza was added. The procedure becomes more complicated if the population in 1300 of the kaza added in 1305 is not known. In that case, an iterative procedure is usually employed in which the rates of increase are calculated a number of times until the rates before and after the addition of the kaza are the same.

## Correction for Underenumeration

Women and children were underenumerated in every Ottoman Anatolian province. In this study, the procedure used to correct this deficiency is in every case the same. Because of deficiencies in recording, records of female and child population were discarded. Only the population of males over 15 was accepted, and total population calculated from it. The male population by age group as entered in the *1313 İstatistik* was entered into a computer program that produced age pyramids of the recorded population and a model stable population from the Coale and Demeny models, mortality level 4, 5, 6, 7, and 8 and Gross Reproduction Rates of 2.5 and 3.0. The Coale and Demeny models are a set of population tables, based on census records, that indicate what the structure of various populations would be if the same mortality and fertility conditions were to exist over a long period of time. Coale and Demeny list age structures which vary according to long-term fertility and mortality rates. The fertility parameter used here is the Gross Reproduction Rate, which can be defined as the average number of female children born to an average woman who completes her fertile period (c. ages 15–45). The mortality parameter used here is dependent on life expectancy at birth ($e_0^0$) and is listed in "levels" (level 4 indicates a life expectancy at birth of 25 years; level 6, 30 years; level 7, 32.5 years; level 8, 35 years). The dotted pyramid is the model population by percentage in each group. The line pyramid is the percentage of the model population by age group, not the percentage of the total recorded population, which is inaccurate. In the line pyramid, each age group is a percentage of the following:

$$RP_{15+}/M_{15+}$$

where $RP_{15+}$ is the recorded population 15+ and $M_{15+}$ the proportion in the model in the 15+ age group. The use of this formula may introduce a slight increase in the population, since some young males under 15 may have stated their ages as over 15, but this is balanced by the fact that a certain percentage of males over 15 may not have been counted at all.

When a representative mortality level and Gross Reproduction Rate for each province were selected all ten pyramids were viewed and the one that best fit the recorded population was chosen by sight. More complicated statistical methods would have been inappropriate, yielding a spurious impression of precision. Figures A4.1 to A4.4 illustrate this process. They are pyramids and population corrections produced by computer for Sivas Vilâyeti. Six more pyramids which were also consulted in the actual analysis (GRR = 2.5 − L = 4, 5, 6, 7; and GRR = 3.0 − L = 8) have not been included, since they are very far from representative of the Sivas population.

The actual Sivas population probably fit between mortality levels 5 and 6. It was felt to be preferable to choose the higher mortality, which resulted in a lower correction factor and thus lower Muslim populations, because the likelihood then was one of understatement of Muslim population, rather than overstatement. This policy was followed throughout the study. Since my conclusions would be better supported by higher numbers of Muslims, it was better to always err on the side of lower Muslim numbers. (The difference in corrected population if a level 5 or 6 mortality was chosen in slight, less than 2%.)

One demographic phenomenon worthy of note is the consistent overstating of age by males in Anatolia. This follows a pattern seen in all records of Turkish population and argues for the continuity of typically Turkish age-reporting errors from Ottoman to modern times. The traditional overstatement of age has been demonstrated in each modern Turkish census. For example, the proportion of males listed as over 70 in the 1935 Turkish census was almost double the expected number. The number giving their ages as over 80 was more than three times the expected number.[1]

## Selection of the Models

Use of the Coale and Demeny stable population tables requires the selection of mortality and fertility parameters. One must first decide which of the "families" of modern tables, styled "North," "South," "East," and "West" is applicable to the data, then select a model population on the basis of the

FIGURE A4.1    1313 ISTATISTIK—SIVAS MALES

LEVEL 4

| AGES | RECORDED POPULATION | CORRECTED POPULATION |
|---|---|---|
| 0 – 4 | 48373 | 80795 |
| 5 – 9 | 40982 | 65115 |
| 10 – 14 | 48919 | 59984 |
| 15 – 19 | 46863 | 55650 |
| 20 – 24 | 42985 | 50747 |
| 25 – 29 | 44128 | 45843 |
| 30 – 34 | 39114 | 41281 |
| 35 – 39 | 39005 | 36720 |
| 40 – 44 | 28013 | 32101 |
| 45 – 49 | 30230 | 27483 |
| 50 – 54 | 18419 | 22979 |
| 55 – 59 | 15747 | 18474 |
| 60 – 64 | 15893 | 13970 |
| 65 – 69 | 13898 | 9579 |
| 70 – 74 | 15006 | 5645 |
| 75 – 79 | 11583 | 2623 |
| 80 – 84 | 3484 | 1083 |
| TOTALS | 502452 | 570186 |

FIGURE A4.2    1313 ISTATISTIK--SIVAS MALES

LEVEL 5

| AGES | RECORDED POPULATION | CORRECTED POPULATION |
|------|---------------------|----------------------|
| 0 - 4 | 48373 | 84921 |
| 5 - 9 | 40982 | 68784 |
| 10 - 14 | 48919 | 62573 |
| 15 - 19 | 46863 | 57349 |
| 20 - 24 | 42985 | 51777 |
| 25 - 29 | 44128 | 46320 |
| 30 - 34 | 39114 | 41270 |
| 35 - 39 | 39005 | 36453 |
| 40 - 44 | 28013 | 31635 |
| 45 - 49 | 30230 | 26333 |
| 50 - 54 | 18419 | 22348 |
| 55 - 59 | 15747 | 17936 |
| 60 - 64 | 15683 | 13583 |
| 65 - 69 | 13888 | 9345 |
| 70 - 74 | 15006 | 5514 |
| 75 - 79 | 11593 | 2612 |
| 80 - 84 | 3484 | 1103 |
| TOTALS | 502452 | 580456 |

FIGURE A4.3    1313 ISTATISTIK—SIVAS MALES

LEVEL 6

| AGES | RECORDED POPULATION | CORRECTED POPULATION |
|---|---|---|
| 0 - 4 | 48373 | 88729 |
| 5 - 9 | 40982 | 72092 |
| 10 - 14 | 48919 | 64954 |
| 15 - 19 | 46863 | 58877 |
| 20 - 24 | 42985 | 52883 |
| 25 - 29 | 44128 | 46724 |
| 30 - 34 | 39114 | 41297 |
| 35 - 39 | 39005 | 36164 |
| 40 - 44 | 28013 | 31209 |
| 45 - 49 | 30230 | 26430 |
| 50 - 54 | 18419 | 21828 |
| 55 - 59 | 15747 | 17463 |
| 60 - 64 | 15693 | 13156 |
| 65 - 69 | 13898 | 9085 |
| 70 - 74 | 15006 | 5428 |
| 75 - 79 | 11593 | 2655 |
| 80 - 84 | 3484 | 1121 |
| TOTALS | 502452 | 589953 |

FIGURE A4.4    1313 ISTATISTIK—SIVAS MALES

LEVEL 7

| AGES | RECORDED POPULATION | CORRECTED POPULATION |
|---|---|---|
| 0 - 4 | 48373 | 92347 |
| 5 - 9 | 40982 | 75219 |
| 10 - 14 | 48919 | 67194 |
| 15 - 19 | 46863 | 60307 |
| 20 - 24 | 42985 | 53480 |
| 25 - 29 | 44128 | 47072 |
| 30 - 34 | 39114 | 41263 |
| 35 - 39 | 39005 | 35873 |
| 40 - 44 | 28013 | 30782 |
| 45 - 49 | 30230 | 25931 |
| 50 - 54 | 18419 | 21380 |
| 55 - 59 | 15747 | 17009 |
| 60 - 64 | 15693 | 12876 |
| 65 - 69 | 13898 | 8923 |
| 70 - 74 | 15006 | 5390 |
| 75 - 79 | 11593 | 2635 |
| 80 - 84 | 3484 | 1198 |
| TOTALS | 502452 | 598878 |

level of fertility and mortality. Alternatively, one can use the level of mortality in conjunction with the observed rate of increase to select an appropriate table.[2] The latter method, however, is very affected by migration and confused by the many border changes between Anatolian provinces and thus has not been used here.

In selecting a family of model populations for Anatolia, the options were either the South (based on the Southern European demographic experience) or the East (based on Central and Eastern Europe). North and West tables were drawn from cultures whose demographic experiences were too different from that of Anatolia. Of the two, the East family was chosen for the following reasons:

1. Both East and South tables were fit to the age-specific data from the *1313 İstatistik.* The East tables better fit the data.

2. Available evidence indicates that Turkish populations typically experience high infant mortality and the East tables better fit such a pattern.[3]

3. Research by other scholars has indicated that the East tables more closely approximate the Turkish demographic experience.[4]

Nevertheless, the choice of the East family of population tables has had little effect on the correction factors used here. For example, using a South model of level 5 (GRR = 3.0) instead of an East model of level 5 (GRR = 3.0) would result in a decrease in the total corrected population of approximately one-tenth of one percent.[5]

Mortality levels of 5 to 8 in the Coale and Demeny tables were chosen because they fit the age pyramids in the *1313 İstatistik.* Levels lower than 5 and higher than 8 were seen to be impossible when graphically compared to the recorded age groups.

It is, of course, possible to make an error in selecting the most representative mortality level, especially when the observed population seems to fit somewhere between two levels. The data did not seem to be accurate enough to support interpolation in such cases and one level or the other was always chosen. Nevertheless, because of the closeness of the mortality levels to one another, choosing a mortality level one removed from the correct mortality would result in only a one to two percent difference in the corrected total population.

The effect of the selection of an incorrect fertility level would be much greater than that of selecting the wrong mortality level. Selecting a Gross

Reproduction Rate of 3.0 instead of 2.5 could mean a difference of seven to nine percent in the corrected population. The choice of the proper GRR is thus very important.

The primary method of selecting a GRR was observation of the correspondence between the model population of that GRR and the recorded age-specific population. Models chosen with a 3.0 GRR were observed to be slightly more representative than models with a 2.5 GRR and much more representative than those with a GRR of 3.5. In every province except Biga, the recorded age pyramid best corresponded to a model GRR of 3.0. This supports the uniform findings of numerous modern surveys of the Turkish population, which have arrived at an average GRR of 3.0 for the Turkish population. Primary among these is the Turkish Demographic Survey,[6] but studies by various scholars,[7] the United States Census Bureau,[8] and the United Nations[9] have supported the finding of the Turkish Demographic Survey that the Turkish GRR is 3.0. In addition, there is evidence that this fertility level has been fairly stable.[10]

The correction rates derived from the age pyramids are described often in the body of the study. Briefly, two correction factors are derived as follows:

$$1. \ \text{C.F.} = (M_c \times 2)/(M_r \times 2)$$
$$2. \ \text{C.F.} = (M_c \times 2)/(M_r + F_r)$$

where $M_r$ is the recorded male population in 1313, $F_r$ is the recorded female population in 1313, and $M_c$ is the corrected male population in 1313 from the age pyramid. (The 1313 recorded populations have occasionally been miscalculated in the 1313 İstatistik and have been recalculated here. Due to this, the total populations as recorded in the 1313 İstatistik may not always agree with the totals entered here.)

Two cautions on the age pyramid analysis must be mentioned. First, the populations in the pyramids are total populations. Populations by age groups for Muslims alone were not available. The presence of minority groups experiencing a higher degree of out-migration undoubtedly affected the age groups and the pyramids. Second, the multiplication of male population by two to obtain total population may result in a slight undercounting of population. Mortality from the pre-1879 wars may very likely have caused there to be more women than men in Anatolia. As before, it was felt better to err here on the side of undercounting.

FIGURE A4.5   1313 ISTATISTIK—HUDAVENDIGAR MALES

LEVEL 7

| AGES | RECORDED POPULATION | CORRECTED POPULATION |
|---|---|---|
| 0 – 4 | 75200 | 126679 |
| 5 – 9 | 83164 | 103183 |
| 10 – 14 | 74593 | 92175 |
| 15 – 19 | 65271 | 82727 |
| 20 – 24 | 72302 | 73362 |
| 25 – 29 | 67072 | 64572 |
| 30 – 34 | 58597 | 56603 |
| 35 – 39 | 41235 | 49209 |
| 40 – 44 | 54528 | 42226 |
| 45 – 49 | 38351 | 35572 |
| 50 – 54 | 32718 | 29328 |
| 55 – 59 | 22478 | 23331 |
| 60 – 64 | 20674 | 17663 |
| 65 – 69 | 12339 | 12241 |
| 70 – 74 | 7496 | 7394 |
| 75 – 79 | 3442 | 3615 |
| 80 – 84 | 3065 | 1643 |
| TOTALS | 732525 | 821523 |

FIGURE A4.6   1313 ISTATISTIK—AYDIN MALES

LEVEL 6

| AGES | RECORDED POPULATION | CORRECTED POPULATION |
|---|---|---|
| 0 - 4 | 58109 | 135078 |
| 5 - 9 | 69858 | 109751 |
| 10 - 14 | 63235 | 98883 |
| 15 - 19 | 68554 | 89633 |
| 20 - 24 | 69164 | 80202 |
| 25 - 29 | 75136 | 71131 |
| 30 - 34 | 63843 | 62869 |
| 35 - 39 | 49845 | 55055 |
| 40 - 44 | 43929 | 47511 |
| 45 - 49 | 41953 | 40236 |
| 50 - 54 | 34838 | 33231 |
| 55 - 59 | 26604 | 26584 |
| 60 - 64 | 23661 | 20028 |
| 65 - 69 | 19246 | 13831 |
| 70 - 74 | 13244 | 8263 |
| 75 - 79 | 9206 | 4042 |
| 80 - 84 | 14549 | 1706 |
| TOTALS | 745614 | 898124 |

FIGURE A4.7    1313 ISTATISTIK—BIGA MALES

| AGES | RECORDED POPULATION | CORRECTED POPULATION |
|---|---|---|
| 0 – 4 | 6623 | 10364 |
| 5 – 9 | 6817 | 8709 |
| 10 – 14 | 7915 | 8106 |
| 15 – 19 | 6512 | 7592 |
| 20 – 24 | 5952 | 7014 |
| 25 – 29 | 5595 | 6427 |
| 30 – 34 | 5575 | 5865 |
| 35 – 39 | 5579 | 5310 |
| 40 – 44 | 4850 | 4732 |
| 45 – 49 | 3568 | 4137 |
| 50 – 54 | 3967 | 3535 |
| 55 – 59 | 2295 | 2916 |
| 60 – 64 | 2977 | 2274 |
| 65 – 69 | 1642 | 1623 |
| 70 – 74 | 1517 | 1004 |
| 75 – 79 | 1381 | 506 |
| 80 – 84 | 1758 | 225 |
| TOTALS | 74523 | 80338 |

FIGURE A4:8    1313 ISTATISTIK—IZMID MALES

LEVEL 7

| AGES | RECORDED POPULATION | CORRECTED POPULATION |
|---|---|---|
| 0 - 4 | 10765 | 21536 |
| 5 - 9 | 11754 | 17542 |
| 10 - 14 | 12977 | 15670 |
| 15 - 19 | 10973 | 14064 |
| 20 - 24 | 10425 | 12472 |
| 25 - 29 | 9959 | 10978 |
| 30 - 34 | 8851 | 9623 |
| 35 - 39 | 8273 | 8366 |
| 40 - 44 | 8411 | 7179 |
| 45 - 49 | 6255 | 6047 |
| 50 - 54 | 5505 | 4986 |
| 55 - 59 | 4067 | 3966 |
| 60 - 64 | 3522 | 3003 |
| 65 - 69 | 2794 | 2081 |
| 70 - 74 | 1492 | 1257 |
| 75 - 79 | 1972 | 615 |
| 80 - 84 | 2630 | 279 |
| TOTALS | 120425 | 139663 |

FIGURE A4.9    1313 ISTATISTIK—KASTAMONU MALES

LEVEL 6

| AGES | RECORDED POPULATION | CORRECTED POPULATION |
|---|---|---|
| 0 - 4 | 42579 | 86094 |
| 5 - 9 | 46702 | 69952 |
| 10 - 14 | 47383 | 63025 |
| 15 - 19 | 42940 | 57129 |
| 20 - 24 | 44906 | 51119 |
| 25 - 29 | 43005 | 45337 |
| 30 - 34 | 37307 | 40071 |
| 35 - 39 | 33694 | 35090 |
| 40 - 44 | 31004 | 30282 |
| 45 - 49 | 25570 | 25845 |
| 50 - 54 | 20618 | 21180 |
| 55 - 59 | 19296 | 16944 |
| 60 - 64 | 15974 | 12765 |
| 65 - 69 | 12758 | 8816 |
| 70 - 74 | 9400 | 5266 |
| 75 - 79 | 6690 | 2576 |
| 80 - 84 | 10203 | 1088 |
| TOTALS | 490029 | 572436 |

FIGURE A4.10  1313 ISTATISTIK--TRABZON MALES

LEVEL 8

| AGES | RECORDED POPULATION | CORRECTED POPULATION |
|---|---|---|
| 0 - 4 | 85886 | 93981 |
| 5 - 9 | 76545 | 76748 |
| 10 - 14 | 76338 | 67981 |
| 15 - 19 | 52936 | 60527 |
| 20 - 24 | 49366 | 53252 |
| 25 - 29 | 42852 | 46514 |
| 30 - 34 | 41809 | 40491 |
| 35 - 39 | 35700 | 35004 |
| 40 - 44 | 32933 | 29876 |
| 45 - 49 | 27512 | 25046 |
| 50 - 54 | 18499 | 20573 |
| 55 - 59 | 14653 | 16339 |
| 60 - 64 | 11653 | 12344 |
| 65 - 69 | 8828 | 8528 |
| 70 - 74 | 6539 | 5188 |
| 75 - 79 | 3571 | 3280 |
| 80 - 84 | 6116 | 1193 |
| TOTALS | 591736 | 596329 |

FIGURE A4.11   1313 ISTATISTIK—SIVAS MALES

LEVEL 5

| AGES | RECORDED POPULATION | CORRECTED POPULATION |
|---|---|---|
| 0 – 4 | 48373 | 84921 |
| 5 – 9 | 40982 | 68784 |
| 10 – 14 | 48919 | 62573 |
| 15 – 19 | 46863 | 57349 |
| 20 – 24 | 42985 | 51777 |
| 25 – 29 | 44128 | 46320 |
| 30 – 34 | 39114 | 41270 |
| 35 – 39 | 39005 | 36453 |
| 40 – 44 | 28013 | 31635 |
| 45 – 49 | 30230 | 28333 |
| 50 – 54 | 18419 | 22348 |
| 55 – 59 | 15747 | 17936 |
| 60 – 64 | 15893 | 13583 |
| 65 – 69 | 13898 | 9345 |
| 70 – 74 | 15006 | 5514 |
| 75 – 79 | 11593 | 2612 |
| 80 – 84 | 3484 | 1103 |
| TOTALS | 502452 | 580456 |

FIGURE A4.12   1313 ISTATISTIK--ANKARA MALES

LEVEL 5

| AGES | RECORDED POPULATION | CORRECTED POPULATION |
|---|---|---|
| 0 - 4 | 39565 | 87856 |
| 5 - 9 | 47869 | 71162 |
| 10 - 14 | 52849 | 64736 |
| 15 - 19 | 49417 | 59331 |
| 20 - 24 | 53372 | 53566 |
| 25 - 29 | 43972 | 47922 |
| 30 - 34 | 39477 | 42697 |
| 35 - 39 | 34646 | 37713 |
| 40 - 44 | 32516 | 32728 |
| 45 - 49 | 29115 | 27864 |
| 50 - 54 | 25417 | 23120 |
| 55 - 59 | 19315 | 18556 |
| 60 - 64 | 15162 | 14052 |
| 65 - 69 | 9762 | 9668 |
| 70 - 74 | 9842 | 5705 |
| 75 - 79 | 8817 | 2702 |
| 80 - 84 | 5937 | 1141 |
| TOTALS | 517050 | 600521 |

FIGURE A4.13    1313 ISTATISTIK—KONYA MALES

LEVEL 6

| AGES | RECORDED POPULATION | CORRECTED POPULATION |
|------|---------------------|----------------------|
| 0 - 4 | 34255 | 97456 |
| 5 - 9 | 39624 | 79183 |
| 10 - 14 | 40730 | 71342 |
| 15 - 19 | 43340 | 64668 |
| 20 - 24 | 44452 | 57864 |
| 25 - 29 | 45267 | 51320 |
| 30 - 34 | 41928 | 45358 |
| 35 - 39 | 40466 | 39721 |
| 40 - 44 | 34012 | 34278 |
| 45 - 49 | 29367 | 29029 |
| 50 - 54 | 27997 | 23975 |
| 55 - 59 | 22454 | 19180 |
| 60 - 64 | 18597 | 14450 |
| 65 - 69 | 15285 | 9979 |
| 70 - 74 | 10947 | 5961 |
| 75 - 79 | 9884 | 2916 |
| 80 - 84 | 16000 | 1231 |
| TOTALS | 514605 | 647977 |

FIGURE A4.14   1313 ISTATISTIK--HALEB MALES

LEVEL 5

| AGES | RECORDED POPULATION | CORRECTED POPULATION |
|---|---|---|
| 0 - 4 | 25689 | 70239 |
| 5 - 9 | 44537 | 56892 |
| 10 - 14 | 40809 | 51755 |
| 15 - 19 | 34183 | 47434 |
| 20 - 24 | 32928 | 42825 |
| 25 - 29 | 34609 | 38312 |
| 30 - 34 | 30073 | 34135 |
| 35 - 39 | 26113 | 30151 |
| 40 - 44 | 26435 | 26186 |
| 45 - 49 | 25315 | 22277 |
| 50 - 54 | 21688 | 18484 |
| 55 - 59 | 18834 | 14835 |
| 60 - 64 | 14480 | 11234 |
| 65 - 69 | 12719 | 7730 |
| 70 - 74 | 7817 | 4561 |
| 75 - 79 | 6519 | 2160 |
| 80 - 84 | 9504 | 912 |
| TOTALS | 412252 | 480104 |

FIGURE A4.15  1313 ISTATISTIK—ADANA MALES

LEVEL 5

| AGES | RECORDED POPULATION | CORRECTED POPULATION |
|---|---|---|
| 0 - 4 | 10631 | 37671 |
| 5 - 9 | 13108 | 30513 |
| 10 - 14 | 16117 | 27757 |
| 15 - 19 | 14561 | 25440 |
| 20 - 24 | 15211 | 22968 |
| 25 - 29 | 16964 | 20548 |
| 30 - 34 | 18697 | 18308 |
| 35 - 39 | 18411 | 16170 |
| 40 - 44 | 18419 | 14033 |
| 45 - 49 | 16949 | 11948 |
| 50 - 54 | 12831 | 9913 |
| 55 - 59 | 9763 | 7956 |
| 60 - 64 | 7461 | 6025 |
| 65 - 69 | 5702 | 4146 |
| 70 - 74 | 2210 | 2446 |
| 75 - 79 | 1412 | 1159 |
| 80 - 84 | 2958 | 489 |
| TOTALS | 201405 | 257490 |

FIGURE A4.16   1313 ISTATISTIK—HALEB MALES

LEVEL 5

| AGES | RECORDED POPULATION | CORRECTED POPULATION |
|---|---|---|
| 0 – 4 | 25689 | 56294 |
| 5 – 9 | 44537 | 47160 |
| 10 – 14 | 40809 | 44325 |
| 15 – 19 | 34183 | 41940 |
| 20 – 24 | 32928 | 39150 |
| 25 – 29 | 34609 | 36180 |
| 30 – 34 | 30073 | 33300 |
| 35 – 39 | 26113 | 30330 |
| 40 – 44 | 26435 | 27225 |
| 45 – 49 | 25315 | 23940 |
| 50 – 54 | 21688 | 20565 |
| 55 – 59 | 18834 | 17010 |
| 60 – 64 | 14480 | 13275 |
| 65 – 69 | 12719 | 9450 |
| 70 – 74 | 8817 | 5805 |
| 75 – 79 | 6519 | 2835 |
| 80 – 84 | 9504 | 1260 |
| TOTALS | 413252 | 449996 |

FIGURE A4.17   1313 ISTATISTIK—ADANA MALES

| AGES | RECORDED POPULATION | CORRECTED POPULATION |
|---|---|---|
| 0 - 4 | 10631 | 30092 |
| 5 - 9 | 13108 | 25209 |
| 10 - 14 | 16117 | 23694 |
| 15 - 19 | 14561 | 22419 |
| 20 - 24 | 15211 | 20927 |
| 25 - 29 | 16964 | 19340 |
| 30 - 34 | 18697 | 17800 |
| 35 - 39 | 18411 | 16213 |
| 40 - 44 | 18419 | 14553 |
| 45 - 49 | 16949 | 12797 |
| 50 - 54 | 12831 | 10993 |
| 55 - 59 | 9763 | 9093 |
| 60 - 64 | 7461 | 7096 |
| 65 - 69 | 5702 | 5051 |
| 70 - 74 | 2210 | 3103 |
| 75 - 79 | 1412 | 1515 |
| 80 - 84 | 2958 | 674 |
| TOTALS | 201405 | 240543 |

FIGURE A4.18    1313 ISTATISTIK—BITLIS MALES

LEVEL 5

| AGES | RECORDED POPULATION | CORRECTED POPULATION |
|---|---|---|
| 0 – 4 | 13649 | 32658 |
| 5 – 9 | 15319 | 26453 |
| 10 – 14 | 20662 | 24064 |
| 15 – 19 | 21563 | 22055 |
| 20 – 24 | 18196 | 19912 |
| 25 – 29 | 15758 | 17814 |
| 30 – 34 | 13927 | 15872 |
| 35 – 39 | 11455 | 14019 |
| 40 – 44 | 10043 | 12166 |
| 45 – 49 | 9172 | 10358 |
| 50 – 54 | 8441 | 8594 |
| 55 – 59 | 6823 | 6898 |
| 60 – 64 | 5648 | 5224 |
| 65 – 69 | 5081 | 3594 |
| 70 – 74 | 4164 | 2121 |
| 75 – 79 | 3446 | 1005 |
| 80 – 84 | 6337 | 424 |
| TOTALS | 189684 | 223229 |

FIGURE A4.19    1313 ISTATISTIK--MAMURETULAZIZ MALES

LEVEL 5

| AGES | RECORDED POPULATION | CORRECTED POPULATION |
|---|---|---|
| 0 - 4 | 13219 | 43134 |
| 5 - 9 | 20128 | 34938 |
| 10 - 14 | 24348 | 31783 |
| 15 - 19 | 22939 | 29129 |
| 20 - 24 | 18528 | 26299 |
| 25 - 29 | 20755 | 23528 |
| 30 - 34 | 20158 | 20963 |
| 35 - 39 | 18726 | 18515 |
| 40 - 44 | 15270 | 16068 |
| 45 - 49 | 14005 | 13680 |
| 50 - 54 | 11281 | 11351 |
| 55 - 59 | 10650 | 9110 |
| 60 - 64 | 9357 | 6899 |
| 65 - 69 | 7749 | 4747 |
| 70 - 74 | 5731 | 2801 |
| 75 - 79 | 4473 | 1327 |
| 80 - 84 | 5356 | 560 |
| TOTALS | 242673 | 294833 |

FIGURE A4.20    1313 ISTATISTIK—DIYARBAKIR MALES

LEVEL 5

| AGES | RECORDED POPULATION | CORRECTED POPULATION |
|---|---|---|
| 0 – 4 | 12163 | 36830 |
| 5 – 9 | 27730 | 29831 |
| 10 – 14 | 23691 | 27138 |
| 15 – 19 | 21275 | 24872 |
| 20 – 24 | 22242 | 22455 |
| 25 – 29 | 19807 | 20089 |
| 30 – 34 | 18921 | 17899 |
| 35 – 39 | 13627 | 15809 |
| 40 – 44 | 13997 | 13720 |
| 45 – 49 | 11384 | 11681 |
| 50 – 54 | 10105 | 9692 |
| 55 – 59 | 7649 | 7779 |
| 60 – 64 | 6230 | 5891 |
| 65 – 69 | 4230 | 4053 |
| 70 – 74 | 2785 | 2392 |
| 75 – 79 | 2692 | 1133 |
| 80 – 84 | 2998 | 478 |
| TOTALS | 221526 | 251741 |

FIGURE A4.21  1313 ISTATISTIK—VAN MALES

LEVEL 6

| AGES | RECORDED POPULATION | CORRECTED POPULATION |
|------|------|------|
| 0 - 4 | 9444 | 11139 |
| 5 - 9 | 9076 | 9050 |
| 10 - 14 | 7102 | 8154 |
| 15 - 19 | 7644 | 7391 |
| 20 - 24 | 7686 | 6614 |
| 25 - 29 | 6388 | 5866 |
| 30 - 34 | 5145 | 5184 |
| 35 - 39 | 4239 | 4540 |
| 40 - 44 | 3875 | 3918 |
| 45 - 49 | 3015 | 3318 |
| 50 - 54 | 2570 | 2740 |
| 55 - 59 | 1658 | 2192 |
| 60 - 64 | 1380 | 1652 |
| 65 - 69 | 828 | 1141 |
| 70 - 74 | 617 | 681 |
| 75 - 79 | 337 | 333 |
| 80 - 84 | 355 | 141 |
| TOTALS | 71339 | 74060 |

FIGURE A4.22   1313 ISTATISTIK—ERZURUM MALES

LEVEL 6

| AGES | RECORDED POPULATION | CORRECTED POPULATION |
|---|---|---|
| 0 - 4 | 31439 | 57232 |
| 5 - 9 | 40287 | 46501 |
| 10 - 14 | 33544 | 41896 |
| 15 - 19 | 27499 | 37977 |
| 20 - 24 | 35694 | 33381 |
| 25 - 29 | 31133 | 30138 |
| 30 - 34 | 26088 | 26637 |
| 35 - 39 | 25435 | 23326 |
| 40 - 44 | 24945 | 20130 |
| 45 - 49 | 19183 | 17048 |
| 50 - 54 | 13679 | 14080 |
| 55 - 59 | 9700 | 11264 |
| 60 - 64 | 7877 | 8486 |
| 65 - 69 | 5043 | 5860 |
| 70 - 74 | 3855 | 3501 |
| 75 - 79 | 1928 | 1712 |
| 80 - 84 | 2842 | 723 |
| TOTALS | 340271 | 380530 |

## Derivation of Correction Factors for Each Anatolian Province

The following series of figures represents the age-specific populations of each Anatolian province, as recorded in the *1313 İstatistik*. The analysis described in the previous section has been applied to each province's age-specific population and a correction factor calculated, using the model stable population that best fits each population.

In the evaluation of their age pyramids, certain provinces presented particular problems. These have been discussed in detail below.

It should be remembered that the correction factors are the number by which the total recorded population (males and females) is multiplied to correct undercounting (twice the corrected male population divided by the uncorrected total population equals the correction factor). If a source gave only male population, the correction factor will be slightly different, since there is no need to account for female underenumeration in the correction factor.

The correction factors for the western Anatolian provinces are uncomplicated results of the analyses of their age pyramids: Hüdavendigâr, 1.1298; Aydın, 1.2150; İzmit, 1.227; Biga, 1.1162.

Trabzon's statistics needed less correction than those of any other province, a factor of 1.0242.

In figure A4.9, Kastamonu is shown to have had the normal Anatolian pattern of male age misrepresentation and undercounting. Children were seriously undercounted (50% of the expected males aged 0 to 5 were unrecorded) and from the young adult ages on the males gave their ages as older than they actually were. The false aging of the population has been corrected by redistributing the population according to the percentages of the model (figure A4.9). Most of the numbers added to the population by the correction factor are a corrective for the undercounting in the 0 to 15 age groups.

The Kastamonu underregistration of females (table A2.3) is also at a normal rate for northern and western Anatolia. It is only a small part of the correction factor (recorded population × 1.1818 = corrected population).

The age pyramid of Sivas Vilâyeti (figure A4.11) is slightly odd. Large numbers in the age groups 35–40 and 45–50 are unexpected, as is the shape of the pyramid in the age groups above 70. The explanation for this probably lies in errors on the part of the registrars. It is even conceivable that those whose ages were listed as 40 or 50 were placed in the wrong age groups, i.e., someone who was listed as 40 should have been placed in the 40–55 age group, but may have been placed in the 35–40 group. Since the ages 40 and 50 were often chosen by those who only approximately knew their own ages, the placement of the 40s and 50s in the wrong age group would surely affect the age pyramid. A man aged 42 might have given his age, only approximately known to him, as 40. If he was mistakenly placed in the 35–40 age group he would have been improperly registered. The correction factor for Sivas is 1.1836.

The male population of Ankara Vilâyeti, like that of Sivas, shared with the eastern provinces of Anatolia a fairly high level of both fertility and mortality. The model portrayed in figure A4.12 fits the upper ages of the Ankara male population (as recorded in the *1313 İstatistik*) well. One can be more sure of the "fit" of the recorded and model populations for Ankara than for Sivas. Comparison with the age pyramid of Sivas (figure A4.11) shows that Ankara registration practices were more precise than Sivas. Ankara age groups form a more satisfactory pyramid.

The main error shown in the Ankara population sources is, as usual, underregistration of children and age misrepresentation—persons stating they were older than their actual ages. Bulges in the 10–15 and 20–25 age groups reflect age-heaping at the "10" ages. (Those who only approximately knew their own ages or those of their children often round their ages out to 10, 20, 30, etc.) These are the errors one would expect to find in a conscientiously run population registration program in a modern developing country. That they are found here indicates that Ankara population officials attempted to provide correct population reports.

The records of Konya's population (figure A4.13) present certain anomalies. At the upper ages, Konya's 1313 recorded population forms a fairly smooth age pyramid, yet the recorded pyramid does not fit any model population very well. The model it best fits (1.6—3.0) indicates that Konya experienced slightly greater mortality than did Ankara or Sivas, and the sex ratios of the Konya population, usually an indicator of accuracy of registration, are very good, i.e., women are only slightly less than half of the recorded population. Yet the enumeration of young males, another indicator of registration accuracy, is very poor, one of the lowest in Anatolia. It is difficult to understand how one type of registration could be so good and another so poor.

One answer to this problem is that, for an unknown reason, males in Konya were even more likely to overstate their ages than males in other parts of Anatolia. This would have the effect of making most men in the Konya population appear in a higher age group and would account for both the preponderance of males in the upper ages and the small number of males at the younger ages. Another answer may be bureaucratic inefficiency in some parts of the province, coupled with efficiency in others.

The pattern of population registration in Konya Vilâyeti can be explained as the result of very accurate registration of adults and children in some areas (thus the fairly accurate sex ratio) and fairly accurate registration of adults and poor registration of children in other areas. This solution is somewhat unsatisfying, since it in no way answers why the Konya registration system would have worked in this way. It is possible, though, that the coastal areas of Konya, closer to communication and transportation lines and government control, might have returned significantly better statistics on population than the interior regions. Konya's large geographic area makes such regional discrepancies all the more likely.

Both solutions probably explain part of the unique Konya age distribution. Whatever the reason for the deficiency, the method of correction readjusts the Konya population to more accurate figures (correction factor equals 1.270). The uniform progression of the population as reported in various years indicates that the population was similarly undercounted in all the Konya population records.

The methods used to find a model population for every other Anatolian province do not work for Adana and Haleb. These methods are fully explained earlier in this appendix, but, briefly, the basic analysis involves comparing the recorded population, by age group as found in the 1313 İstatistik, with models of various fertility and mortality levels until a proper "fit" is found. By this method, both provinces (figures A4.14 and A4.15) seem to fit best a mortality level of 5 in the Coale and Demeny tables, fairly low, and a Gross Reproduction Rate of 2.5. The mortality level, 5, is the same as that of eastern and central Anatolia, reflecting the demographic dominance of the interior sections of the two provinces. However, analysis of the population sources for each vilâyet reveals that a Gross Reproduction Rates of 2.5 is impossible.

A model population of mortality level 5 and a Gross Reproduction Rate of 2.5 is expected to increase at a rate of .005 per year. No matter what analyses and changes are applied to them, the various populations in the sources for Adana and Haleb consistently show rates of increase of slightly over .010. Only a massive and constant in-migration could account for such increases, unless the choice of model is incorrect. In the absence of any reason to believe that great amounts of in-migration occurred, one must assume, despite the "fit" of the two age pyramids, that a Gross Reproduction Rate of 2.5 is wrong. The fertility parameter that seems obvious from the age pyramids is incorrect.

Figures A4.16 and A4.17 give the age pyramids for a Gross Reproduction Rate of 3.0. This model has a growth rate of .0155 per year, almost exactly the same as the rates indicated by the populations as they appear in the sources. The pyramids also indicate that age misrepresentation was great. Males in Haleb consistently overstated their ages. The Haleb correction factor is 1.1722.

The Adana age pyramid (figure A4.17) is so unusual that one is tempted to speculate that the figures for the middle years are misprints. This is not the case.[11] Another explanation could be migration; a small possibility does exist that young males left their villages and the province for work or the military and returned when they were older. Such movement was somewhat common on the Black Sea,[12] though large movements of young men from Adana have not been mentioned in the literature and such a large-scale migration should have been noticed. Migration of minority group members at young ages could not have been great enough to account for the situation.[13] A more tenable hypothesis than any of these would be in-migration of males in the middle years, 35 to 50, but such migration would probably have occurred mainly in the cities, and the most urban kaza of Adana actually increased at a lesser rate than the rest of the province.[14]

Unless more evidence appears, the answer must be assumed to lie in faulty records. Many speculations on this point are possible, but, without documentation, one must assume for the present that the bulges at the middle ages are a product of age misrepresentation, i.e., the young adult males stated their ages as older than they were and did it more consistently than in other provinces. (Females in Adana reported the same type of age pyramid, a fact that discounts the idea of male migration for jobs, etc. Any in-migration would have had to have been one of adult married couples, aged 35–50, without their children. This appears to be highly unlikely.) The correction factor applied to Adana total Muslim population (recorded population × 1.2913 = corrected population) supplies most of its added numbers from the much undercounted younger ages.

The recorded sex ratio in Adana Vilâyeti is one of the best in Anatolia (.507 males), equal to the Hüdavendigâr ratio. This may be the result of the great underregistration in the younger ages—the ages in which the underregistration of females usually occurs. By underregistering both young males and young females the usual effects of female undercounting are diminished.

The Bitlis age groups from the 1313 İstatistik demonstrate either massive out-migration at the middle ages or large-scale underreporting of the Bitlis male population. The former is unlikely. The evidence of the existence of underenumeration is supported by the low percentage of females reported (table A2.3). The low registration of both females and males forces one to use, for Bitlis Province, the largest correction factor used for any Anatolian province (total population × 1.3184 = corrected population).

Mamuretülaziz, with more accurate statistics than Bitlis, had a 1.2638 correction factor.

The ratio of males in the recorded Diyarbakır population is high (.536), falling between the Bitlis (.560) and Mamuretülaziz (.520) figures. The age pyramid also indicates very considerable miscounting. This is especially true of the youngest ages. Only one-third of the expected young males aged 0 to 5 are recorded. A deficiency of this magnitude must indicate more than just incomplete responses by villagers asked by the local registrar "How many sons have you, and what are their ages?" It is more likely that the registrars simply did not record very young children in many areas, despite their orders from Istanbul.[15] Since the age pyramid is of total, and not only Muslim, population, it is possible that the lack of young males was partially caused by minority inhabitants of the province not reporting their children in order to escape present or future taxation.

The Diyarbakır correction factor is 1.2172.

As explained in chapter 2, Van's age pyramid is unusable for the type of analysis made for the other provinces.

Figure A4.21, if the data were correct, would indicate that the undercounting of children in Van was very slight. Since some age misrepresentation must have taken place between the ages 5 and 30, it would appear from figure A4.21 that males in the 5 to 30 age groups were not undercounted at all. The only significant underenumeration seems to be in the 0 to 5 age group, and even here the lack is very small. Could such accuracy be possible, in one of the most underdeveloped Ottoman provinces? Also, could the recorded population of the upper age groups be as small a proportion of the population as is indicated? Such small proportions in the upper ages go against all Ottoman statistical traditions. The upper ages were usually much over-, not undercounted, as has been seen in earlier chapters on the other Ottoman provinces.

If undercounting of females and undercounting of children go together and are directly related, as they seem to have been in other Anatolian vilâyets, then table A2.3 further demonstrates the problems with the Van age pyramid. Undercounting of females as serious as that in Van should have been part of a syndrome in which children were undercounted, as well.

It must be assumed that the population officials did not record the ages of the population properly. Those who recorded the Van population must have changed the data they received, probably because age registration was so bad as to be obvious to any observer. Perhaps the bureaucrats knew that, uncorrected, the information in their records would appear to their masters in Istanbul to be examples of poor work. The difficulty this presents for analysis is that by rearranging the data the Van officials obliterated evidence of the undercount of children. By redistributing the population age groups, the Van officials made the percentages in the lower age groups seem larger than they were.

For Van, due to the inaccuracy of age-specific date, it has been necessary to construct an artificial correction factor, one that has no relation to the recorded age-specific population of the province. A factor of 1.3 has been selected as representing the approximate average correction factor for the area (the factor for Mamuretülaziz is 1.2638 and that for Bitlis 1.3184). Given the state of Van's population records it is doubtful if application of this correction factor can result in anything but an underestimation of the total population. This is in keeping with the general policy of this study— to underestimate rather than overestimate Muslim population.

The Erzurum male age distribution shown in figure A4.22 has two odd features: the large number of males in the middle years, 35–50, and the unexpectedly small numbers in the upper age groups. These phenomena were most likely the result of the 1877–78 war with the Russians, much of which was fought in the territory of the Erzurum Vilâyeti. The upper age groups most likely reflect the losses of the population during the war, whereas

Table A4.1

Summary of Stable Models and Correction Factors

| Province | Gross Reproduction Rate | Mortality Level | Life Expectancy at Birth | Correction Factor* | Under-enumeration° |
|---|---|---|---|---|---|
| Hüdavendigâr | 3.0 | 7 | 32.5 | 1.1298 | .1149 |
| Aydın | 3.0 | 6 | 30.0 | 1.2150 | .1770 |
| Biga | 2.5 | 6 | 30.0 | 1.1162 | .1041 |
| İzmit | 3.0 | 7 | 32.5 | 1.2227 | .1821 |
| Kastamonu | 3.0 | 6 | 30.0 | 1.1816 | .1537 |
| Trabzon | 3.0 | 8 | 35.0 | 1.0242 | .0236 |
| Sivas | 3.0 | 5 | 27.5 | 1.1836 | .1551 |
| Ankara | 3.0 | 5 | 27.5 | 1.1788 | .1517 |
| Konya | 3.0 | 6 | 30.0 | 1.2709 | .2132 |
| Haleb | 3.0 | 5 | 27.5 | 1.1722 | .1469 |
| Adana | 3.0 | 5 | 27.5 | 1.2913 | .2256 |
| Bitlis | 3.0 | 5 | 27.5 | 1.3184 | .2415 |
| Mamuretülaziz | 3.0 | 5 | 27.5 | 1.2638 | .2087 |
| Diyarbakır | 3.0 | 5 | 27.5 | 1.2172 | .1784 |
| Van | 3.0 | 6 | 30.0 | 1.3000 | .2308 |
| Erzurum | 3.0 | 6 | 30.0 | 1.1947 | .1364 |

*To arrive at the corrected population, the recorded total population is multiplied by this number.
°The proportion of the total corrected population not included in the recorded figures.

the middle age groups are swelled by migrants from the areas lost to the Ottomans as a result of that war.[16] The percentage of males (table A2.3) in the Erzurum Province partially reflects this migration and partially reflects, as in all provinces, the underenumeration of women.

The correction factor for Erzurum is 1.1947.

## Analysis Using Life Table Values

It is possible to compare the numbers in a population who live from one period to another by comparing $L_x$ values from a model life table. These single-year $L_x$ values are the numbers of the stable population from a life table who would be alive during a year (i.e., age x to x−1). Thus (table A4.2), of the 10,000 who are born, 8,991 will be alive during age 0, 7,060 will be alive during age 10, etc. By summing $L_x$ values one can fine how many members of age groups survive over a period of time. For example, if the 77,682 ($\sum_9^0 L_x$) who are alive between ages 0 and 9 are aged 10 years, 69,024 will have survived. In a situation such as that of the 1927 and 1935 censuses, taken eight years apart, the 394,580 ($\sum_9^0 L_x$) who were alive in

Table A4.2

Single Year Life Table Value

| Ages | $l_x$ | Summed | $L_x$ | Summed |
|---|---|---|---|---|
| 0 | 10000 | 10000 | 8990.6 | |
| 1 | 8558 | 18558 | 8287.5 | 18287.5 |
| 2 | 8017 | 26575 | 7883.5 | 26171 |
| 3 | 7750 | 34325 | 7673 | 33844 |
| 4 | 7596 | 41921 | 7539 | 41383 |
| 5 | 7482 | 49403 | 7431 | 48814 |
| 6 | 7380 | 56783 | 7334.5 | 56148.5 |
| 7 | 7289 | 64072 | 7249 | 63397.5 |
| 8 | 7209 | 71281 | 7174.5 | 70572 |
| 9 | 7140 | 78421 | 7110 | 77682 |
| 10 | 7080 | 85501 | 7060.5 | 84742.5 |
| 11 | 7041 | 92542 | 7025 | 91767.5 |
| 12 | 7009 | 99551 | 6995 | 98762.5 |
| 13 | 6981 | 106532 | 6967.5 | 105730. |
| 14 | 6954 | 113486 | 6940.5 | 112671. |
| 15 | 6927 | 120413 | 6905 | 119576. |
| 16 | 6883 | 127296 | 6859.5 | 126435. |
| 17 | 6836 | 134132 | 6810.5 | 133246. |
| 18 | 6785 | 140917 | 6758 | 140004. |
| 19 | 6731 | 147648 | 6702.5 | 146706. |
| 20 | 6674 | 154322 | 6642.89 | 153349. |
| 21 | 6611.77 | 160934. | 6579.48 | 159928. |
| 22 | 6547.19 | 167481. | 6514.06 | 166442. |
| 23 | 6480.93 | 173962. | 6447.3 | 172890. |
| 24 | 6413.66 | 180376. | 6379.83 | 179270. |
| 25 | 6346 | 186722. | 6313.73 | 185583. |
| 26 | 6281.46 | 193003. | 6249.36 | 191833. |
| 27 | 6217.25 | 199220. | 6185.27 | 198018. |
| 28 | 6153.29 | 205374. | 6121.4 | 204139. |
| 29 | 6089.52 | 211463. | 6057.76 | 210197. |
| 30 | 6026 | 217489. | 5994.58 | 216192. |
| 31 | 5963.16 | 223452. | 5931.67 | 222123. |
| 32 | 5900.18 | 229352. | 5868.57 | 227992. |
| 33 | 5836.97 | 235189. | 5805.16 | 233797. |
| 34 | 5773.35 | 240963. | 5741.17 | 239538. |
| 35 | 5709 | 246672. | 5676.4 | 245215. |
| 36 | 5643.8 | 252316. | 5610.76 | 250825. |
| 37 | 5577.72 | 257893. | 5544.18 | 256370. |
| 38 | 5510.64 | 263404. | 5476.54 | 261846. |
| 39 | 5442.44 | 268846. | 5407.72 | 267254. |
| 40 | 5373 | 274219. | 5337.66 | 272591. |
| 41 | 5302.32 | 279522. | 5266.31 | 277858. |

Table A4.2 (continued)

| | | | | |
|----|---------|----------|---------|----------|
| 42 | 5230.29 | 284752. | 5193.38 | 283051. |
| 43 | 5156.48 | 289908. | 5118.58 | 288170. |
| 44 | 5080.68 | 294989. | 5041.84 | 293212. |
| 45 | 5003 | 299992. | 4962.91 | 298175. |
| 46 | 4922.83 | 304915. | 4881.3 | 303056. |
| 47 | 4839.78 | 309755. | 4796.88 | 307853. |
| 48 | 4753.98 | 314509. | 4709.61 | 312562. |
| 49 | 4665.25 | 319174. | 4619.12 | 317181. |
| 50 | 4573 | 323747. | 4525.08 | 321707. |
| 51 | 4477.16 | 328224. | 4427.6 | 326134. |
| 52 | 4378.04 | 332602. | 4326.84 | 330461. |
| 53 | 4275.64 | 336878. | 4222.8 | 334684. |
| 54 | 4169.96 | 341048. | 4115.48 | 338799. |
| 55 | 4061 | 345109. | 4005.62 | 342805. |
| 56 | 3950.24 | 349059. | 3892.83 | 346698. |
| 57 | 3835.43 | 352894. | 3776.15 | 350474. |
| 58 | 3716.88 | 356611. | 3655.64 | 354129. |
| 59 | 3594.39 | 360206. | 3530.69 | 357660. |
| 60 | 3467 | 363673. | 3400.34 | 361061. |
| 61 | 3333.67 | 367006. | 3264.71 | 364325. |
| 62 | 3195.75 | 370202. | 3125.11 | 367450. |
| 63 | 3054.47 | 373257. | 2982.41 | 370433. |
| 64 | 2910.35 | 376167. | 2836.68 | 373269. |
| 65 | 2763 | 378930. | 2689.72 | 375959. |
| 66 | 2616.45 | 381546. | 2541.98 | 378501. |
| 67 | 2467.51 | 384014. | 2392.46 | 380894. |
| 68 | 2317.42 | 386331. | 2241.97 | 383136. |
| 69 | 2166.53 | 388498. | 2090.26 | 385226. |
| 70 | 2014 | 390512. | 1936.84 | 387163. |
| 71 | 1859.69 | 392372. | 1782.96 | 388946. |
| 72 | 1706.22 | 394078. | 1630.42 | 390576. |
| 73 | 1554.62 | 395632. | 1480.24 | 392056. |
| 74 | 1405.87 | 397038. | 1333.44 | 393390. |
| 75 | 1261 | 398299. | 1190.64 | 394580. |

1927, aged forward eight years, would total 331,452 in 1935 ($\sum_{17}^8 L_x$). Any age groups or totals of all ages can be examined in this way and the percentages of survivors found by simple division.

For this type of analysis, the life tables developed by Brass and presented by Carrier and Hobcraft,[17] are convenient, since certain $L_x$ values for certain single years of age are given by Carrier and Hobcraft and the remainder can be found using their methods. Table A4.2 is a combination of their single-year $L_x$ values, given only for ages 0–19, and $L_x$ values calculated for this study. Only five-year $L_x$ values for ages 20+ are given in the Brass tables, so single-year $L_x$ values for ages 20+ must be taken from $l_x$ values. Single-year $l_x$ values are calculated by fitting a third-degree polynomial curve to a 15-year period for each five years of single-year $l_x$ values, e.g., for $l_{35-40}$ the curve is fitted to $l_{30}$, $l_{35}$, $l_{40}$, and $l_{45}$. The $L_x$ values are computed from $l_x$ values using a separation factor of .5.[18]

## NOTES

1. Recorded in 1935: .01226 of the population was over 70, .065 over 80. In the model (East, GRR = 3.0): over 70 in level 14—.0135 over 80—.0020; over 70 in level 10—.0146, over 70 in level 12—.014; over 70 in level 16—.0139; over 70 in level 18—.0122. No matter which level is chosen, the overstatement of age in the 1935 census is obvious.

2. Substituting for the intrinsic rate of increase in the model stable population.

3. The mortality under 1 in Turkey as listed in the Turkish Demographic Survey (p. 78) was 155 per thousand. The TDS lists the life expectancy at birth ($e_0^0$) of Turkey in 1968 as 54.89 years (p. 80), which corresponds to a Coale and Demeny mortality level of 16 in both East and South tables. The South table, however, gives an $m_0 - 1$ of 124.75, whereas the East is 136.28. The higher East figure comes closer to the 0–1 mortality observed in the TDS.

4. Frederic C. Shorter, "Information on Fertility, Mortality, and Population Growth in Turkey," in Shorter and Bozkurt Güvenç, *Turkish Demography: Proceedings of a Conference* (Ankara, 1969), p. 35; Aysu Oral, "Techniques for Mortality Estimation in Turkey," *Turkish Demography*, p. 111.

5. South—proportion under age 15: .3722; East—proportion under age 15: .3726. Since the population under 15 is, in essence, the entire correction, the change would be .001 if the South table was chosen.

6. Ankara, 1969. Contains extensive information on Turkish fertility, broken down by regions that roughly correspond to the regions in chapter 2. The 3.0 GRR reflects today's rural fertility experience in the Turkish Republic.

7. See, for example, Shorter, *Turkish Demography*, pp. 34–37, and Paul Demeny and Frederic Shorter, *Estimating Turkish Mortality, Fertility, and Age Structure* (Istanbul, 1968), pp. 46–52, among others.

8. U.S. Department of Commerce, Bureau of the Census, A *Compilation of Age-Specific Ferility Rates for Developing Countries*, under "Turkey" (Washington, DC, 1979). See also *Country Demographic Profiles—Turkey* (various years).

9. U.N. Department of Economic and Social Affairs, Population Studies No. 52, *Interim Report of Conditions and Trends of Fertility in the World, 1960–65* (New York, 1972), p. 79.

10. Shorter, *Turkish Demography*, pp. 34–37.

11. The handwritten and typeset editions of the *1313 İstatistik* both show this age structure. It is very difficult to believe that misprints could have taken place in both editions and in all the middle years.

12. Justin McCarthy, "Age, Family, and Migration in the Black Sea Provinces of the Ottoman Empire," *IJMES* 10(1979), pp. 309–323.

13. These pyramids, it must be remembered, are of total, not Muslim population.

14. From statistics in the Adana salnames, the 1311 Census and the *1330 Nüfus-i Umumî.*

15. See appendix A2, "Reliability and Accuracy."

16. See W. E. D. Allen and Paul Muratoff, *Caucasian Battlefields* (Cambridge, 1953).

17. Norman Carrier and John Hobcraft, *Demographic Estimation for Developing Societies* (London: Population Investigation Committee, London School of Economics, 1971).

18. This is the same method used by Carrier and Hobcraft to compute their single-year $L_x$ values (p. 46).

# Appendix 5.
## Ottoman and Republican Provinces

THE FOLLOWING are the 1927 provinces of the Turkish Republic that made up the geographic area of each of the vilâyets of Ottoman Anatolia. The Ottoman provinces are those listed in chapter 6, and independent sancaks have been included in their "mother" provinces. Also given is the area of each province in square kilometers, as listed in the 1927 Turkish census.

Republican provinces are listed in three ways:

1. The province was completely enclosed within the boundaries of the Ottoman vilâyet (e.g., Erzincan).

2. The province was within the Ottoman vilâyet's borders, except for certain Republican kazas (e.g., Erzurum [−Oltu]).

3. Only certain kazas of the Republican province were within the borders of the Ottoman vilâyet (e.g., Gümüşhane [Bayburt]).

## APPENDIX 5

### Table A5.1

Ottoman and Republican Provinces

| Province | Area (square kilometers) |
|---|---|
| Adana | 36,800 |
|     Adana | 16,160 |
|     Cebelibereket | 6,180 |
|     İçel | 9,845 |
|     Mersin | 4,615 |
| Ankara | 71,965 |
|     Ankara | 23,385 |
|     Kırşehir | 9,090 |
|     Çorum (-Mecidözü) | 9,850 |
|     Yozgad | 13,950 |
|     Eskişehir (Sivrihisar, Mihalıççık) | 6,930 |
|     Kayseri (Kayseri, Develi, İncesu) | 6,760 |
| Aydın | 57,842 |
|     Aydın | 7,580 |
|     Muğla | 12,760 |
|     Denizli | 11,150 |
|     İzmir | 12,502 |
|     Manisa | 13,850 |
| Biga | 7,560 |
|     Çanakkale (-İmroz, -Bozcaada, -Gelibolu, -Eceabat) | 7,560 |

Table A5.1 (continued)

| | |
|---|---|
| Bitlis | 32,274 |
| | |
| Bitlis | 16,507 |
| Elaziz (Çapakçur, Genç) | 3,437 |
| Diyarbakır (Kalp) | 1,010 |
| Siirt | 11,320 |
| | |
| Diyarbakır | 36,670 |
| | |
| Diyarbakır (-Kalp) | 13,865 |
| Mardin | 13,045 |
| Elaziz (Palu, Maden) | 4,150 |
| Urfa (Siverek, Viranşehir) | 5,160 |
| | |
| Erzurum | 54,521 |
| | |
| Erzurum (-Oltu) | 23,870 |
| Erzincan | 14,276 |
| Gümüşhane (Bayburt) | 3,430 |
| Bayazıt (-İğdir, -Kulp) | 10,305 |
| Artvin (Yusufeli) | 2,640 |
| | |
| Haleb | 31,705 |
| | |
| Maraş | 13,465 |
| Gaziantep (-Besni) | 7,970 |
| Urfa (-Siverek, -Viranşehir) | 10,270 |
| | |
| Hüdavendigâr | 66,090 |
| | |
| Bursa | 13,565 |
| Bilecik | 4,730 |
| Kütahya | 14,415 |
| Afyon | 12,660 |
| Balıkesir | 14,315 |
| Eskişehir (Eskişehir, Seyitgazi) | 6,405 |
| | |
| İzmit | 8,450 |
| | |
| Kocaeli | 8,450 |

Table A5.1 (continued)

| | |
|---|---|
| Kastamonu | 47,780 |
| Kastamonu | 14,610 |
| Sinop | 5,755 |
| Çankırı | 8,665 |
| Bolu | 11,140 |
| Zonguldak | 7,610 |
| | |
| Konya | 103,425 |
| Konya | 48,990 |
| Aksaray | 10,101 |
| Niğde | 9,965 |
| Antalya | 19,479 |
| Burdur | 6,615 |
| Isparta | 8,275 |
| | |
| Mamuretülaziz | 29,186 |
| Malatya | 15,730 |
| Elaziz (-Çapakçur, -Genç, Palu, -Maden) | 10,226 |
| Gaziantep (Besni) | 3,230 |
| | |
| Sivas | 59,920 |
| Sivas | 26,930 |
| Şebin Karahisar | 5,140 |
| Tokat | 10,415 |
| Amasya | 5,550 |
| Samsun (Havza, Ladik, Vezirköprü) | 3,075 |
| Kayseri (Bunyan, Pinar Başı) | 7,150 |
| Çorum (Mecitözü) | 1,390 |
| | |
| Trabzon | 31,221 |
| Trabzon | 4,630 |
| Ordu | 5,026 |
| Giresun | 4,170 |
| Rize | 4,590 |
| Gümüşhane (-Bayburt) | 6,670 |
| Samsun (-Havza, - Vezirköprü) | 6,135 |
| | |
| Van | 37,110 |
| Van | 21,605 |
| Hakkâri | 15,505 |

# Selected Bibliography

Volumes published in Ottoman or modern Turkish and a European language are listed in the European language. Ottoman authors are listed by their first names (i.e., Ahmed Cemal, not Cemal, Ahmed). Ottoman Turkish words and names are transcribed into the modern Turkish orthography.

## SECONDARY SOURCES

Ahmed Emin (Yalman). *Turkey in the World War*. New Haven: Yale University Press, 1930.

Ahmed Cemal. *Coğrafya-yi Askerî*. Istanbul, 1314.

Ali Cevat. *Memalik-i Osmaniye'nin Coğrafya Lugatı*. Istanbul, 1313.

Ali Saib. *Mufassal Coğrafya-yi Memalik-i Devlet-i Osmaniye*. Istanbul, 1304.

Allen, W.E.D. and Paul Muratoff. *Caucasian Battlefields*. Cambridge, 1953.

Antoniades, Alexandre. *Le Developpement Economique de la Thrace*. Athens, 1922.

Aysel, Alpay. "Abridged Life Tables for Three Metropolitan Cities and Selected Regions of Turkey by Sex." In *Turkish Demography: Proceedings of a Conference*, edited by Frederic Shorter and Bozkurt Güvenç, pp. 83–108. Ankara, 1969.

Belen, Fahri. *Türk Kurtuluş Savaşı* Ankara: Başbakanlık Basimevi, 1973.

Bolu Vilâyeti. *Bolu Livası Salnamesi*. Bolu, 1922.

Bulutoğlu Yakut. *La Structure Par Age et la Mortalite de la Population de la Turquie*. Paris: Librairie General de Droit et de Jurisprudence, 1970.

Carrier, Norman and John Hobcraft. *Demographic Estimation for Developing Societies*, London: Population Investigation Committee, London School of Economics, 1971.

Coale, Ansley J. and Paul Demeny. *Regional Model Life Tables and Stable Populations*, Princeton: Princeton University Press, 1966.

Cuinet, Vital. *La Turquie d'Asie*, 4 vol. Paris, 1890–94.

Danişmend, İsmail Hamî, *İzahlı Osmanlı Tarihi Kronolojisi*, 6 vols. 2nd ed. Istanbul: Türkiye Yayınevi, 1971.

Demeny, Paul, and Frederic Shorter. *Estimating Turkish Mortality, Fertility, and Age Structure*. Istanbul, 1968.

Duran, Faik Sabri. *Türkiye 1:2,000,000: Two Maps—Physical and Political*. Istanbul: Kanaat Yayınevi, n.d.

Eldem, Vedat. *Osmanlı İmparatorluğunun İktisadi Şartları Hakkında Bir Tetkik*, Istanbul: İş Bankası Kültür Yayınları, 1970.

Hüseyin. *Memalik-i Osmaniye'nin Ziraat Coğrafyası*. Istanbul, 1303.

Hovannisian, Richard G. *Armenia on the Road to Independence*. Berkeley and Los Angeles: University of California Press, 1967.

Hovannisian, Richard G. "The Ebb and Flow of the Armenian Minority in the Arab Middle East." *Middle East Journal* 28, no. 1, Winter, 1974.

Hovannisian, Richard G. *The Republic of Armenia*. v. I. Berkeley and Los Angeles: University of California Press, 1971.

Issawi, Charles. "Population and Resources in the Ottoman Empire and Iran." In *Studies in Eighteenth Century Islamic History*, edited by T. Naff and R. Owen, pp. 152–164. Carbondale, Southern Illinois University Press, 1977.

Karal, Enver Ziya. *Osmanlı İmparatorluğunda İlk Nüfus Sayımı, 1831*. Ankara, 1943.

Karal, Enver Ziya. *Osmanlı Tarihi*, VIII Cilt. Ankara: Türk Tarih Kurumu, 1962.

Karamürsel, Ziya. *Osmanlı Malî Tarihi Hakkında Tetkikler*. Ankara: Türk Tarih Kurumu, 1940.

Kalopothakes, D. [Polybius]. *Greece Before the Conference*. London, 1919.

Karpat, Kemal. "Ottoman Population Records and the Census of 1881/2–1893." *IJMES* 9 (2), May, 1978.

Ladas, Stephen P. *The Exchange of Minorities: Bulgaria, Greece, and Turkey*. New York: Macmillan, 1932.

Larcher, M. *La Guerre Turque dans la Guerre Mondiale*. Paris, 1926.

Lynch, H.F.B. *Armenia, Travels and Studies*. vol. 2. London, 1901.

Maccas, Leon. *L'Hellenisme de l'Asie Mineure*. Paris, 1919.

McCarthy, Justin. "Age, Family, and Migration in the Black Sea Provinces of the Ottoman Empire." *IJMES*, 1979.

McCarthy, Justin. *The Arab World, Turkey, and the Balkans: A Handbook of Historical Statistics*. Boston: G.K. Hall, 1982.

McCarthy, Justin. "Greek Statistics on Ottoman Greek Population." *International Journal of Turkish Studies*, I (2) 1980, pp. 66–76.

McCarthy, Justin and J. Dennis Hyde. "Ottoman Imperial and Provincial Salnames." *IJMES*, 1978.

Mehmed Eşref. *Tarih-i Umumî ve Osmani Atlası*. Istanbul, 1329.

Mehmed Hikmet. *Coğrafya-i Umran*. Istanbul, 1312.

Mehmed Nasrullah, Mehmed Rüşdi, and Mehmed Eşref. *Memalik-i Mahruse-i Şahane'ye Mükemmel ve Mufassal Atlası*. Istanbul, 1325.

Michoff, Nikola. *La Population de la Turquie et de la Bulgarie au XVIIIe et XIXe s.: recherches bibliographico-statistiques*. Sofia, 1915–1935.

Mirak, Robert. "Armenian Emigration to the United States to 1915 (I): Leaving the Old Country." *Journal of Armenian Studies* I, no. 1, 1975, pp. 5–42.

Mostras, C. *Dictionaire Geographique de L'Empire Ottoman*. St. Petersburg, 1873.

Nubar, Boghos. *The Pre-War Population of Cilicia*. Paris, 1920.

Ormanian, Malachia. *L'Eglise Armenienne*. Paris, 1910.

Özalp, Kâzim. *Milli Mücadele, 1919–22*. 2 vol. Ankara: Türk Tarih Kurumu, 1971.

Pallis. *Greece's Anatolian Venture—and After*. London, 1937.

Patriarcat Armenien de Constantinople. *Population Armenienne de la Turquie Avant la Guerre*. Paris, 1920.

Pentzopoulos, Dimitri. *The Balkan Exchange of Minorities and Its Impact Upon Greece*. Paris, 1962.

Poladian, Terenig, ed. *The Church of Armenia* (Translation of *L'Eglise Armenienne* by Ormanian, with additions by Poladian). London, 1955.

Ravenstein, E.G. "The Populations of Russia and Turkey." *Journal of the Royal Geographic Society*, September, 1877.

Representatives of Armenia. *The Armenian Question Before the Peace Conference*. Paris, 1919.

Semseddin Sami. *Kamusülalam*. 6 vols. Istanbul, 1306–1316.

Shaw, Stanford J. and Ezel Kural Shaw. *History of the Ottoman Empire and Modern Turkey*. Vol. II. New York: Cambridge University Press, 1977.

Shaw, Stanford J. "The Nineteenth-Century Ottoman Tax Reforms and Revenue Systems." *IJMES* 6 (4), October, 1975.

Shaw, Stanford J. "The Ottoman Census System and Population." *IJMES* 9 (3), August, 1978.

Shorter, Frederic C. "Information on Fertility, Mortality, and Population Growth in Turkey." *Population Index* 34, no. 1 (1968), 3–21.

Shorter, Frederic C. "The Population of Turkey after the War of Independence." In *Regional Papers*, Giza, Egypt: West Asia and North Africa Region. 1983.

Shorter, Frederic C. and Bozkurt Güvenç, eds. *Turkish Demography: Proceedings of a Conference*. Ankara: Hacettepe University Press, 1969.

Shryock, Henry S., Jacob Siegel, and associates. *The Materials and Methods of Demography*. 2nd ed. 2 vols. Washington: Washington: United States Department of Commerce, 1973.

Soteriadis, George. *An Ethnological Map Illustrating Hellenism in the Balkan Peninsula and Asia Minor*. London, 1918.

Tansel, Selahattin. *Mondros'tan Mudanya'ya Kadar*. 4 vols. Ankara: Başbakanlık Basımevi, 1973.

Timur, Serim. *Türkiye'de Aile Yapısı*. Ankara: Hacettepe University Press, 1972.

Trak, Selçuk. *Türkiye Ait Coğrafî Eserler Genel Bibliografyası, I*. Ankara, 1942.

Ubicini, A. and Pavet de Courteille. *Etat Present de l'Empire Ottoman*. Paris, 1876.

United Nations, Department of Economic and Social Affairs. Population Studies, no. 42, *Methods of Estimating Basic Measures From Incomplete Data*. New York, 1967.

Uras, Esat. *Tarihte Ermeniler ve Ermeni Meselesi*. Ankara, 1950.

Yücetürk, Alper. "Sex Ratios at Birth and Monthly Distribution of Births." In *Turkish Demography*, pp. 167–174. Ankara, 1969.

ARCHIVAL SOURCES

*Turkey—Baş Bakanlık Arşivi, Istanbul.*

Cevdet. Dahiliye
Cevdet. Mahsus
İrade. Dahiliye
İrade. Mahsus

İrade. Vala
Kepeci
Yıldız

Certain archival sources, all from the Yıldız Tasnifi, are quoted in the text
and identified only as "Archival Document #1–10." They are as follows:

1. Yıldız 18-553/49-93-33.
2. Yıldız 18-553/45-93-33.
3. Yıldız 18-553/47-93-33.
4. Yıldız 18-553/37-93-33.
5. Yıldız 18-553/217-93-33.
6. Yıldız 18-553/50-93-33.
7. Yıldız 18-553/41-93-33.
8. Yıldız 18-553/48-93-33.

*Great Britain—Public Record Office, London*

F.O. 78. Turkey, General Correspondence
F.O. 96. Toynbee
F.O. 97. Turkey
F.O. 608. Peace Conference, 1919–20.
F.O. 369. Sections of Turkey (Consular)
F.O. 371. Sections on Turkey (Political)
F.O. 195–8. Consular. Turkey
F.O. 222. Consular. Anatolia
F.O. 525–6. Consular. Trabzon
F.O. 626. Consular. Izmir
F.O. 732. Consular. Ankara and Konya
F.O. 785. Consular. Bursa

GOVERNMENT PUBLICATIONS

*Ottoman*

Dahiliye Nezâreti, Sicil-i Nüfus İdare-i Umumiyesi Müdüriyeti. *Memalik-i
Osmaniye'nin 1330 Senesi Nüfus İstatistiği.* Istanbul, 1330 M.

Dahiliye Nezâreti, Sicil-i Nüfus İdare-i Umumiyesi Müdüriyeti. *Sicil-i Nüfus Nizamnamesi.* Istanbul, 1300.

Dahiliye Nezâreti. *Teşkilat-i Hazre-yi Mülkiye'ye Havi Cedvel.* Istanbul, 1331.

Dette Publique. *Tableau des divisions administratives de l'Empire Ottoman avec les agences correspondantes de la Dette Publique.* Istanbul, 1911.

Erkân-i Harbiye. *1:200,000 Maps of Anatolia, Istanbul, 1333 and 1334.*

Maliye Nezâreti. *İhsaiyat-i Maliye, 1326, 1327.* Istanbul, 1328, 1329, 1330.

Nezâret-i Umur-i Ticaret ve Nafia. *Devlet-i Aliye-i Osmaniye'nin 1313 Senesine Mahsus İstatistik-i Umumisi.* Istanbul, 1315.

*Tableau indiquant le nombre des divers elements de la population dans l'Empire Ottoman au 1er Mars 1330 (14 Mars 1914).* Constantinople, 1919.

*Van ve Bitlis İstatistaği.* Mehmet Sadik, translator. Istanbul, 1330.


Ottoman Salnames


*Salname-i Devlet-i Aliye-i Osmaniye.* Volumes used: 1277 to 1328, 52 volumes.

Adana Vilâyeti. *Adana Vilâyeti Salnamesi.* Volumes used: 1294, 1312, 1316, 1320.

Ankara Vilâyeti. *Ankara Vilâyeti Salnamesi.* Volumes used: 1293, 1300, 1307 M., 1308, 1311, 1318, 1325, 1329.

Aydın Vilâyeti. *Aydın Vilâyeti Salnamesi.* Volumes used: 1301, 1304, 1305, 1306, 1308, 1309, 1310, 1311, 1312, 1313, 1315, 1316, 1317, 1320, 1321, 1323, 1326.

Bitlis Vilâyeti. *Bitlis Vilâyeti Salnamesi.* Volumes used: 1310, 1316.

Diyarbakır Vilâyeti. *Diyarbakır Vilâyeti Salnamesi.* Volumes used: 1293, 1294, 1297, 1300, 1312, 1317, 1321.

Erzurum Vilâyeti. *Erzurum Vilâyeti Salnamesi.* Volumes used: 1293, 1294, 1299, 1304, 1310, 1312, 1315, 1317, 1318.

Haleb Vilâyeti. *Haleb Vilâyeti Salnamesi.* Volumes used: 1299, 1302, 1305, 1307, 1309, 1310, 1313, 1315, 1316, 1317, 1318, 1319, 1321, 1322, 1323, 1324.

Hüdavendigâr Vilâyeti. *Hüdavendigâr Vilâyeti Salnamesi.* Volumes used:

1292, 1296, 1301, 1302, 1306, 1311, 1312, 1313, 1314, 1315, 1316, 1317, 1318, 1319, 1320, 1321, 1322, 1323, 1324.
Kastamonu Vilâyeti. *Kastamonu Vilâyeti Salnamesi.* Volumes used: 1293, 1294, 1295, 1306, 1311, 1312, 1314, 1317, 1321.
Karası Vilâyeti. *Karası Vilâyeti Salnamesi.* Volume used: 1305.
Konya Vilâyeti. *Konya Vilâyeti Salnamesi.* Volumes used: 1298, 1299, 1310, 1312, 1317, 1324.
Mamuretül aziz Vilâyeti. *Mamuretülaziz Vilâyeti Salnamesi.* Volumes used: 1301 1305, 1307, 1312.
Sivas Vilâyeti. *Sivas Vilâyeti Salnamesi.* Volumes used: 1293, 1321, 1325.
Trabzon Vilâyeti. *Trabzon Vilâyeti Salnamesi.* Volumes used: 1295, 1296, 1305, 1307, 1311, 1313, 1318, 1319, 1320, 1321, 1322.
Van Vilâyeti. *Van Vilâyeti Salnamesi.* Volumes used: 1315.


*Turkish*


Başbakanlık İstatistik Umum Müdürlüğü. *Annuaire Statistique, 1938–39.* Ankara, 1939 (?).
Başvekâlet İstatistik Genel Direktorluğu. *Recensement General de la Population au 20 Octobre, 1935.* 67 vol. Ankara, 1937.
Basvekâlet İstatistik Umum Müdürlüğü. *Recensement General de la Population au 28 Octobre, 1927.* 3 vols. Ankara, 1929.
Dahiliye Vekâleti. *Köylerimiz.* Istanbul, 1933.
Devlet İstatistik Enstitüsü. *1965 Census of Population, Social and Economic Characteristics.* Ankara, 1969.
Devlet İstatistik Enstitüsü. *Alfabetik İl ve İlçeler.* Ankara, n.d.
Devlet İstatistik Enstitüsü. *Statistical Yearbook of Turkey, 1971.* Ankara, 1973.
Devlet İstatistik Enstitüsü. *Statistical Yearbook of Turkey, 1973.* Ankara, 1974.
İçişleri Bakanlığı. *Köylerimiz.* Ankara, 1968.
İcisleri Bakanlığı. *Türkiye'de Meskün Yerler Kılavuzu.* 2 vols. Ankara, 1947.
İmar ve İskan Bakanlığı. *İl ve İlçelerin Nüfus Düzeltmeleri (1935–1965).* Ankara: Bölge Planlama Dairesi, 1968.
Maarif Vekâleti. *Tanzimat I.* Istanbul, 1941.

Sağlık ve Sosyal Yardım Bakanlığı. *Vital Statistics from the Turkish Demographic Survey, 1965–1966.* Ankara, 1967.

Turkish Demographic Survey. *Vital Statistics from the Turkish Demographic Survey, 1966–1967.* Ankara: Hacettepe Basımevi, 1970.

Urfa Vilâyeti. *Urfa Salnamesi, 1927.* Istanbul, n.d.


*Other*


Bulgaria. *Annuaire Statistique du Royaume de Bulgarie, 1931.* Sofia, 1931.

Cyprus, Ministry of Finance, Statistics and Research Department. *Statistical Abstracts, 1968.* Nicosia, 1969.

Egypt, Ministry of Finance, Statistical and Census Department. *Population Census of Egypt, 1937.* Cairo, 1942.

France, Statistique generale. *Resultats statistiques du recensement general de la population, 1926 and 1931.* Paris, 1928 and 1933.

Great Britain. *Documents on British Foreign Policy, 1919–1936,* First series. Various volumes. London.

Great Britain, Foreign Office, Historical Section, no. 59. *Anatolia.* London: H.M. Stationery Office, 1920.

Greece, Genikē Statistikē Hypēresia. *Resultats statistiques du recensement de la population de la Grece du 15–26 mai 1928.* Various volumes. Athens, 1929–1933.

League of Nations, International Labor Organization. *Report by Dr. Fridtjof Nansen.* A41.1925 (Annex); also A29.1926 and A33.1927. Lausanne, 1925–7.

Palestine, Superintendent of the Census. *Census of Palestine, 1931.*

Republic of Cyprus, Ministry of Finance, Statistics and Research Department. *Statistical Abstracts, 1968.* Nicosia, 1968(?).

Russia, Comite central de statistique. *Premier recensement de la population de l'empire de Russie, 1897.* Various volumes. St. Petersburg, 1899.

Syrian Republic, Ministry of National Economy, Directorate of Statistics. *Statistical Abstract of Syria, 1953.*

United States, Department of Commerce. *Historical Statistics of the United States.* Part I. Washington, DC:1975.

United States, Department of Labor, Bureau of Immigration. *Annual Re-*

port of the Commissioner General of Immigration. Various years, especially 1928. Washington, DC: 1928.

United States, Defense Mapping Agency Aerospace Center, 1:1,000,000 maps of the Middle East. Four cover Anatolia: F-3, F-4, G-3, G-4. St. Louis, 1972.

# Index